FIRST CERTIFICATE
Avenues
COURSEBOOK

David Foll & Anne Kelly

Plan of the book

READING	LISTENING	WRITING	SPEAKING
Electronic dreams (*variety of short texts*)	Speaking from experience (*students of English speak*)		English in our lives (*exchanging experiences*)
Fatal mistakes / Two views of the English language (*newspaper articles*)			
	Getting it across (*radio interview*)	Message in a bottle (*getting ideas*)	

Test exercises: *Paper 1* **Vocabulary** *Paper 3* **Dialogue completion**

READING	LISTENING	WRITING	SPEAKING
Food in India (*cookery book*)		Food in my country (*using a foreign word; organising ideas*)	
	The perfect blend of coffee (*interview*)		Personal preference
Different angles (*variety of short texts*)			Agreeing and disagreeing (1)

Test exercises: *Paper 1* **Vocabulary** *Paper 3* **Gap-filling; word set**

READING	LISTENING	WRITING	SPEAKING
	Come properly dressed (*conversation*)		Clothes (*exchanging experiences*) / Emphasising words
Mr McElroy (*autobiography*)		Description of a person (*getting and organising ideas*)	
A modern heroine? (*novel*)	Who am I? (*TV game show*)		My hero (*discussion*)

Test exercises: *Paper 1* **Vocabulary** *Paper 3* **Dialogue completion; word sets; phrasal verbs**

READING	LISTENING	WRITING	SPEAKING
Japan (*encyclopaedia*)		Description of my country (*organising ideas*)	
	Living in a city (*monologue and interview*)		Describing a photo
Interpreting diagrams (*variety of charts*)		Working on a farm (*directed writing*)	Pronouncing numbers and symbols / Guided visit (*simulation*)

Test exercises: *Paper 1* **Vocabulary** *Paper 3* **Gap-filling; word set**

READING	LISTENING	WRITING	SPEAKING
Questionnaire		Personal health and fitness (*topic sentences*)	
	Taking exercise (*recorded telephone message*)		Advice
My left foot (*autobiography*)			Disability (*discussion*) / Expressing opinion / Individual sounds

Test exercises: *Paper 1* **Vocabulary** *Paper 3* **Gap-filling; rewriting sentences**

READING	LISTENING	WRITING	SPEAKING
	Clive comes home (*radio soap opera*)		Home surroundings (*exchanging experiences*) / Episode 94 (*role play*)
Give him an inch (*newspaper article*)		A burglar's point of view (*directed writing*)	
	A beautiful memory (*monologue*)	Description of a place (*getting and organising ideas*)	

Test exercises: *Paper 1* **Vocabulary** *Paper 3* **Gap-filling; rewriting sentences**

READING	LISTENING	WRITING	SPEAKING
Safe drivers (*newspaper article*)	Motoring (*variety of short radio items*)		
		A letter to a friend	Airport (*discussion*)
Penang, Pearl of the Orient (*magazine article*)	A good holiday? (*interview*)		Discussing a photo

Test exercises: *Paper 1* **Vocabulary** *Paper 3* **Dialogue completion; rewriting sentences; word formation**

READING	LISTENING	WRITING	SPEAKING
The news (*teleprinter and newspaper items*)	The news (*variety of short news items*)		Stop press (*discussion*) / Weak forms
Turning point (*novel*)	Assassination! (*radio programme*)		Historic moments (*discussion*)
		Telling a story	

Test exercises: *Paper 3* **Gap-filling; rewriting sentences; phrasal verbs**

READING	LISTENING	WRITING	SPEAKING
	First job (*radio interviews*)		Jobs (*discussion*) Asking politely
Monthly budget (*magazine article*)	What shall we get her? (*conversation*)		Money and me (*exchanging experiences*)
What makes young people commit crimes? (*opinion composition*)		Opinion composition	Crime and punishment (*discussion*)

Test exercises: *Paper 1* **Vocabulary** *Paper 3* **Rewriting sentences; word formation**

READING	LISTENING	WRITING	SPEAKING
When your best friend suddenly isn't (*magazine article*)			My best friend (*discussion*)
	A new baby (*radio phone-in programme*)		Conversation skills (1)
A Japanese experiment (*magazine article*)		'For and against' composition	

Test exercises: *Paper 1* **Vocabulary** *Paper 3* **'Telegram' letter; rewriting sentences**

READING	LISTENING	WRITING	SPEAKING
Making a connection (*variety of short texts*)			What's in a sport? (*discussion*) Agreeing and disagreeing (2) Question tags Sports school (*simulation*)
	Scuba diving (*interview*)	A talk (1)	Passing the time (*discussion*)
Party politics (*novel*)	Cinema attendance (*talk*)		Giving a party (*simulation*)

Test exercises: *Paper 1* **Vocabulary** *Paper 3* **Gap-filling; rewriting sentences; word formation**

READING	LISTENING	WRITING	SPEAKING
Fact or opinion? (*newspaper article*)	Logic problems (*radio programme*)		
School days (*newspaper articles and prospectus*)		Further education (*directed writing*)	
		A talk (2)	Museums (*discussion*) Conversation skills (2) Word linking Our museum (*simulation*)

Test exercises: *Paper 1* **Vocabulary** *Paper 3* **'Telegram' letter; phrasal verbs; rewriting sentences**

READING	LISTENING	WRITING	SPEAKING
	Easy to operate (*answerphone messages*)	A formal letter	
	First step to the stars (*radio discussion*)	Space diary (*telling a story*)	Exclamations
Fire is fire (*newspaper article*)			Conversation skills (3)

Test exercises: *Paper 1* **Vocabulary** *Paper 3* **Gap-filling; rewriting sentences**

READING	LISTENING	WRITING	SPEAKING
	The sea – sink or swim? (*radio discussion*)		Adding something extra
Strange but true (*textbook and newspaper article*)		Different composition types	
Away from their homes (*travel books*)			Near and far (*discussion*) Telling a story

Test exercises: *Paper 1* **Vocabulary** *Paper 3* **'Telegram' letter; rewriting sentences; word set**

READING	LISTENING	WRITING	SPEAKING
	A faraway kingdom (*radio talk*)		Our culture (*simulation*)
Picture choice (*newspaper articles*)	Chi wara (*conversation*)		My favourite work of art (*talk*)
A traditional wedding (*novel*)	A traditional festival (*radio programme*)		A celebration (*talk*)

Test exercises: *Paper 1* **Vocabulary** *Paper 3* **Gap-filling; rewriting sentences**   End of course (*simulation*)

Language

1 Learning English

Speaking *English in our lives*

How big a part does English play in your lives?

Find out by:
– filling in the questionnaire for yourself.
– comparing your answers with those of your classmates.

QUESTIONNAIRE

English and me

If you tick a YES box, write a short answer to the question that follows.

A ENTERTAINMENT

	NO	YES	
1 Have you seen a film in English in the last three months?	☐	☐	→ Which one?
2 Have you seen a TV programme in English in the last three months?	☐	☐	→ Which one?
3 Have you read a book / magazine / newspaper in English in the last three months?	☐	☐	→ Which one?
4 Have you got a favourite song in English?	☐	☐	→ Which one?

B FRIENDS

5 Do you have any English-speaking friends?	☐	☐	→ Who?
6 Is there a good place near where you live for meeting English-speaking people?	☐	☐	→ Where is it?
7 Have you ever written a letter to someone in English?	☐	☐	→ Who? Why?
8 Have you ever been to an English-speaking country?	☐	☐	→ Which one? When?

C STUDY

Write short answers to these questions.

9 How long have you been learning English?

10 Why are you learning English?

11 What do you like about learning English?

12 What do you dislike about learning English?

Reading *Electronic dreams*

1 *Look quickly through these texts (A–E). What do they all have in common?*

A They are all trying to sell technological items.
B They are all connected with modern communication.
C They are all taken from TV magazines.
D They are all written for learners of English.

A

B

ELECTRONIC DREAMS

Telephones, TV sets and personal computers. The dream of linking these commonplace household items into a single Super-System has come a long way toward reaching reality. With the vital support of communications satellites, optical-fiber and laser transmission systems, Very-Large-Scale-Integrated-Circuit "chips" and the like, we are on the verge of a terrific "electronic revolution" of immense proportions. This is history in the making, and it is already changing our lives.

C

Dictionary

ENGLISH – FRENCH DICTIONARY

A portable Harraps English / French dictionary, essential for the business traveller, tourist and language student.

❑ Instant English–French and French–English translation.
❑ 29,000 entry translations per language.
❑ Direct / wild card / blank word search.
❑ Memory feature for regularly used translated words.
❑ Alphabetical word list and verb conjugation display.
❑ Can be used with organizer functions, e.g. memo.

D

BBC ENGLISH

BBC English is the largest English-teaching organisation in the world. It teaches English to millions of learners in 120 countries through radio, television and a wide range of published courses in the form of books, audio and video cassettes. Lessons are broadcast to all parts of the world with explanations in English and some 30 other languages.

EUROPE'S AWARD WINNING NEWSPAPER UK 75p

PEAN

● MOSCOW

E

MTV - ROCKING EUROPE

Since its launch in August 1987 MTV Europe, the 24-hour youth entertainment channel, has become the fastest-growing cable & satellite channel in Europe and has gained an enviable reputation in the European television arena. MTV has overcome the cultural barriers which restrict traditional broadcasters by communicating through music, an international language which transcends national boundaries and unites young people throughout the world.

2 *Find the answers to these questions as quickly as possible. Write the letter of the correct text in each gap.*

Which text(s) could you show:

– a young person who liked pop music?   **1** .....

– a speaker of English who was travelling
  on business in France?   **2** .....

– someone who wanted to practise their
  English, but who didn't have a television?   **3** .....
          4 .....

– someone who enjoyed using sophisticated
  technology?   **5** .....
          6 .....

3 *Which examples of the 'electronic dreams' shown here are available to you? Do you use any to help you learn English? How can they help? In your opinion, how do these compare with the traditional method of books and blackboard?*

Listening 🔲 *Speaking from experience*

1 *Listen to six students talking about what helps them improve their English. Write the number of each student (1–6) in the correct gap.*

To help improve his/her English, this student:

– tries not to be nervous about speaking
  English.   **a** .....

– makes an effort to practise out of school.   **b** .....

– listens to the radio and watches videos.   **c** .....

– sometimes speaks English with her boyfriend
  and her father.   **d** .....

– makes an effort to use a dictionary to check
  the meaning of new vocabulary.   **e** .....

– tries to enjoy studying English.   **f** .....

2 *Which of the different points the students make do you think is:*

● the most sensible?
● the easiest to do?

Grammar *Questions*

1 YES/NO QUESTIONS

Have you ever written a letter to someone in English?
Do you have any English-speaking friends?

These are questions which expect either a 'yes' or 'no' answer. The auxiliary verb or modal verb comes before the subject. The auxiliary verb 'do' is used if there is no other auxiliary or modal verb present.

2 'TAG' QUESTIONS

It isn't necessary to look up every new word in the dictionary, is it?
We should only speak English in class, shouldn't we?
You enjoy watching MTV, don't you?

'Tag' questions are a special type of yes/no question. They are formed by adding a question tag to a statement. The tag repeats the auxiliary verb or modal verb in the statement, or uses the auxiliary verb 'do'. If the statement is positive, then the tag is negative; if the statement is negative, then the tag is positive.

3 QUESTION-WORD QUESTIONS

These questions begin with a question word:
Why are you learning English?
How long have you been learning English?
When are you going to take First Certificate?
Where can you buy a good English dictionary?

If the question begins with 'why', 'how', 'when' or 'where', you put the auxiliary or modal verb before the subject. You also use this word order with 'who', 'what' or 'which' if the question word is the *object* of the sentence:
Who can I practise speaking English with?
What do you particularly like about learning English?
Which English magazines have you read?

When 'who', 'what' or 'which' is the *subject* of the sentence, the question word comes first, then the verb, and you do not use the auxiliary 'do':
Who gave you your first English lesson?
What will happen if I don't do my homework?
Which cinema shows English films?

4 INDIRECT QUESTIONS

Could you tell me what English magazines you have read?
I wonder if you understood every word on page 9?

An indirect question is introduced by a phrase like 'Could you tell me' or 'I wonder'. After the introductory phrase, there is a question word (for indirect question-word questions) or 'if' or 'whether' (for indirect yes/no questions). Indirect questions do *not* have the word order of direct questions.

Indirect questions usually sound more polite than direct questions.

5 Complete this dialogue. A television interviewer is speaking to Barry Spinaker, a famous footballer.

INTERVIEWER: Barry, you have played football for Liverpool and for England, and you've also played for a Spanish team. Why (1) .... ?

BARRY: Well, a Spanish club bought me from Liverpool. Also my wife thought it would be nice to spend a few years in a warm country!

INTERVIEWER: Could (2) .... ?

BARRY: No, not a word! But I started having Spanish lessons as soon as I arrived.

INTERVIEWER: Who (3)................................. ?

BARRY: The sister of one of my team-mates. She was a very good teacher.

INTERVIEWER: I wonder if (4)................................. ?

BARRY: My wife was a better one! But she had more time for studying than I did.

INTERVIEWER: But you spoke quite fluently after a few months, (5)... ?

BARRY: Not exactly fluently, no! But I could make myself understood, both on and off the football field. It was great to be able to really communicate with Spanish people.

INTERVIEWER: But now you've left Spain. Can you tell me where (6) .... ?

BARRY: Japan. I've got a contract with a Japanese club.

INTERVIEWER: So you've got to pack your suitcases again. What (7) .... ?

BARRY: Top of the list, after my football gear of course, is a Japanese dictionary and a Japanese grammar book. I want to learn the language as soon as possible!

2 English in the world

Reading *Fatal mistakes*

When do you think it could be dangerous to speak bad English?

Quickly read this newspaper report to find out:
- the situation
- the kind of mistake that is made
- a possible result

Text A

Bad language on the airways may be fatal

AIR travellers are at risk because of poor standards of radio English, according to a team of experts in three countries. Some pilots and air traffic
5 controllers are inadequately trained and many cannot communicate in a crisis.

The claims are made by language and aviation specialists in Britain, France and Australia. A team, organised
10 from Cambridge University, says that although English is accepted as the international language of the air, people are failing seriously when it comes to using it:
15 ● There are wide variations in the ability of controllers and pilots who do not have English as their first language.
● Conversations stray from the standard phrases (drawn up by the
20 International Civil Aviation Organisation) into idiom and inexact, everyday use of English. This has been a factor in numerous aircraft accidents.
● Controllers and flight crews, because they know only the routine phrases, 25 resort to their own language in a crisis.

Have you ever been in a situation where someone made a dangerous, embarrassing or amusing language mistake?

Grammar *Grammar terms*

You need to know some basic grammar terms in order to be able to talk about and improve your command of English grammar. Underline one example of each of the following in Text A.

adjective	adverb
pronoun	noun
preposition	conjunction
present participle	past participle
modal verb	auxiliary verb
main clause	subordinate clause

Reading *Two views of the English language*

Quickly read the next two texts.

1 Choose the most appropriate title for each one:
  a Learning English
  b Working with English
  c A World Language
  d Language Sandwich
  e Language Pollution

Text B

ENGLISH is losing its political and cultural associations and becoming the property of all cultures. Over 70 countries in the
5 world use English as the official or semi-official language, and in 20 more English occupies an important position. It is the main foreign language taught within
10 most school systems. Worldwide, many newspapers are published in English and it is the language of much radio and television broadcasting. English is the
15 language of international business, the main language of airports, air traffic control and international shipping. It is the language of science, technology
20 and medicine, and it is estimated that two-thirds of all scientific papers today are first published in English. It is the language of diplomacy and sport; it is one of
25 the working languages of the United Nations and the language used by the International Olympic Committee. International pop culture and advertising are also
30 dominated by English. 70% of the world's mail is written in English, and 80% of all information in electronic retrieval systems is stored in English.

Text C

ENGLISH infiltration of foreign languages is often regarded with horror. The late President Pompidou of France
5 recommended a return to totally unpolluted French with an abolition of all anglicisms. In official documents 'fast food' and 'jumbo jet' were to
10 be referred to by French expressions instead. But it would be difficult to eradicate the use of such familiar 'French' terms as 'le
15 weekend', 'le sandwich', or 'le parking'. French is not the only 'polluted' language. In German we find 'der Babysitter', 'der Bestseller' and 'der Teenager'.
20 'Il weekend' turns up again in Italian, where we can also find 'la pop art' and 'il popcorn'. 'Jeans' is found in both Italian and Spanish, and in Spanish
25 we also have 'pancakes', and 'suéter' (sweater). Russian young people like to wear the latest trainer-style 'shoozy',

while Japanese young people like to eat 'eisucurimu' (ice 30 cream). But this invasion is not one-sided. Other languages have quietly been getting their own back for a long time. Native English speakers may 35 think they are speaking 'pure' English when they talk about the alphabet, the traffic, a mosquito, a sofa, a garage, their pyjamas or their boss, but 40 Greek, Italian, Spanish, Arabic, French, Hindi and Dutch speakers know better!

2 In Text B, what do these figures refer to?

  70   two-thirds   70%   80%

3 In what fields is English used in your country?

4 How often do you come across English in your daily life?

5 Can you think of any examples of:
  ● English words which have become part of your language?
  ● words from your language which have become part of English?

Dictionary skills

1 *Read the dictionary entry for 'retrieval' and find the following information about the word:*

- its pronunciation
- which syllable is stressed
- its grammar (i.e. Is it a noun? a verb? an adjective? etc. A countable or uncountable noun? A transitive or intransitive verb?)
- its meaning or meanings
- any words that often go with it

punishment: *retributive measures*
re·triev·al /rɪˈtriːvəl/ *n* [U] *fml* the act or process of re-
trieving: *The court ordered the retrieval of the confiscat-
ed funds.* | *a computerized* **retrieval system** *that will en-
able you to find the information you want within a few
seconds.* | *I'm afraid the situation is* **beyond/past re-
trieval.** (=cannot now be put right)
re·trieve /rɪˈtriːv/ *v* **1** [T (from)] *usu. fml or tech* to
find and bring back; regain: *I went and retrieved the bag
I had left on the train.* | *This computer can retrieve stored
information in a matter of seconds.* | *Wreckage from the
crashed plane was retrieved from the ocean.* **2** [T] to
put right; make up for (a mistake, loss, defeat, etc.): *She
tried to retrieve the situation by making profuse apolo-
gies.* **3** [I;T] (of a dog) to bring back (shot birds) —**re-
trievable** *adj*
triev·er /rɪˈtriːvə/ *n* a type of middle-sized hunting

(from *Longman Dictionary of Contemporary English*)

2 *Do the following exercises, which are based on words from Texts A–C, and check your answers in your dictionary.*

1 PRONUNCIATION: SOUNDS AND SPELLINGS

These words all contain a vowel sound spelt 'or'. But in standard British English 'or' can be pronounced in four different ways.

Group these words according to their pronunciation. The word which contains more than one 'or' may need to be put in more than one group.

**according   factor   foreign   horror
information   more   organised   sport   stored
working   world**

How many of the following words contain the same vowel sound as the one in 'sport'? Underline the relevant syllables.

**also   Australia   broadcasting   drawn   global
taught   totally**

2 PRONUNCIATION: STRESS

'Retrieval' has this stress pattern: oOo. Which of these words have the same stress pattern?

**alphabet   broadcasting   committee   controllers
medicine   occupies   pyjamas**

3 GRAMMAR

property (Text B, line 3) – Is this noun countable or uncountable in this context? Could it be a different kind of noun in another context?

stray (Text A, line 18) – Is this a transitive or intransitive verb in this context? Is 'stray' always a verb, or can it sometimes be another kind of word?

4 MEANING AND USE

at risk (Text A, line 1) – What is the meaning of this prepositional phrase? What verbs are usually used with the noun 'risk'?

claims (Text A, line 7) – What does this word mean in this context? There should be several entries in your dictionary for this word. Which one applies to the word here?

turns up (Text C, line 20), *drawn up* (Text A, line 19) – What do these phrasal verbs mean in these contexts? Remember to look for an entry for the complete verbs (i.e. 'turn up', not just 'turn').

Other languages have quietly been getting their own back for a long time (Text C, lines 32–3) – Express this idea in your own words as far as possible. Does the word 'own' stand alone or is it part of an idiomatic phrase? If it is part of a phrase, which word(s) complete(s) the phrase?

3 Unspoken messages

Vocabulary *Ways of communicating*

1 *What can you see in each photo? In what way are the people communicating? Why are they not speaking?*

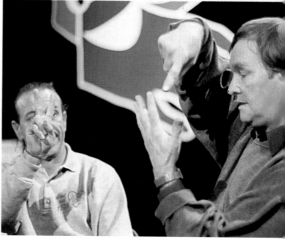

2 *Which part(s) of the body do you use to communicate in the following ways? Use the words in the box to help you.*

1	clap	6	smile
2	cry	7	wave
3	laugh	8	whisper
4	scream	9	whistle
5	shout	10	yawn

> eyes   hands   lips   lungs   mouth   voice

3 *How could you communicate these messages without speaking?*

1 Well done!
2 I feel very unhappy.
3 I'm bored.
4 Come here!
5 I'd like to talk to you.
6 Help!

Listening 📼 *Getting it across*

1 *Listen to this extract from an interview in which Dervla Murphy talks about a journey in Cameroon. What topic is she discussing with the interviewer?*

2 *Listen again and mark if each statement is True or False. Correct the statements you think are False.*

	True	False
1 Dervla Murphy praises herself for being good at languages.	☐	☐
2 In some villages on her last journey an interpreter would have been useful.	☐	☐
3 The speakers agree with each other about one advantage of being bad at languages.	☐	☐
4 When Dervla Murphy travels, she doesn't trust anybody she meets.	☐	☐
5 She thinks it's a weakness to trust people when you travel.	☐	☐

3 *The interviewer says that not being able to speak foreign languages is also 'slightly a strength in that it develops a muscle of communication in other ways'. What does she mean? Do you agree? Can you think of any examples?*

Dervla Murphy, traveller and writer

Grammar *Pronouns*

1 *You use these pronouns to refer back to someone or something that has already been mentioned.*

I	you	he	she	it	we	you	they
me	you	him	her	it	us	you	them
mine	yours	his	hers	its	ours	yours	theirs
myself	yourself	himself	herself	itself	ourselves	yourselves	themselves

this	these	that	those
one	ones		
each other / one another			
anyone/anybody	everyone/everybody		
someone/somebody	no one/nobody		
anything	everything	something	nothing

Which of these pronouns should you use instead of the nouns in italics?

EXAMPLE: 'yours' instead of *your idea*

1 Is that idea *your idea* or *Dervla Murphy's idea*?
2 The interviewer asks Dervla Murphy to talk about *Dervla Murphy*.
3 She's bad at languages. *Being bad at languages* is her greatest weakness.
4 The speakers agree with *the speakers* about one advantage of not being good at languages.
5 When Dervla Murphy travels, she trusts *all the people she meets*.
6 There were several travel programmes on the radio last week, but the *travel programme* with Dervla Murphy was the most interesting.

Here are some points about pronouns to remember:

1 You can use 'you' and 'they' to talk *impersonally*:
- You can use 'you' to talk about people in general:
  Being bad at languages, you do miss out a lot.
- You can use 'they' if it is not important to name the person or people you are referring to:
  They say communication prevents wars.

2 You use 'this' and 'that' to identify yourself on the phone, or to introduce people:
This is Dervla speaking.
Who was that on the phone?
This is Ms Murphy. She will be travelling with us.

3 You can use reflexive pronouns after nouns or pronouns for emphasis:
The topic itself was interesting but the film made it seem boring.
Henry himself had never been abroad.
You can also use a reflexive pronoun at the end of a clause to indicate that someone did something without any help from other people:
I baked this bread myself.
You use 'by' + a reflexive pronoun to indicate that someone did something without any help from other people, or to indicate that someone is alone:
She decorated the whole house by herself.
He sat by himself on the cliff top and looked out to sea.
'On' + 'my/your/his/her/its/our/their' + 'own' has the same meaning:
Do you like travelling on your own?

4 Indefinite pronouns are always used with a singular verb:
No one knows who started the fire.
There's something in the cupboard.
Everyone is invited to the party.

2 **Correct the mistakes in these sentences.**

1 You don't have to introduce me to Sally. She's an old friend of me.
2 Let me introduce me. My name's Tim Tracy.
  Your husband and I went to school with ourselves.
3 Everybody in my class do their Latin homework on their own.
4 The teacher has ten dictionaries, so there are enough for the students to borrow each one.
5 It was Smiley by himself who worked out the meaning of the coded message.

Writing *Message in a bottle*

1 **Before you can write anything you have to have ideas to write about. Here are three different ways of getting ideas.**

Imagine you are one of these people shipwrecked on a desert island and you want to send a message in a bottle to the outside world. Use one of these methods to get ideas for your message.

1 MIND MAP
Write 'island' in the middle of a piece of paper. Write down all the other ideas which this suggests at suitable places on the mind map.

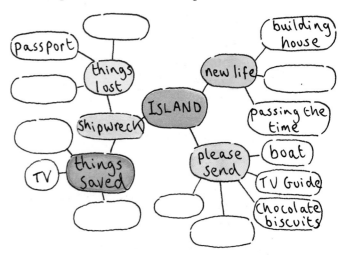

2 BRAINSTORMING
Make quick notes about anything that comes into your head about the situation on the island.

Can't swim... don't like fish... tell mother... wonderful suntan

3 ASKING QUESTIONS
Write down the questions that a reader of your message might want to ask.

How long have you been on the island? Are you alone? Is it dangerous there? What do you eat?

2 **Look at the ideas you have collected. Decide which ones you will use in your message.**
Decide which order you will write them in.
Write the message (50–100 words).

4

Exam skill *All about the exam*

1 Students often ask these questions at the beginning of a First Certificate Exam course:

1 What do I have to do in the exam?
2 How many papers are there?
3 How long are they?
4 How many marks do you get for each paper?

Are there any other questions you would like to ask? Find the answers in this information about the exam.

PAPER 1 Reading Comprehension (1 hour)   40 marks

This paper is in two sections. Section A tests your knowledge of vocabulary and your grammatical accuracy (25 multiple-choice questions). Section B tests your comprehension of both the main idea and the details of three or more texts (15 multiple-choice questions).

PAPER 2 Composition (1½ hours)   40 marks

You have to write two compositions, one of which may be a letter. There is a choice of descriptive, narrative or discussion topics, including one based on the set books. Your compositions are marked for organisation, grammatical accuracy, fluency and range of language.

PAPER 3 Use of English (2 hours)   40 marks

This paper tests your knowledge of the rules and systems of English grammar. There is a variety of exercises (e.g. gap-filling, rewriting sentences, word formation, dialogue completion). There is also a directed writing exercise, which tests your ability to interpret and present information.

PAPER 4 Listening Comprehension (approx. 30 mins)   20 marks

This paper tests accurate comprehension of spoken English. There are three to four listening texts recorded on cassette. There is a variety of exercises (e.g. blank-filling, true/false, multiple-choice, labelling).

PAPER 5 Interview (approx. 10–12 mins if individual, 18–25 mins if group)   40 marks

Your spoken English is tested in an interview with an examiner. You can have this by yourself, or, if you choose, in a pair or a group of three. The interview is based on a photograph, related passages and other materials. It may also be based on one of the set books. Your English is marked for fluency, communicative ability, pronunciation, grammatical accuracy and use of vocabulary.

There are three pass grades (A–C) and two fail grades (D–E).

2 Look at what these four FCE students say about their English.

"I have no problem communicating with people, but I know I make lots of mistakes. And I don't really know many useful words."

ANA

"Where I live I don't hear much English. I can understand written English well, but I'm not so good at understanding people when they speak."

MARIE   ALI

"I'm studying economics, so I have to read books in English. My grammar and vocabulary are good, but I can't write very well. And I never speak English."

"I know the grammar rules and I have a wide vocabulary. But I'm no good at speaking because I don't get much chance to practise."

WON-SUL

Which paper(s) do you think each student should do well in? And what should each pay particular attention to, if he or she doesn't want to fail the exam?

3 Do any of these students sound like you? Which paper(s) could you do well in? And which should you pay particular attention to?

Test exercises

1 *Claudia is in England and wants to do a summer course in English. Complete her conversation with the director of the Central Language College.*

DIRECTOR: What can I tell you about our college?
CLAUDIA: Well, I can't stay in England very long. When (1) .... ?
DIRECTOR: Would Monday suit you? We have a few free places then.
CLAUDIA: That would be fine. How long (2) .... ?
DIRECTOR: Exactly four weeks. It ends on the second of September.
CLAUDIA: Could you tell me how many (3) .... ?
DIRECTOR: Three in the morning and two in the afternoon. You'll have to work hard!
CLAUDIA: Are (4) .... ?
DIRECTOR: Well, the average number is 12. Our teachers find that the best size.
CLAUDIA: I don't have to (5) .... ?
DIRECTOR: I'm afraid you do. Your marks will tell us which is the best class for you.
CLAUDIA: What about accommodation? Can you (6) .... ?
DIRECTOR: We'll do our best. But most of our regular families are fully booked at the moment.
CLAUDIA: Well, I think I'll do the course. Shall I write you a cheque now?

2 *Choose the word or phrase (A–D) which best completes each sentence.*

1 On Friday afternoons it is often difficult to .... attention to the lesson.
   A give   B lend   C pay   D put

2 Verbs like 'can', 'will' and 'may' are all .... verbs.
   A main   B modal   C passive   D subordinate

3 The politicians are trying to .... out a solution to the country's economic problems.
   A cross   B read   C rub   D work

4 She asked .... whether she really wanted to take the exam.
   A anyone else   B each other   C herself   D one

5 I .... the mistake of leaving my car in a dark street, and the radio was stolen.
   A committed   B did   C had   D made

6 The romantic film made her .... so much her handkerchief was completely wet.
   A clap   B cry   C wave   D whisper

7 Through .... the foreigner was able to indicate that he wanted food and drink.
   A signals   B signatures   C signposts   D signs

8 The circus performer .... her dogs to jump through rings of fire.
   A coached   B educated   C showed   D trained

9 Could you tell me what 'yawn' .... ?
   A does mean   B mean   C meaning   D means

10 When she answers the phone, she often .... in a funny accent, which annoys me.
   A repeats   B says   C speaks   D tells

11 Are Jon and Liz in love? They've been looking into .... eyes all evening!
   A each other's   B the other's   C their   D their own

12 I'm going to .... all my clothes and decide which to keep and which to give away.
   A get on   B go through   C hand in   D look up

13 Her .... is that she never gives up.
   A ability   B quality   C skill   D strength

UNIT TWO

2 *Eating and drinking*

1 National food

Reading *Food in India*

1 ***Before you read, can you answer these questions?***

1 What does a typical Indian meal consist of?
2 How do Indians serve and eat their food?

Read the passage quickly to check your ideas.

Generally speaking, an Indian meal consists of a meat dish, a vegetable dish, bread and/or rice, a pulse dish, a yoghurt relish (or plain yoghurt), and a fresh chutney or small, relish-like salad. Some pickles and preserved chutneys may be added if you have them. Fruit rather than desserts is served at the end of a meal, although on festive occasions sweets would not be at all amiss. Sometimes, when the meat dish is particularly elegant and rich, we don't serve any pulses but serve instead an equally elegant *pullao* rice. Vegetarians – of whom there are millions in India – increase the number of vegetable and pulse dishes and always serve yoghurt in some form.

Within this general framework, we try to see that the dishes we serve vary in colour, texture and flavour. If our meat, for example, has a lot of sauce, then we often serve a 'dry' vegetable that doesn't have any sauce with it. If the vegetable we are serving is very soft – such as spinach – we make sure that there is a crunchy relish around on the table.

Most Indians like to eat with their hands, although more Westernised ones may use knives and forks or spoons and forks, or just forks. It is only the right hand that is used for eating, the left being considered 'unclean'. With the right hand, we break pieces of bread and then use the pieces to scoop up some meat or vegetable. With it, we also form neat morsels out of rice and other accompanying dishes and then transport them to our mouths. Needless to say, hands must be washed before and after eating. Even the humblest of roadside stalls will have a *lota* (water vessel) of water for washing first.

When we serve ourselves, we put most foods beside each other on our plates. Only very wet, flowing dishes are sometimes ladled on top of the rice but not on top of all the rice. Some of the rice is left plain to enable us to eat it with other dishes.

2 ***What does each highlighted word mean? Before looking it up in your dictionary, consider:***

- what the general meaning of the context is.
- if the word is similar to another word you know in English, or to a word in your language.
- what kind of word (e.g. noun, verb, adjective) it is.

Use these ideas to help you check the correct meaning in your dictionary.

3 ***What similarities and differences are there between food in India and in your country?***

Think about:
- kinds of food.
- serving and eating food.

Grammar *Nouns*

1 ***There are two types of noun:***

1 COUNTABLE NOUNS

These nouns can be either singular or plural, and are used with verbs in either the singular or the plural:

a meal, meals   this dish, those dishes
one colour, several colours
An Indian meal consists of a variety of dishes.
The dishes vary in colour, texture and flavour.

2 UNCOUNTABLE NOUNS

These are always used with a singular verb:

beauty   bread   fruit   greed   hunger   milk
oil   water
Fruit is served at the end of a meal.

If you want to talk about separate, countable pieces or quantities of uncountable nouns, you use an expression like:

a bit of   a bottle of   a piece of   a slice of

The following nouns are uncountable:

advice   equipment   evidence   furniture
homework   information   knowledge   luggage
news   work

COUNTABLE AND UNCOUNTABLE

Some nouns can be either countable or uncountable:

UNCOUNTABLE	COUNTABLE
Do you prefer coffee or tea?	*Let's stop and have a coffee or a tea.*
His hair is black.	*The detective found two black hairs on the knife.*
In most jobs experience is rewarded.	*My trip to India was full of wonderful experiences.*

2 ***The plural of most countable nouns is '–s'. But what is the plural of these nouns?***

bus   bush   box   match   country   knife
potato   child   foot   man   mouse   person
tooth   woman

Some nouns only exist in the plural:

clothes   scissors   sunglasses   trousers

3 ***You use 'some' and 'any' in front of*** **plural countable *nouns* and uncountable *nouns.***

'Some' is usually used in positive statements:
Some pickles and preserved chutneys may be added.
Here is some information about Indian food.

'Any' is usually used in negative statements and questions:
We don't serve any pulses.
Is there any milk left?

'Some' can also be used in questions when you expect the answer to be 'yes', or you want to encourage someone to say 'yes':
Could you get me some lemons?
Would you like some orange juice?

'Any' can also be used in positive statements when you don't want to mention a specific person or thing:
Any bank will accept these traveller's cheques.
Call me any time this evening. I'll be in the whole time.

4 ***Make any necessary corrections to these sentences.***

1 Is there a bread left?
2 My kitchen equipment are very old.
3 I haven't got some sharp knife.
4 How many sugars would you like in your coffee?
5 There isn't a meat because this is a vegetarian restaurant.
6 Have you got some green tomatos?
7 Can you give me an information about traditional recipes?
8 I broke a teeth eating any peanut.
9 I'd like to make some cake. I've got some flour, but I haven't got some eggs. Could you go and buy some for me?
10 The news are bad, I'm afraid: the price of a cooking oil has gone up again.

Writing *Food in my country*

1 ***What foreign words are used in the passage on page 19? How were you able to find them? What do they mean? Why are English words not used instead?***

2 ***Prepare answers to these questions about food in your country:***

1 What is commonly eaten? What ingredients and flavourings are commonly used?
2 How is food commonly prepared?
3 When is food eaten? When is the main meal of the day? Who is food eaten with?
4 How is food served and how is it eaten?

3 ***Write four short paragraphs about food in your country. Remember to:***

– use the four categories above as your four main topic areas.
– decide on the order in which to write about the topic areas.
– try to include and explain some words from your own language.

2 Some like it hot

Speaking *Personal preference*

1 *Read this magazine article, and see if you agree with the connection it makes between your food preferences and your character.*

2 *Underline the expressions which are used in the article to show likes, dislikes and preferences.*

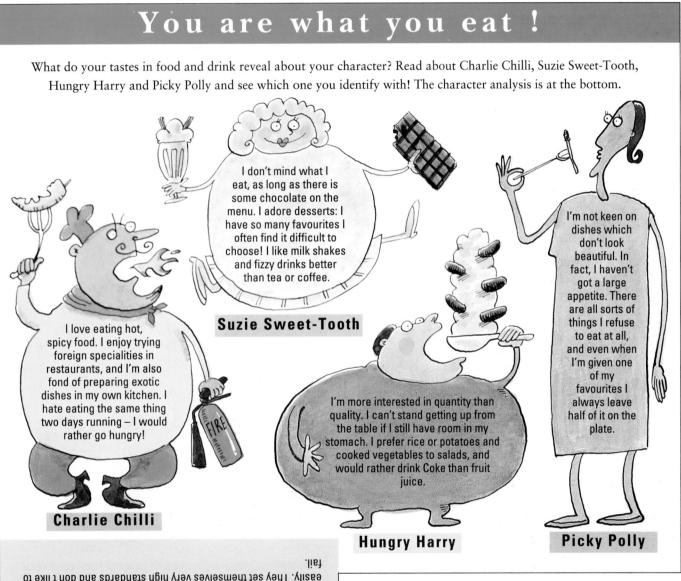

You are what you eat !

What do your tastes in food and drink reveal about your character? Read about Charlie Chilli, Suzie Sweet-Tooth, Hungry Harry and Picky Polly and see which one you identify with! The character analysis is at the bottom.

Suzie Sweet-Tooth
I don't mind what I eat, as long as there is some chocolate on the menu. I adore desserts: I have so many favourites I often find it difficult to choose! I like milk shakes and fizzy drinks better than tea or coffee.

Charlie Chilli
I love eating hot, spicy food. I enjoy trying foreign specialities in restaurants, and I'm also fond of preparing exotic dishes in my own kitchen. I hate eating the same thing two days running – I would rather go hungry!

Hungry Harry
I'm more interested in quantity than quality. I can't stand getting up from the table if I still have room in my stomach. I prefer rice or potatoes and cooked vegetables to salads, and would rather drink Coke than fruit juice.

Picky Polly
I'm not keen on dishes which don't look beautiful. In fact, I haven't got a large appetite. There are all sorts of things I refuse to eat at all, and even when I'm given one of my favourites I always leave half of it on the plate.

CHARACTER ANALYSIS
Chilli eaters are brave and adventurous; they like to shock, but they get bored and restless very easily.
Sweet eaters are easy-going and sociable but they lack confidence. They are kind and sympathetic but not always reliable.
Hungry eaters are hard-working and generous; they aren't ambitious and hate changes of any sort. They worry about the future.
Picky eaters are artistic and sensitive but they lose their tempers easily. They set themselves very high standards and don't like to fail.

3 *What is your favourite in each of the following categories? And what do you like least? Use the expressions you underlined above.*

ice cream flavour   party drink
pizza topping   sandwich filling
chocolate centre   breakfast dish
appetiser   pasta/noodle dish

How similar are your tastes to other people's?

Vocabulary *Taste*

1 *How would you describe the taste of:*

– honey?
– sea water?
– black coffee without sugar?
– lemon?
– beer?
– unripe fruit?

2 *Here are other words used to describe taste. Can you think of an example of a food or drink for each?*

aromatic   fresh   fruity   hot   nutty   rich
sharp   spicy   strong

Listening 📼 *The perfect blend of coffee*

1 *You are going to listen to a coffee-taster talking about:*

● a typical coffee-tasting session
● the basic kinds of coffee

Prepare some questions which you would like to hear him cover in his talk.

2 *Listen once to the whole talk. Which of your questions did the coffee-taster answer?*

3 *Listen again to the talk, section by section. Look at each exercise before you listen.*

Section 1

Mark whether each statement is True or False.

		True	False
1	The tasters must swallow the coffee they are tasting.	☐	☐
2	The tasters need to know where the coffee they are tasting comes from.	☐	☐
3	The tasters shouldn't know the name of the supplier.	☐	☐
4	The tasters compare the coffee they are tasting with a standard.	☐	☐
5	The coffees the tasters select taste exactly the same as the standard.	☐	☐
6	One way of tasting coffee more easily is to draw air into the mouth with the coffee.	☐	☐

Section 2

1 Match the description of the coffee bush to its name.

   a 'much finer, much more aromatic'   **i** Arabica
   b 'relatively coarse, woody, earthy'   **ii** Robusta

2 Note the main adjectives the taster uses to describe the coffee from:

   a Kenya
   b Colombia
   c Costa Rica
   d India

4 *Would you make a good coffee-taster? Why (not)? What other drink, or food, would you like to be a taster for?*

Grammar *Adverbs*

 1 Most adverbs are formed by adding '-ly' to an adjective:

useful → *usefully*   *slow* → *slowly*

Note these spelling changes:
-le becomes *-ly*   *terrible* → *terribly*
-y becomes *-ily*   *easy* → *easily*
-ic becomes *-ically*   *tragic* → *tragically*

A few common adverbs have the same form as adjectives:
early   far   fast   hard   late   next

It was a hard decision to make.
You must work hard.

The adverb related to the adjective 'good' is 'well':
He's a good cook.   *He cooks well.*

2 Two common types of adverb are:

1 ADVERBS OF MANNER

The coffees will turn slowly.
We choose the standard carefully.
These tell us something extra about verbs (as if in answer to 'How?').

2 ADVERBS OF DEGREE

Kenya coffee tends to be quite *acid.*
That standard we select very *carefully.*
These tell us something extra about adjectives or adverbs (as if in answer to 'How much?').

Some adverbs of degree strengthen an adjective or adverb:
We select it extremely *carefully.*
Others make an adjective or adverb less strong:
It just makes it a little *easier to register.*

What is the effect of these adverbs of degree, to strengthen or to make less strong?
Much *finer*, much *more aromatic.*
It's fairly *acid.*

And what is the effect of these?
absolutely   quite   rather   really   slightly

 3 Make an adverb of manner from the adjective in brackets and put it in a suitable place in the sentence.

1 She answered three of the four questions. (successful)
2 When he arrived, the children were playing together. (happy)
3 The kettle switches itself off after it has boiled. (automatic)
4 She picked up her pet rabbit. (gentle)
5 They walked home and arrived in time for supper. (fast)
6 Please cook that meat. (good)

4 Choose the correct adverb of degree to complete this extract from a letter.

I'm (**1** fairly / really) sorry you couldn't come to the picnic on Saturday. The weather was (**2** much / rather) cold but we kept (**3** a little / very) warm thanks to Sofia's (**4** absolutely / extremely) delicious home-made soup. The picnic basket was (**5** completely / quite) heavy on the way there, but it was (**6** fairly / much) lighter when we carried it home! As it was cold and the beach was deserted, we played games (**7** slightly / very) energetically – and (**8** much / quite) more noisily than usual!

3 Food for thought

Reading *Different angles*

Look quickly at the following texts to find the answers to these questions. You don't have to read every word to do this.

1 **IDENTIFYING TOPIC**
What common topic do these texts have? What is the particular topic of each text?

2 **IDENTIFYING PURPOSE**
The purpose of each text is to inform, but to inform in order to do which of these?

- persuade
- educate
- shock
- entertain
- a combination of these

EXAMPLE: The purpose of Text A is to educate, possibly also to entertain (because people enjoy reading statistics like these) and possibly also to shock (because people in these countries eat many more calories than they actually need).

3 **IDENTIFYING SOURCE**
Where is each text from?

- a newspaper article
- a specialist magazine
- a campaign leaflet

4 **REACTING**
How do you react to each of these texts? Which ones:

- tell you something new?
- surprise you?
- shock you?
- amuse you?
- irritate you?
- make you want to do something?

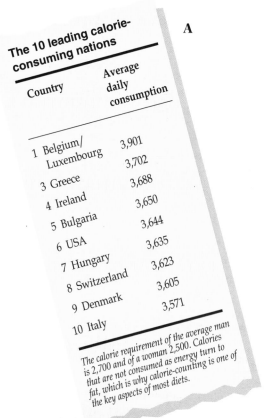

A

The 10 leading calorie-consuming nations

Country	Average daily consumption
1 Belgium/ Luxembourg	3,901
	3,702
3 Greece	3,688
4 Ireland	3,650
5 Bulgaria	3,644
6 USA	3,635
7 Hungary	3,623
8 Switzerland	3,605
9 Denmark	3,571
10 Italy	

The calorie requirement of the average man is 2,700 and of a woman 2,500. Calories that are not consumed as energy turn to fat, which is why calorie-counting is one of the key aspects of most diets.

B

Turkey - A Cruel Tradition

If you are planning your Christmas dinner why not have a change this year – choose not to buy turkey. Unless you are buying free range your turkey will have grown up in a dark, smelly, overcrowded shed, having to fight for food, water and living space. Most turkeys spend the last 6 minutes of their lives hanging upside-down on the way to the automatic knife.

If you would rather celebrate Christmas without a blood-bath choose another meal. An alternative cruelty-free recipe is on the reverse of this leaflet. BE COMPASSIONATE THIS CHRISTMAS – CHOOSE ANOTHER MEAL – DON'T BUY TURKEY.

C

Food for thought

Each year 40 million people die from hunger and hunger-related diseases. This is the equivalent of more than 300 jumbo jet crashes a day with no survivors, with children as almost half the passengers.

D **LIFE AFTER MEAT**

15-year-old Tom Stanmore became vegetarian over a year ago.

Tom's sudden conversion took his family by surprise. While she'd been aware of his views on hunting and vivisection, his mother had usually cooked a roast lunch on Sundays which Tom had always put away with gusto. His vegetarianism called for changes in the Stanmores' eating habits.

'Right from the beginning my parents accepted my views, even though I turned vegetarian so suddenly. Now my mother makes a lot more vegetarian meals than she used to, and my father has given up red meat – I've persuaded him it isn't very healthy.'

E

FAST FOOD is a fact of life

The big three fast food giants – McDonald's, Kentucky Fried Chicken and Wimpy – sell more than £500 million of food a year in Britain.

But junk food junkies risk saturating their systems with fat and running short of essential fibre and vitamins if they fail to heed the warnings published by nutritionist Dr Tim Lobstein.

Nearly two ounces of fat in a halfpounder burger and up to 12 teaspoons of sugar in a large cola are just two of the facts revealed by the author in Fast Food Facts published today by the London Food Commission.

The author argues that many takeaways are a poor source of essential nutrients.

A double-burger, fries and milkshake provide half the day's total calorie needs for an average woman, but just 18 per cent of the vitamin A needed, 26 per cent of the vitamin C and 31 per cent of the iron.

Speaking *Agreeing and disagreeing (1)*

1 *When we read or hear another person's opinion we can agree or disagree, strongly or not so strongly. Look at these expressions for agreeing and disagreeing. Which are the strongest? Which disagreement expressions are more polite?*

Agree	*Disagree*
I quite agree.	I don't agree at all.
I agree.	I see what you mean, but ...
That's absolutely true.	You must be joking!
That's right.	That's a good point, but ...
I couldn't agree more.	I'm not sure about that.

2 *Here are some things people said when they read Texts A–F. Tell a partner whether you agree or disagree with each opinion, using the expressions in* **1** *.*

a 'Western society is very wasteful: food which is thrown away, or given to pet animals, could save hundreds of dying children.'

b 'There have always been starving people and there always will be, so there's not much point in trying to do anything about it.'

c 'When you eat meat, it is crazy to think about whether the animal had a happy life, or whether it was killed humanely.'

d 'Everybody who eats in a hamburger restaurant should demand to know exactly what the hamburgers contain.'

e 'Junk food eaters are more likely to put on weight than vegetarians.'

f 'Children can't be forced to eat things they don't like.'

Which opinion do you agree with most strongly?
Which opinion do you disagree with most strongly?

F

WHAT CHILDREN ATE FOR BREAKFAST

University of Nottingham researchers have found large numbers of schoolchildren going without breakfast before attending school.

Staff in the faculty of Agriculture and Food Sciences surveyed nearly 500 secondary schoolchildren and asked them what they had eaten for breakfast.

The table shows the sort of breakfast the children reported. High proportions – including more than a quarter of the older girls – said they had eaten nothing at all. The proportion eating no breakfast tended to be higher among children in urban schools.

Per cent of each group of children (some ate more than one type of breakfast)

	Toast	Cereal	Cooked meal	Other food	Nothing
Boys 11–13	31	63	4	0	12
Girls 11–13	26	59	6	1	21
Boys 14–16	31	71	12	2	6
Girls 14–16	29	46	2	4	25

Grammar *Phrasal verbs*

1 *A phrasal verb is a combination of a verb and an adverb or preposition (or both an adverb and a preposition) which together have a single meaning.*

The meanings of some phrasal verbs can be understood by adding together the meanings of the separate parts:

Junk food eaters are more likely to put on *weight than vegetarians.*

But others have meanings which are quite different from the individual parts:

My father won't put up with *bad table manners.*

Match the phrasal verbs in **A** with the correct meanings in **B**:

A	B
put off	connect (by phone)
put away	tolerate
put out	place something tidily in its proper place
put through	apply for
put aside	raise
put up	extinguish (a fire)
put in for	postpone
put up with	reserve

2 *The position of the object of a phrasal verb depends on what kind of phrasal verb it is. Phrasal verbs can be divided into three kinds:*

1 INTRANSITIVE PHRASAL VERBS

These verbs do not have an object, so there is no word order problem.
The milk has gone off.

2 SEPARABLE PHRASAL VERBS

These are made up of verb + adverb. A noun object may come either *before* or *after* the adverb:

Junk food eaters put on *weight.*

Junk food eaters put *weight* on.

But when the object is a *pronoun*, it comes *before* the adverb:
Junk food eaters put *it* on.

3 INSEPARABLE PHRASAL VERBS

These are made up of verb + preposition, or verb + adverb + preposition. Both noun and pronoun objects come *after* the preposition:
She asked for *a vegetarian dish.*
She asked for *it.*
My father won't put up with *bad table manners.*
My father won't put up with *them.*

3 *Fill each of the gaps with the correct form of one of the phrasal verbs in the box.*

clear up	cut up	drink up	wipe up
cut off	go off		
feel like	throw away		
cut down on	run out of		

1 We've .... lemons. Could you go and buy some more?
2 That cheese looks delicious. Can you .... a small piece for me too?
3 Cream .... quickly even when it's kept in the fridge.
4 She's trying to .... the number of cups of coffee she drinks every day.
5 .... your milk. You'll be late for school.
6 That was a great party but I'm too tired to .... now. I'll do it in the morning.
7 It's so hot I .... a really long cool drink.

Where should the words in brackets come in these sentences?

8 If you spill anything, make sure you .... (it) immediately.
9 The dog will eat the meat bones. Don't .... (them).
10 I'm using these apples in the fruit salad. Can you .... (them) for me?

4

Exam skill *Gap-filling*

The first exercise in Paper 3 is a passage with 20 gaps. You have to fill each gap with one word. Follow these steps to help you do this well.

1 Read the passage through a couple of times, until you have 'seen the whole picture'. Give the passage a title which summarises the content.

In Medieval Europe, spices from the Far East like cloves and nutmeg were literally worth their weight in gold. Take, for example, Magellan's trip (**1**) .... the world (**2**) .... the sixteenth century. His trip (**3**) .... for three years and only a (**4**) .... people survived the dangers of the expedition. But they came home with just over one ton (**5**) .... cloves. These cloves paid (**6**) .... the Spanish king for his huge investment (**7**) .... the expedition and made (**8**) .... eighteen survivors rich for life.

Spices (**9**) .... highly valued. (**10**) .... made badly preserved meat taste better. People also used them (**11**) .... make medicines and magic drinks. At that time these were (**12**) .... to be able to cure anything (**13**) .... a serious disease to a lover's heartache.

The islands (**14**) .... the spices grew are hardly visible (**15**) .... any world map. But they attracted adventurers from all over Europe (**16**) .... hoped to make (**17**) .... fortunes. In this way men who were mainly (**18**) .... in money became known (**19**) .... discoverers of a new world. That is (**20**) .... Europeans call the sixteenth century the Age of Discovery.

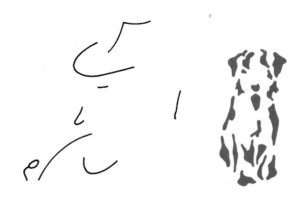

2 Begin filling in the gaps. Do the easy ones first – don't be afraid to move backwards and forwards through the passage.

3 Work at the difficult gaps. Think about the grammar and the meaning of the missing word.

EXAMPLE:

His trip (**3**) .... for three years and only a (**4**) .... people survived the dangers of the expedition.

(3) You need a verb after 'His trip'. It is followed by 'for three years', so it must be something to do with time. 'For' suggests duration. What about 'lasted', 'spent' or 'took'? Which is right? Why?

(4) What sort of word would fit grammatically before 'people'? What about 'couple', 'few' or 'some'? Which is right? Why?

4 Check your ideas. When you have filled in a gap, read the sentence through and ask yourself:
- Does it make sense?
- Does it sound like good, correct English?

Remember
1 Only ONE word per gap. Never put in two, even if they make sense.
2 If you have no idea what to put, guess. You don't lose marks for a wrong answer – and you might just be right!

Test exercises

1 *Complete this passage. Use only **one** word in each gap.*

Isabella Beeton, who (**1**) .... born in London in 1836, is the most famous British woman cookery writer. She was well educated and finished (**2**) .... education in Heidelberg, (**3**) .... she learnt French and German. In 1856 she married Sam Beeton, an enterprising young publisher, and the following year (**4**) .... contributing a column on various household matters to his 'The Englishwoman's Domestic Magazine'. (**5**) .... was the first of the cheap women's magazines. It pioneered the problem page and medical columns, and introduced dress-making patterns (**6**) .... France to British readers. (**7**) .... she was only 23 she edited 'Beeton's Book of Household Management'. This was first (**8**) .... as a serial in 30 monthly parts, and (**9**) .... in book form in 1861. It was an immense work, containing more (**10**) .... 3,000 recipes as well (**11**) .... advice on instructing servants, nursing, legal matters, good manners and bringing (**12**) .... babies. Many of the recipes (**13**) .... contributed by the readers of 'The Englishwoman's Domestic Magazine' and others were simply taken (**14**) .... previous cookery writers. The chapters on specialist topics were (**15**) .... anonymously by a doctor, a lawyer and (**16**) .... experts. But even (**17**) .... Mrs Beeton herself was not (**18**) .... creative cook, the editing work that she did on the book is a great achievement for (**19**) .... so young. She died (**20**) .... the age of 28 after the birth of her fourth son.

Mrs Isabella Beeton

2 *Complete each sentence with a word or phrase connected with **food**.*

EXAMPLE: We have soup as a starter and then chicken pie or fish for the
.*main course*. .

1 We can't cook at the moment. We're still waiting for a new
.... to be delivered.
2 I made this pudding using a .... I found in an old cookery book.
3 We've .... sugar again. Can you borrow some from Mrs Jones next door?
4 If you want a .... between meals, an apple is better for you than a bar of chocolate.
5 Steak and kidney pie is a famous British ....

3 *Choose the word or phrase (A–D) which best completes each sentence.*

1 If the coffee is still too .... put some more sugar in it.

A bitter   B hot   C sour   D sweet

2 He likes to .... butter thickly over his bread.

A slice   B spread   C stir   D swallow

3 Traditional English cooking does not use many spices to .... a dish.

A cook   B eat   C flavour   D taste

4 There was no meat left in the fridge, so we had to .... and eat only vegetables.

A feel like   B go without   C throw away   D try out

5 The girls in this class are as keen .... metalwork as the boys.

A at   B for   C in   D on

6 He's .... his driving test next week.

A making   B passing   C revising   D taking

7 Spoken English is usually less .... than written English.

A fluent   B foreign   C formal   D friendly

8 If you come across a new English word written down, you can't always be sure how to .... it.

A declare   B pronounce   C spell   D write

9 The child carefully carried the bowl of water across the room without .... a drop.

A dripping   B falling   C pouring   D spilling

10 I left my briefcase on the train, but I found it in the railway Lost .... department.

A Belongings   B Goods   C Possessions   D Property

11 She often .... him off helping in the house while he was studying for his exam.

A cut   B gave   C let   D went

12 They're fond .... gardening and grow a wide variety of plants and flowers.

A for   B in   C of   D with

13 I can't stand .... on the underground when it is busy.

A travel   B travelling   C to travel   D to travelling

14 We had .... perfect day sailing round the island.

A an absolutely   B an extremely   C a fairly   D a very

15 He always sees that the children .... up their toys before they go to bed.

A clear   B give   C wash   D wipe

3 UNIT THREE
People

1 Judging by appearances

Speaking *Clothes*

1 What clothes do you wear when you:

1 go to work or school?
2 spend a lazy day at home?
3 go out in the evening?
4 play your favourite sport?
5 have a family celebration?
6 do physical work (e.g. cleaning, decorating, gardening)?

Use the words in the box to help you, and give some examples.

casual	comfortable	elegant	formal	old
scruffy	smart	trendy		

2 What sort of clothes do you like best? What sort do you like least?

30

Listening 🔊 *Come properly dressed*

1 **Listen to this conversation between Julia and her brother Philip.**

1 What are they talking about?
2 What do you learn about their:
   a characters?
   b age?
   c interests?

2 **Listen again and mark if each statement is True or False.**

	True	False
1 Philip is excited about going to the party.	☐	☐
2 Julia tells Philip to stop reading and get dressed for the party.	☐	☐
3 Julia wants Philip to wear something nice for the party.	☐	☐
4 Julia has decided to wear her blue dress.	☐	☐
5 Julia wants to borrow Philip's belt.	☐	☐
6 Philip would prefer Julia not to mention Helen's name.	☐	☐
7 Julia says they are going to leave at seven o'clock.	☐	☐

3 **Do you think Julia is going to enjoy the party? What about Philip?**

Grammar *Conditional sentences (1)*

1 **When you want to talk about a possible situation and its result, you use a conditional sentence:**

If people invite you to a party, they expect you to come properly dressed.
If I wear the green dress, it'll go with my beautiful new belt.

In this kind of conditional sentence there is a real possibility that what is described will happen. There are two main types:

1

Conditional clause	Main clause
If + present simple	present simple

You use this type of conditional sentence to talk about something that is always true. It is like a law. In this type of condition 'if' has a similar meaning to 'when':
If people invite you to a party, they expect you to come properly dressed.
If you heat ice, it melts.

2

Conditional clause	Main clause
If + present simple	will / 'll / won't + infinitive

You use this type of conditional sentence to talk about a probable future result:
If I wear the green dress, it'll go with my beautiful new belt.
If you don't study, you won't pass the exam.

2 **In these conditional sentences we can usually use 'unless' instead of 'if ... not':**

Unless you study, you won't pass the exam.
Unless you get out of those jeans and put some decent clothes on, you won't be going at all. (= If you don't get out of those jeans ...)

3 **The examples above show two patterns for this kind of condition. But other combinations of verb forms and modal verbs are possible. Here are some of them:**

If you get the chance, visit Delphi.
If you have finished, you may go.
If you're feeling ill, you ought to see a doctor.
If she can do that, she can do anything.
If you're not nervous, why is your hand shaking?

4 **Put the verbs in brackets in the correct form.**

1 I always (get) bad-tempered if my shoes (be) uncomfortable.
2 If you (borrow) my jacket, what I (wear)?
3 She (not be able to) wear her new belt if she (wear) the blue dress.
4 Unless he (change) his clothes, he (have to) stay at home.
5 If I (finish) knitting this sweater, you (take) it on holiday with you.
6 If you (want) to see the latest fashions, (buy) 'Teen Dream Weekly'!

Pronunciation 🔲 *Emphasising words*

When people want to emphasise a word in a sentence, they say that word more loudly and also use a higher pitch (i.e. they move their voice up).

1 *Listen to these sentences. Underline the word(s) the speaker wants to emphasise.*

1 If I wear the green one, it'll go with my beautiful new belt.
2 But if I wear the blue one, it'll go with my new Manyuki shoes.

3 The green one is smarter, but I prefer the blue one.
4 And shall I wear shoes or sandals?

2 *Which words do you think should be emphasised here? Underline them.*

1 I said skirt, not shirt.
2 This coat or that one?
3 Are you going to wear jeans or trousers?
4 You should wear a white shirt and a black tie.

Practise saying the sentences. Check your pronunciation against the examples on the tape.

Vocabulary *Describing people's appearance*

1 *Put these words used to describe age in chronological order.*

elderly	teenage	youngish	retired
middle-aged	in her early thirties		
in his teens	in their mid-twenties		

2 *Which of these words used to describe body size and shape have:*

– a positive meaning?
– a neutral meaning?
– a negative meaning?

broad-shouldered
fat
large
of medium height
overweight
short
skinny
slim
tall
thin
well-built

3 *Which of the adjectives can go with these nouns? (Note that many can go with more than one.)*

blond(e)	curly	dark
fair	large	long
pale	round	straight

complexion	eyes	face
hair	mouth	nose

Can you add any more adjectives to your list for each noun?

4 *Which of these words would you use to describe the people in the photo? Can you say why?*

beautifully-dressed	good-looking	plain
pretty	strange-looking	striking
unattractive	unusual	

2 Quite a character

Writing *First ideas*

1 Write a few sentences describing a person from your childhood who you remember well.

2 Look at the sentences you have written. What kind of information about the person do they contain? How many of these things do they describe?

– RELATIONSHIP to you
– OCCUPATION
– APPEARANCE: age, attractiveness, figure, complexion, hair, eyes, face, nose, other special facial features (e.g. moustache, glasses)
– CLOTHES: person's usual style
– BEHAVIOUR: voice, smile, walk, gestures
– CHARACTER: positive and negative aspects

Choose some interesting aspects you left out of your description, and make some notes. You will have a chance to write up the notes later.

Reading *Mr McElroy*

1 This description of Mr McElroy comes from an account by Maya Angelou of her childhood in the 1930s in Arkansas, USA. Read it to see how much information the writer gives us about Mr McElroy's:

– relationship to her
– occupation
– appearance
– clothes
– behaviour
– character

2 Which two statements best describe the writer's technique in giving a picture of Mr McElroy?

a She gives detailed information about the man's appearance.

b She describes only a few aspects of the man's appearance, choosing things which make him different from other people.

c She describes him objectively.

d She includes both her childhood and adult feelings about the man.

Mr McElroy, who lived in the big rambling house next to our Store, was very tall and broad, and although the years had eaten away the flesh from his shoulders, they had not, at the time of my knowing him, gotten to his high stomach, or his hands or feet.

He was the only Negro I knew, except for the school principal and the visiting teachers, who wore matching pants and jackets. When I learned that men's clothes were sold like that and called suits, I remember thinking that somebody had been very bright, for it made them look less manly, less threatening and a little more like women.

Mr McElroy never laughed, and seldom smiled, and to his credit was the fact that he liked to talk to poor lame Uncle Willie. He never went to church, which my brother Bailey and I thought also proved he was a very courageous person.

I watched him with the excitement of expecting him to do anything at any time. I never tired of this, or became disappointed or disenchanted with him, although from the perch of age, I see him now as a very simple and uninteresting man who sold patent medicine and tonics to the less sophisticated people in villages surrounding the metropolis of Stamps.

One greeting a day was all that could be expected from Mr McElroy. After his "Good morning, child," or "Good afternoon, child," he never said a word, even if I met him again on the road in front of his house or down by the well, or ran into him behind the house escaping in a game of hide-and-seek.

He remained a mystery in my childhood. A man who owned his land and the big many-windowed house with a porch that clung to its sides all around the house. An independent Black man. A near anachronism in Stamps.

Grammar *Relative clauses*

1   *A relative clause adds information about one of the nouns in the main clause. The relative clause comes immediately after the noun it relates to:*

Mr McElroy, who lived in the big rambling house next to our Store, *was very tall and broad.*
His big many-windowed house had a porch that clung to its sides.

2   *A relative pronoun goes at the beginning of a relative clause.*

WHO, WHOM
'Who' and 'whom' are used for people. 'Whom' is only used when the relative pronoun is the object of the relative clause; nowadays in informal English it is usually replaced by 'who' or 'that':
He was a simple man who sold patent medicine.
The lawyer whom you requested is unavailable.

WHICH
'Which' is used for things:
I enjoyed the book which you lent me.

THAT
'That' may often be used instead of 'who', 'whom' or 'which':
I enjoyed the book that you lent me.
The lawyer that you requested is unavailable.

WHOSE
You use 'whose' in a relative clause to show who something belongs to. It may be used for people or things:
Mr McElroy, whose garden I enjoyed playing in, hardly ever spoke to me.
That's the house whose garden is open to the public.

3   *The relative pronoun may be the subject or the object of the relative clause.*
Is 'who' the subject or the object in these sentences?

Mr McElroy was a neighbour who Maya enjoyed watching.
He was a simple man who sold patent medicine.

When the relative pronoun is the *object* of the clause it may be left out:
Mr McElroy was a neighbour Maya enjoyed watching.

4   *There are two main types of relative clause:*

1 DEFINING RELATIVE CLAUSE
The information in a defining relative clause is *essential* to the meaning of the main clause. If the defining relative clause is taken away, the meaning of the main clause is not clear:
He was the only Negro I knew who wore matching pants and jackets.

In defining relative clauses:
– you may leave out the relative pronoun if it is the object of the relative clause.
– you should not use commas to separate the relative clause from the rest of the sentence.

2 NON-DEFINING RELATIVE CLAUSE
The information in a non-defining relative clause is *extra*. If the non-defining relative clause is taken away, the meaning of the main clause is still clear:

Mr McElroy, who lived in the big rambling house next to our Store, was very tall and broad.

In non-defining relative clauses:
– you must not leave out the relative pronoun, even if it is the object of the clause.
– you must not use the relative pronoun 'that'.
– you must use a comma or commas to separate the clause from the rest of the sentence.

5   *Rewrite the following sentences as one sentence, using relative clauses, and making any other necessary changes.*

EXAMPLE: My aunt was an adult. She impressed me a lot as a child.
My aunt was an adult who impressed me a lot as a child.

1 She had a short plump figure. Her figure made it difficult to find attractive clothes.
2 In spite of this, she had a large wardrobe. I was allowed to help her select something colourful from her wardrobe. She would brighten up the dark day with something colourful.
3 She had two habits. These two habits fascinated me and worried my mother.
4 Hanging from her mouth she kept a lighted cigarette. Her mouth was generously painted bright red or orange. The cigarette was never removed to embrace a child or to talk.
5 She was a great talker. Her favourite subject was the lives and loves of friends, relatives and neighbours.
6 She recounted scandals to my mother. My mother tried to change the subject if she saw me listening.

Writing *Description of a person*

Look back at what you wrote in First ideas. Expand those sentences into a composition with four paragraphs. Write a full and interesting description of a person you knew when you were a child.

Paragraph 1: Introduction. Briefly describe where or how you knew the person.
Paragraph 2 and 3: Select some of your impressions, and organise them in two paragraphs.
Paragraph 4: Conclusion. Summarise what knowing this person meant to you.

3 Heroes and heroines

Listening 🔊 *Who am I?*

Joan of Arc

Gandhi

Gary Lineker

Elizabeth I

Madonna

Superman

Monica Seles

Cleopatra

Julius Caesar

1 *Look at the faces. Which ones do you know? Why are they famous?*

2 *Listen to this extract from a television game show. What information do you find out about the mystery personality? Tick (✓) the boxes.*

The mystery personality:	Yes	No
female	☐	☐
contemporary	☐	☐
fought against his/her country	☐	☐
had an unexciting love life	☐	☐
married a close relative	☐	☐
died a natural death	☐	☐
liked unconventional introductions	☐	☐

3 *Cleopatra's story has been retold in books, plays and films. Why do you think this is?*

Grammar *Making deductions*

1 *'Must' may indicate either obligation, or a deduction/certainty. Which of these two meanings does 'must' have in each of these sentences?*

You must give me your final answer before the three-minute bell rings.
It must be a political figure of some sort.
It must be a woman – men don't marry their brothers.
It must be Cleopatra.

OBLIGATION
The negative is 'mustn't' and the past is 'had to':
The chairman mustn't reveal the answer until the celebrity guests have tried to work it out.
Last week he had to give them the answer because they couldn't guess it.

DEDUCTION/CERTAINTY
The negative is 'can't' and the past is 'must have' + past participle:
I'm sure it's a political figure. So it can't be Madonna or Monica Seles.
It can't be Elizabeth I, because she never married.
Cleopatra must have ruled her country bravely; and she can't have been afraid of dying.

2 *Rewrite these sentences using 'must' or 'can't'.*

1 I'm sure Hillary Clinton works hard.
2 I'm certain Boris Becker is feeling disappointed after losing the match.
3 I don't think Madonna is shy.
4 I'm sure Superman is admired by all children.
5 I'm sure Neil Armstrong liked being famous.
6 I'm certain Columbus didn't get seasick.
7 I'm sure Cleopatra wasn't scared of snakes.
8 I'm certain Romeo was exaggerating about dying of love.

Reading *A modern heroine?*

1 *Read this paragraph and make deductions to answer the questions which follow.*

Just as she was thinking she would have to stop soon to rest and eat, she noticed a slight thinning out of the trees and a small increase of light and realised she must be coming to a clearing. There, she thought, she
5 would take a break, out in the reassuring openness. As she pushed through the last of the vines and stared into the blinding light, she saw an Indian village. In the centre of the encampment stood a long hut. There were other, smaller huts dotted about. A fire smoked
10 in the middle of the clearing, which was about 200 metres wide. But there was no one there. She stood in the shadows of the jungle, knowing that she must have been trailed for many miles by the Indians, moving like ghosts through their own underworld, and that
15 now as she stood there, feeling alone, she must be watched by many eyes.

1 Where does the passage come from?
2 Where does the action take place?
3 Why is 'she' there?
Now read on.

And, across the clearing, on the other fringe of forest, there was the tree, tall and spindly, reaching for the light, dark-leaved and covered with the purple
20 flowers she was looking for. She almost laughed as she stood there, expecting an arrow to hit her, or a body holding a knife to hurl itself at her at any moment. She took a few deep breaths and walked into the centre of the clearing, dropped her pack near the fire, knelt
25 down, unbuckled it and began to take out the gifts. Her left arm suddenly jumped. She looked down slowly at the arm. An arrow, just a stick of wood, jutted from the back of the arm, a little above the elbow. She waited, expecting more arrows to follow,
30 or a crowd to come out of the forest behind her. She said to herself, "Oh, God. Don't let me die here, now." She saw her children's faces clearly, even Fran's grin and the missing top front tooth. Then, because nothing happened, she twisted her right arm, set her
35 teeth and pulled. The arrow eased slowly out through the flesh. A gush of blood stained her jacket. She thought the arrow could be poisoned. That would be why no one had emerged and no further arrows had been fired. They would stay under cover, watching her
40 until she dropped.

4 Do you want to change any of your previous answers?
5 Why is she carrying gifts, and why does she take them out?

Now read on.

Then the noise began. It was a gentle clatter, which grew slowly louder. It took her some time to work out what it was. Slowly, she looked up and around. The helicopter came low across the clearing
45 and landed not far from the forest edge. The rotation of the propellers stopped. The noise died away. She looked at the purple flowers swinging on the branches of the tree opposite her. Then, slowly, she stood up, clutching the bleeding wound in her arm with her
50 right hand and walked towards the helicopter. She was not curious as to who was in the helicopter, or why. She merely saw it as safety. An elderly man with a shock of white hair stepped out of the door. He gave her an unfriendly stare and shouted back, "Martin –
55 chuck the stuff out quickly!" He said to Hannie, "Are you alone?" She nodded.

6 Why is the helicopter there?
7 Do Hannie and the elderly man know each other?

Answer these questions about all three paragraphs.
8 What deductions can you make about Hannie's character?
9 Is she a heroine?

2 *What do these words in the passage refer to?*

1 There (1.4)   **4** itself (1.22)   **7** They (1.39)
2 which (1.10)   **5** it (1.25)   **8** it (1.52)
3 their (1.14)   **6** That (1.37)   **9** He (1.55)

3 *Answer these questions on the passage by choosing the best alternative (A–D).*

1 When Hannie entered the clearing she was
   A completely alone.
   B without a companion.
   C surrounded by friends.
   D part of a group.

2 She saw her children's faces clearly because
   A she was looking at a photograph.
   B she was having a dream.
   C she was missing them.
   D she thought she was going to die.

3 She thought the Indians did not fire again because
   A they did not want to kill her.
   B they wanted to remain hidden.
   C they knew she would die soon.
   D they were frightened of the helicopter.

4 How did the elderly man greet Hannie?
   A with displeasure
   B with relief
   C with curiosity
   D with excitement

Speaking *My hero*

> A hero does dangerous things which other people aren't brave enough to attempt.

> My idea of a hero is someone who protects the poor and the weak.

> A hero is a person in the news doing exciting and glamorous things.

1 *Which definition do you agree with most? Or do you think a hero/heroine has other kinds of characteristics?*

2 *Choose candidates for these titles:*

- Contemporary world hero
- Contemporary world villain
- Greatest hero in my country's history
- Worst villain in my country's history
- Greatest fictional hero
- My personal hero

"Excuse me, that's where I sit."

4

Exam skill *Directed writing*

The final question in Paper 3, Use of English, is a directed writing exercise. You are given some information in note form (e.g. advertisement, diary, message, programme), or in a visual form (e.g. map, chart, diagram, graph, illustration), or in a combination of these. Your task is to use this information to solve a 'problem', and finish writing some paragraphs which have been started for you. There is not a 'right' answer to the problem, but you should be able to give good reasons for the solution you have chosen.

Your answer should:
- be as long as the instructions indicate (usually about three paragraphs with 50 to 60 words in each paragraph).
- continue logically and grammatically from the sentence (or part of a sentence) which is given to you.
- be well organised, with your ideas and reasons clearly linked (see *Useful language* below).
- be in your own words as far as possible, not just a copy of the words in the notes.

EXAMPLE QUESTION

Every year a famous person comes to your school to make a speech and to give out certificates and prizes to successful students. The director of the school has asked you to decide which of these people should be invited this year. Complete the paragraphs on page 39, giving reasons for your choices.

Useful language

because
since   } *for giving reasons*
as

Also,
In addition,   } *for linking a list of reasons*
As well as that,

must/can't – *for making deductions*
e.g. He must have some exciting stories to tell.

Irina Ratushinskaya

Born 1954 in Odessa, Soviet Union
Scientist and poet
Married to human rights activist, Igor Geraschenko
Sentenced to 7 years hard labour for her poetry
Spent 3 years in prison camp
Now living with her husband in London

Eve Adam

Born in London in 1956 into Greek Cypriot family
Performs Anglo-Greek cabaret act with a partner
Won awards for her act
Specialises in music and comedy
Stage name: Donna and Kebab

Sir Ranulph Twistleton Wykeham Fiennes

Born 1944
Explorer
Walked across Antarctica without help
Suffered severe frostbite many times

Mauro Carraro

Born 1960
Photographer
Photographs the rich and famous in embarrassing situations
Once made £70,000 for one photo of Prince Charles
Has been beaten up many times

I think the students at my school will be most interested in listening to ....

....

....

....

....

My second choice is ....

....

....

....

....

....

....

The students will probably **not** want to listen to ....

....

....

....

....

....

Test exercises

1 *Catherine is talking to an archaeologist, Dr Blake, about some ancient jewellery he has recently dug up. Complete their conversation.*

CATHERINE: Tell me about this object. It's very decorative, but (1) ....

.... ?

DR BLAKE: Not really. It was just a personal ornament. Its only function was to show the status of the wearer, a bit like diamonds show status today.

CATHERINE: What (2) .... ?

DR BLAKE: Gold, and these beautiful red stones are garnets.

CATHERINE: How (3) .... ?

DR BLAKE: Like a brooch, probably pinned on the shoulder.

CATHERINE: It looks very modern. Could you tell me when (4) .... ?

DR BLAKE: Probably at the end of the seventh century.

CATHERINE: Where (5) .... ?

DR BLAKE: In a woman's grave in south-east England.

CATHERINE: So that woman must have owned the brooch. What sort (6) ....

.... ?

DR BLAKE: Well, it can't have been an uncomfortable one, because she must have been quite wealthy. I'll know more about her life when I've dug up more of the site.

CATHERINE: The brooch doesn't look as if it's been buried in the earth for hundreds of years. Was (7) .... ?

DR BLAKE: No, not at all. We've had to do a lot of cleaning and restoration work on it.

CATHERINE: It's certainly a beautiful piece. I'd love to wear it! Thank you for showing it to me.

2 *Complete each sentence with a word or phrase connected with* **clothes.**

EXAMPLE: It was so cold in the snow that he wore two pairs of ...... *socks* ...... inside his boots.

1 To protect her hands from being scratched when she's gardening, Lucy always wears ....

2 Jack .... his wife's necklace for her as she couldn't do it herself.

3 After dropping his key down the drain, Ian rolled up his shirt-.................. and reached down to get it.

4 I have to wear a belt with these trousers because the .... is so loose.

5 Even though she was going to India, Liz packed a thick woollen .... in case it was cold at night.

3 *Complete these sentences with a word that means the opposite of the word in capitals.*

EXAMPLE: The twins both have a weight problem: but whereas George is OVERWEIGHT, Jack is ......*skinny*.......

1 Sarah's hair is naturally .... but she'd prefer it to be CURLY.
2 They make an interesting-looking couple: her complexion is DARK while his is ....
3 How WRINKLED my skin is now! And when I was young it was so ....
4 The two faces are very different: this one is round and BROAD, that one long and ....
5 My aunt is GENEROUS and always gives me expensive presents, but my uncle is .... and never spends any money on me.

4 *Complete these sentences with a phrasal verb that includes the word* **put.**

EXAMPLE: Please return to your seats and ...*put*... ...*out*... all cigarettes.

1 Before leaving her study the teacher .... the books and files she had been working on.
2 Because several people are ill, the party has been .... till next weekend.
3 If you need somewhere to sleep in London, just give me a call – I can easily .... you ....
4 She was .... studying medicine by watching a heart operation on TV.
5 My boss has .... a transfer – and we're all hoping she gets it!

5 *Choose the word or phrase (A–D) which best completes each sentence.*

1 The man .... coat was stolen from the library is a well-known writer.
   A that   B which   C whom   D whose

2 I'm always too .... to talk to people I don't know at parties.
   A brave   B modest   C reliable   D shy

3 That politician never stops attacking people – why is he so .... ?
   A aggressive   B adventurous   C confident   D outgoing

4 Let's have dinner together: would next Friday .... you?
   A agree   B fit   C match   D suit

5 The unemployed man .... out his shoes walking in search of work.
   A broke   B burst   C knocked   D wore

6 My .... aunt is coming to live with us because she has no one else to look after her.
   A ancient   B antique   C elderly   D old-fashioned

7 When she had showered and .... on her best clothes, she came down to dinner.
   A dressed   B put   C worn   D used

8 It .... be time to leave already – we've only just arrived!
   A can't   B hasn't   C isn't   D mustn't

9 The .... age of the pupils in this class is sixteen.

    A average   B equal   C middle   D ordinary

10 I'd rather .... to a concert than a film, if you don't mind.

    A go   B going   C gone   D to go

11 On a .... summer weekend we go to our beach house and have a barbecue.

    A general   B medium   C plain   D typical

12 During the storm, the electricity suddenly .... off and we were left in the dark.

    A broke   B set   C turned   D went

13 As the waitress laid the table she checked that the wine glasses were spotlessly ....

    A clean   B neat   C smart   D tidy

14 My colleague is very .... – nice to your face and horrible behind your back.

    A bad-tempered   B cautious   C insincere   D moody

15 Our German teacher often talked about his experiences in Germany, ... we found interesting.

    A that   B this   C what   D which

16 The instructions reminded the candidates not to .... out any questions.

    A leave   B let   C make   D think

Town and country

1 On the map

Vocabulary *Geographical features*

Match these words for geographical features with the pictures.

bay   canal   dam   delta   desert   forest
glacier   jungle   plain   valley   volcano
waterfall

Which of them can be found in your country?

a   b   c   d   e   f   g   h   i   j   k   l

Reading *Japan*

1 *Read this extract from an encyclopaedia and then fill in the column for Japan in the chart, using information from the text.*

JAPAN A country of eastern Asia in the north Pacific Ocean. Japan is made up of a chain of more than 1,000 islands, but the main ones are Hokkaido, Honshu, Shikoku and Kyushu. The capital, Tokyo (population: 16 million), is in Honshu. Japan is separated from its nearest neighbour, Korea, by the Sea of Japan.

About 85% of Japan is mountainous, and the country is crossed from the north to the south west by a mountain range. The highest peak in this range is Fujiyama (3,778 m). Japan has a large number of volcanoes, 67 of which are considered active. There are many rivers and lakes. The longest river is the Ishikari (645 km) in Hokkaido. Earthquakes, usually harmless, are common.

Japan is a long country north to south, so the weather and climate vary widely. In the northern island of Hokkaido several metres of snow fall in the winter, and the summer is pleasantly warm, while in the southern island of Okinawa it is as hot and as humid as the tropics most of the year. In Honshu the winters are cold with snow in the mountains, but it is not as cold nor as snowy as in Hokkaido. The Honshu summers are hot and humid, but the mountains are generally fresher than the cities. The rainy season is in June and July. In the east, autumn typhoons are frequent. Most people consider the most beautiful seasons to be spring with its cherry blossoms, and autumn with its fiery autumn leaves.

The traditional products of Japan used to be rice, silk and fish. But since the 1960s Japan has been one of the leading industrial nations: steel, ships, cars, cameras, electronic equipment, plastics, chemicals, etc. are produced.

	Japan	*Your country*
1 Position		
2 Bordered by		
3 Capital city		
4 Type of scenery		
5 Important geographical features		
6 Climate		
7 Main products		

2 *Now fill in the column for your country.*

Grammar *Comparatives and superlatives*

1 FORM
Underline the examples of comparatives and superlatives in these sentences:

The mountains are generally fresher than the cities.
The central region is more mountainous than the coast.
The longest river is the Ishikari.
Most people consider the most beautiful seasons to be spring and autumn.

What is the rule for forming the comparative and superlative of adjectives in English? Use the adjectives *cold, hot, noisy, beautiful* and *good* to illustrate your rule.

2 SIMILARITY
You can use 'as ... as ...' to show similarity:

In the southern island of Okinawa it is as *hot* as *the tropics most of the year.*

You can put 'nearly', 'almost' or 'just' in front of 'as ... as ...':
London is nearly as *expensive* as *Tokyo.*
In summer, Tokyo is just as *hot* as *the desert.*

3 DIFFERENCE
You can show difference in several ways:

a 'not as/so ... as'
  Life in the countryside is not as *fast* as *it is in Tokyo.*

  You can add 'nearly' to 'not as/so ... as':
  Kyoto isn't nearly as *busy* as *Tokyo.*

b 'as ... as ...' with 'twice', 'three times', etc., 'half', 'a third', etc.:
  Japan's car exports are twice as *high* as *Britain's.*
  Rice-growing is only half as *important* as *it used to be.*

c '-er than ...', 'more/less ... than ...':
  The mountains are generally fresher than the cities.
  Most people think spring is more *beautiful than summer.*
  England is less *mountainous than Japan.*

  You can put 'much', 'far', 'a lot', 'lots', 'a little' or 'a bit' in front of the comparative form of the adjective:
  The south of the country is a lot *warmer than the north.*
  Traditional products are much less *important than they used to be.*

4 Complete the second sentence so that it means the same as the first.

1 The Suez Canal is longer than the Panama Canal.
   The Panama Canal ....

2 The Corinth Canal isn't nearly as long as the Panama Canal.
   The Corinth Canal is much ....

3 No other island is as big as Greenland.
   Greenland is .... in the world.

4 In my opinion, Niagara Falls isn't as spectacular as Iguaçu Falls.
   In my opinion, Iguaçu Falls ....

5 Is any other city as crowded as Mexico City?
   Is Mexico City .... in the world?

6 Mont Blanc is roughly half as high as Mount Everest.
   Mount Everest is roughly ....

Grammar *Passive*

1 Underline the verbs in the passive in these sentences:

Japan has a large number of volcanoes, 67 of which are considered active.
Since the 1960s Japan has been one of the leading industrial nations: steel, ships, cars, cameras, electronic equipment, plastics, chemicals, etc. are produced.

The passive form of the verb is made with the verb 'to be', in the appropriate tense, followed by the past participle:
Traditional products have been replaced *by industrial ones.*
European trade with Japan was begun *in 1542.*
Japan was being ruled *by a 'shogun' when the Portuguese came in 1542.*
Japanese working methods will be studied *by foreign businessmen.*

2 The object of an active verb becomes the subject of a passive verb:

Active sentence: *Industrial products have replaced traditional ones.*
Passive sentence: *Traditional products have been replaced by industrial ones.*

In sentences like 'Japan was being ruled by a shogun', the part of the sentence introduced by 'by' is called the agent. The agent in a passive sentence is the same person or thing as the subject of an active sentence:
A shogun was ruling Japan.

In many passive sentences there is **no** agent, because in these sentences it is usually not important to say who or what something is done by:
Sixty-seven volcanoes in Japan are considered active.

3 *Read this paragraph about the economy of Sweden, and put all the verbs in the passive.*

In the south of Sweden farmers grow cereals, potatoes and sugar beet, and rear cattle and pigs. The Swedes exploit the northern forests for their timber. They can export timber products indefinitely because they have managed the forests well and not destroyed them with uncontrolled cutting. They mine iron inside the Arctic Circle. They established the first mines in the 1890s, and the high salaries attracted workers to move to this inhospitable region. But they have recently had to close many mines because of a fall in demand. Competition from Third World countries has damaged the once prosperous steel and shipbuilding industries, but industrialists manufacture a variety of profitable goods, including aircraft, cars, domestic equipment and textiles.

Writing *Description of my country*

Write a short geographical description of your country. Use the information you have added to the chart on page 43.

Before you start to write, make a paragraph plan. Organise the information in the chart about your country into topic areas. Each topic area will represent one paragraph.

Somewhere in your description include these phrases:
   ... the most beautiful part of my country ...
   ... the most serious problem for my country ...
   ... In this respect, my country is different from her neighbour(s) ...

In which paragraph will they be most appropriate?

2 In the city

Speaking *Describing a photo*

1 *Look at these two photos and give your first*
impression of each:

> This is a photo of ... and that's a photo of ...

2 *Say what is happening in each photo. Use the*
words in these columns to make sentences:

There is/are	a
	a couple of
	a few
	some
	several
	a lot of
		people
		woman
		street vendor
		stalls
		man
		palm trees
			with blonde hair
			with a child
			with things for sale
			with shoulder bags
			in traditional
			  costume
			with tall smooth
			  trunks
				sitting
				standing
				walking
				planted
				waiting
				set up
					across the road.
					under an umbrella.
					at the side of the road.
					in a pedestrian zone.
					on a stool.
					along the pavement.

Make some more sentences like these about the photos.

3 *Compare the two photos:*

The city in this photo ...
    ... looks cleaner than that one.
    ... doesn't have many skyscrapers, but that one ...
    ... must be nice to live in if you like a calm way of
    life, whereas that one ...

4 *Guess where each photo was taken:*

I think this photo was This must have been	taken in ...	because (of) ...

Listening 🔊 *Living in a city*

1 **Here are some reasons people give for living in a city rather than the country:**

- higher standard of living
- more work opportunities
- better health services
- better transport

1 Do you think these reasons are good?

2 What other reasons can you think of? Add them here:

....

....

3 In your opinion, which are the three best reasons for living in a city?

2 **Listen to David and Barbara talking about living in London and how they feel about it.**

Section 1

David mentions three reasons why he likes living in a city. Make a short note of each reason (about five words for each). Are these included in your list of reasons above?

Section 2

Barbara mentions six reasons why she doesn't like living in London. Put a tick (✓) beside each point on the list below:

1 the noise ☐
2 the dirt ☐
3 the pollution ☐
4 the crowds ☐
5 the unreliability of the bus system ☐
6 the hours the underground runs ☐
7 the crime ☐
8 the cost of accommodation ☐
9 the cost of public transport ☐
10 the cost of food ☐

Section 3

Barbara talks about whether she would live in the country if she had the choice.

What do you think she would miss about living away from a city? What would she not miss? Listen to check.

3 **Do you sympathise more with David or Barbara?**

Grammar *Conditional sentences (2)*

1 **Barbara lives in a city but she imagines how she would feel about living in the country:**

I'd get very bored if I lived in the country all the time. I'd miss the stimulus of city life. But if I lived somewhere that was within easy reach of the city, I'd be quite happy living in the country.

These are *unreal* or *hypothetical* conditional sentences. You use this kind of conditional sentence to talk about imaginary situations in the present or future, or things that could happen but probably will not happen:
If I were very rich, I would have one house in the country and another in the city, and a third on a tropical island!

Conditional clause	Main clause
if + past simple	would / 'd + infinitive

In the conditional clause, you may use either 'was' or 'were' with I, he, she or it:
If I were rich ... or *If I was rich ...*

But you usually use 'were' in the expression 'If I were you ...':
If I were you, I'd look for a flat in the suburbs.

You may also use 'could' or 'might' instead of 'would' in the main clause, depending on the meaning:
You could live with me if you paid half the rent.
If I had £100,000, I might buy a house in the country.

2 **Complete each of the following sentences so that it means the same as the sentence before it.**

1 She doesn't live in London because she doesn't know anybody there.
She'd ....

2 My travel expenses are low because I live and work in the city centre.
If I ....

3 Most people go to work by car because the public transport system is inefficient.
If the public transport system ....
....

4 The standard of living in the provinces is low because the government gives them little money.
If the government ....
....

5 Few people want to live in that part of the city because there is so much crime there.
More ....

6 I can't live in the country because I can't find a job there.
I'd ....

3 On the land

Reading *Interpreting diagrams*

1 ***What kind of work has to be done on a farm? In your country, are these activities done by men, or by women, or by both?***

Look at what the chart says about farm work in Malawi. Is the situation similar in your country?

Malawi

housework	95	5
processing crops	85	15
weeding	70	30
harvesting	60	40
looking after animals	50	50
planting	50	50
ploughing	30	70

◼ women   ◻ men

2 ***Look at the information about rainfall and temperature in Malawi.***

1 Which is the hottest, driest month?
2 Which is the wettest month?
3 How is the weather different in June and December?

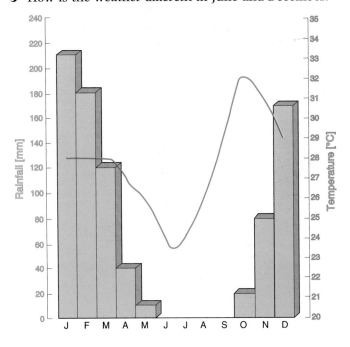

3 ***Look at the information about crops in Malawi.***

1 What is the major food crop?
2 Would a diagram about crops in your country look the same?

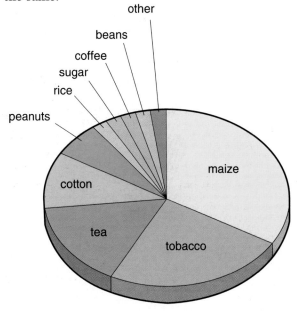

4 ***Look at the information about farm animals in Malawi.***

1 Which is the most popular animal? Why do you think this animal is so popular?
2 Would a diagram about farm animals in your country look the same?

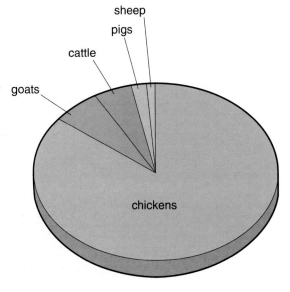

Directed writing *Working on a farm*

1   *Look at the information about Grace and Sally, two farming women. How are their lives similar, and how are they different?*

2   *Write two paragraphs (about 80 words each) comparing the two women's daily activities. The first sentence of each paragraph has been done for you.*

1 There are many similarities in the way Grace and Sally spend their day ...

2 On the other hand, there are some great differences between the ways the two women spend their time ...

Grace Malinki, her husband and five children live on a small farm in the southern part of Malawi, not far from the Liwonde National Park, where tourists love to go to take photographs of the wild animals. The Malinkis grow maize, beans and peanuts; they also have 20 chickens and one cow.

Grace Malinki's day

5 am   gets up; milks cow; feeds chickens; sweeps house; fetches water from pump; prepares breakfast

7 am   wakes up husband and children; gives them breakfast; sends older children to school; cleans up

8 am   works in fields, taking younger children with her

1 pm   brings children home to give them a drink; takes snack to husband in fields; does more work in fields

5 pm   comes home; milks cow; feeds chickens, collects eggs; prepares dinner; cleans up and does other housework

10 pm goes to bed

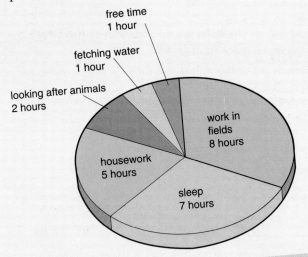

- free time 1 hour
- fetching water 1 hour
- looking after animals 2 hours
- work in fields 8 hours
- housework 5 hours
- sleep 7 hours

Sally Langdon, her husband and two children live on a small farm in Somerset in the west of England. Tourists enjoy driving through this beautiful countryside on their way to the nearby beaches. The Langdons have 70 cows and 20 chickens; they also grow some wheat and barley.

Sally Langdon's day

5.30 am	wakes up when husband goes to do mechanised milking
6 am	gets up; feeds chickens; prepares breakfast; takes cows out to fields after milking; separates the cream from the rest of the milk
8.30 am	drives children to school
9 am	supervises collection of milk by milk tanker from the regional dairy
9.30 am	processes cream; hand feeds calves which have been taken from their mothers;
12 noon	collects eggs; does housework; deals with phone calls about farm business
1 pm	gives lunch to husband and farm worker
3.30 pm	does farm accounts and other paper work
5.30 pm	collects children from school
7.30 pm	calls in cows from fields for milking; feeds chickens; prepares dinner; cleans up
10 pm	takes part in village social life or watches television
	goes to bed

driving children
3/4 hour

looking after animals
2 hours

free time
3 1/4 hours

sleep
7 1/2 hours

processing cream
2 1/2 hours

farm 'office' work
4 hours

housework
4 hours

Pronunciation 📼 *Numbers and symbols*

Practise saying these numbers and symbols. Then check your pronunciation against the examples on the tape.

1 How do you say these figures?

85%   28°C $3\frac{1}{4}$ $7\frac{1}{2}$ $\frac{3}{4}$ £3.50 $9.28

2 Where do you put the word 'and' when you say these numbers? Where do you *not* use it?

420   701   1,362   25,500   57,251   638,959

3 How do you say 'O' in each of these cases?

Phone number: 071 749 0445
Mathematical figure: $2 - 2 = 0$
Countdown: $5-4-3-2-1-0!$
Football score: 2–0
Tennis score: 15–0

4 Which of these symbols (, or . or –) can you use with each figure below? What different figures do you get, and how do you say them?

25   110   1635   170431
EXAMPLE: $\frac{2}{5}$, 2.5

Speaking *Guided visit*

Do visitors from other countries like looking at the countryside and farms in your area, or do they prefer sightseeing in the cities?

You have been asked to arrange a three-day tour of your area (either your home area or the area where you are now studying) for one of these foreign groups: tourists, businessmen and women, or students. You want to give your foreign group a balanced view, so you must plan to show them things which illustrate all aspects of life in your area. For example:

- town and country
- industrial and agricultural
- picturesque and ugly
- well-known and unknown to foreigners
- man-made and natural
- commercial and cultural
- historic and modern
- serious and light-hearted

Decide on ten specific places which the group of foreigners should visit.

4

Exam skill *Interview (1)*

In the first part of the interview you have to talk about one or more photographs with the interviewer. You need to be able to:
- say what you can see in the photo(s), by describing the people, the place and what is happening.
- develop a conversation with the interviewer related to the topic of the photo(s).

This part takes about four minutes (individual interview) or seven minutes (group interview).

(*Note:* The other parts of the interview are described in Unit 11 Lesson 4 and Unit 13 Lesson 4.)

INTERVIEW PRACTICE

This language will help you do well in the first part of the interview.

1 SAYING WHAT YOU CAN SEE IN THE PHOTO

1 Describe what the people in photo **a** are doing, and say where they are. Use either:
   - the sentence structure 'There is/are ...' practised in *Describing a photo* on page 46
   or:
   - the present progressive
   together with the appropriate phrase from round the photo.

   EXAMPLES:
   In the background there are some tall modern buildings towering over the scene.
   In the middle of the photo a train is moving along the track.

2 Say how the people and things in photo **a** look.

He/She It/This They	look(s)	adjective
	seem(s) (to be)	
	look(s) like	noun
	seem(s) to be	

   EXAMPLES:
   He seems determined.
   They look like professional runners.
   It doesn't look very busy.

in the background —

on the right

up here —

in the middle of the photo

in the foreground

down there

on the left

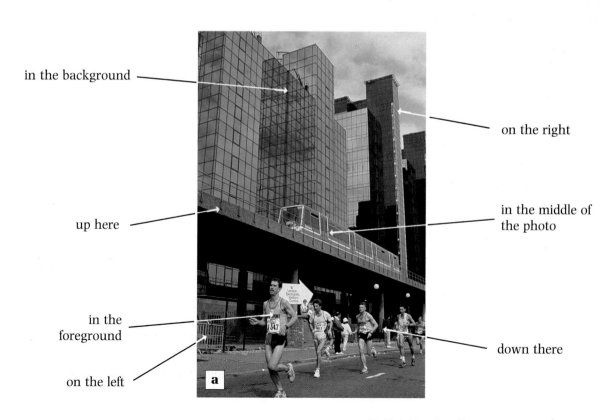

a

2   MAKING GUESSES ABOUT THE PHOTO

1   Say what the people in photos **b** and **c** might be doing.

She He It They	could may might seem(s) to	be	-ing
	look(s) as	if though	pronoun + 'be'	

EXAMPLES:
He might be waiting for someone.
They seem to be inspecting the food.
She looks as if she's trying to touch the dog.

2   Make some deductions about photos **b** and **c**. Use 'can't' or 'must'.
EXAMPLES:
This can't be the USA because ...
They must be on an expedition because ...

3   If you can't see very well, or don't know, use one of these expressions:

It's hard to see. Perhaps ...
I can't make out what he's doing. Maybe he's ...
I've never seen anything like this before – is it perhaps ... ?

3   PARAPHRASING
When you can't remember, or don't know, a word, try to explain what you mean.

It's a	kind sort type	of ...
It's	something you use used	for -ing
	what you do how you feel what happens	when you ...

Use photos **a**–**c** to help you practise this language.

4   DEVELOPING A CONVERSATION FROM THE PHOTO
Look at photos **a**–**c**. What topics related to each photo:
- do you have experience of?
- do you know about?
- are you interested in talking about?

Make a list for each photo.

b

c

Here are some ways of introducing your own ideas to the conversation:

You	can can't	see things like this in my	town. country.
This	reminds me makes me think	of ...	
I don't know much about this, but I *do* know			about ... that ...

Practise developing a conversation that interests you about one of the photos.

Test exercises

1 *Complete this passage. Use only **one** word in each gap.*

Four groups of peoples – the Australian Aborigines, the Indians of North and South America, and the Bushmen of South Africa – are not often considered together, but they have certain things in common.

First, all four human groups were (1) .... original inhabitants of their part (2) .... the world. (The word *aborigine* means the people (3) .... were there from the beginning.) However, none thought (4) .... the land where they (5) .... belonged to them. On the contrary, (6) .... felt that *they* belonged to the land. The land (7) .... where they lived, along with all the (8) .... creatures of nature.

They were hunters, so they had a (9) .... detailed knowledge of the natural world around them. They (10) .... every animal and every part of the landscape, and made stories, dances, pictures and songs (11) .... them.

(12) .... people thought it was important to fit into their surroundings. They took (13) .... place beside all other living things, and lived in balance (14) .... them.

But then the outsiders arrived and changed everything. At (15) ...., the original inhabitants welcomed the white people, helping them (16) .... find food and shelter in the new land. (17) .... they soon (18) .... that the new people lived by a totally different set of beliefs. (19) .... example, unlike the original inhabitants, they thought that land was something which could be (20) .... by one person or group, not shared by all.

2 *Complete each sentence with a word connected with **geography**.*

EXAMPLE: I was in an ...*earthquake*... once: the walls moved, the floor shook and the windows cracked.

1 The land round the volcano is so .... that the farmers can grow three crops a year.
2 Tropical plants need a hot, humid .... to grow well.
3 Britain was not always an ....: once it was connected to the mainland of Europe.
4 The .... in Switzerland is beautiful: mountains, valleys and lakes all round.
5 This region is mostly .... – sand, hardly any rain, little life.

3 *Choose the word or phrase (A–D) which best completes each sentence.*

1 Mexico City lies at about 3,000 metres .... sea level.

   A above   B along   C on   D over

2 The River Thames .... from Oxford to London.

   A floats   B flows   C moves   D passes

3 Italy is famous for its leather goods, ... as shoes and bags.

   A including   B like   C same   D such

4 The old houses were .... down and a new office block was built in their place.

   A cut   B pulled   C set   D taken

5 It's a very pretty rug with flowers round the ....

   A boundary   B edge   C frontier   D margin

6 The President is going to .... a tree to mark the start of the project.

   A cultivate   B grow   C plant   D sow

7 We spent our holiday in a hotel which had a private ....

   A beach   B coast   C seaside   D shore

8 Another problem has .... for the company – new tax laws have just been introduced.

   A arisen   B raised   C risen   D rose

9 Bread is made by .... it in the oven.

   A baking   B boiling   C grilling   D roasting

10 The new teacher is very young: she looks .... a student herself.

   A as   B as if   C like   D to be

11 Even if the rains .... now, there won't be a harvest this year.

   A came   B come   C didn't come   D will come

12 His daughter has been .... the family business for the last five years.

   A commanding   B governing   C making   D running

13 The waiters .... the table for the anniversary dinner and then arranged the flowers and candles.

   A laid   B lay   C lie   D lied

14 She's decided to .... up mountaineering as a hobby.

   A bring   B get   C make   D take

15 Now that we have moved to the city our standard of living is ....

   A bigger   B finer   C higher   D stronger

5 UNIT FIVE
A question of health

1 Health and fitness

Reading *Questionnaire*

1 *How healthy and fit are you? To find out, do this questionnaire. Tick either the Yes or No box. Then look at the Appendix on page 190.*

	YES	NO
1 Do you take some energetic exercise for at least 20 minutes three times a week?	☐	☐
2 Do you usually take the lift rather than walk up two floors?	☐	☐
3 Have you walked at least one and a half kilometres at any time in the last week?	☐	☐
4 Do you usually fry rather than grill food?	☐	☐
5 Do you try not to eat too much sugary, salty or fatty food?	☐	☐
6 Do you eat a piece of fresh fruit every day?	☐	☐

	YES	NO
7 a Do you usually drink more than 10 cups of coffee a day?	☐	☐
b If No, is it 3–5 cups?	☐	☐
8 What sort of smoker are you? (Tick one box.)		
a Never smoked	☐	
b Ex-smoker	☐	
c 1–10 a day	☐	
d 11–20 a day	☐	
e 21–40 a day	☐	
f More than 40 a day	☐	
9 Do you often fall asleep while watching TV?	☐	☐
10 Do you usually wake up looking forward to the day?	☐	☐

2 *Read these two accounts of personal health and fitness. Both people answered the questionnaire. Can you work out how?*

Sue Thorne

I get quite a lot of exercise. The tube station is about ten minutes from my flat, so of course I do that walk twice a day, five times a week. Then I go to aerobics two or three times a week. Sometimes I miss a week or two, but I always pick it up again. I avoid taking lifts if I can – I'll walk up about four floors. Unfortunately, where I'm working at the moment I'm on the sixth floor, so I have to take the lift.

I'm generally very careful about what I eat. I don't eat sugary or fatty foods if I can possibly help it, because of my weight and my teeth. But I don't worry about salty foods much. At home I usually grill rather than fry food. If I'm eating out I never have anything fried, always grilled. I eat fruit every day for lunch: an orange and a banana, and sometimes an apple as well. But one thing that's bad is that I drink an awful lot of coffee, always more than twelve cups a day.

I think I lead quite a healthy life. I don't smoke. I have tried it but I didn't like it. Once in a blue moon I fall asleep in front of the television. I usually wake up looking forward to the day, but at the moment I don't because I don't like the girl I work with. I certainly do at the weekends!

José Augusto Rodrigues

Ten years ago I did a lot of exercise. I went to the beach and played football for seven or eight hours. But since I started working and studying at the same time I just haven't had time for that sort of thing. I'm afraid I'm getting fat. I like walking, but in Brazil we don't really have the right climate for it, so I usually take buses or taxis. I always walk up stairs rather than take the lift. It's the only gymnastics I do!

I know sugary, salty and fatty foods aren't good for me, but I never worry about what I eat. My mother does all the cooking; she usually fries things and hardly ever grills. But I eat lots of fresh fruit every day: apples, oranges, bananas. I love strawberries, but we don't often have them in Santos. Even though I'm Brazilian I don't drink much coffee – just a cup between classes.

I never think about my lifestyle, but I don't think it's unhealthy. I don't smoke because I get bronchitis frequently. At the weekends I don't usually come home until 2 or 3 in the morning. Then I sometimes turn the television on, and immediately fall asleep!

3 *Who is healthier and fitter: Sue or José Augusto? Is your lifestyle like either of theirs?*

Grammar *The present*

1 *You use the present simple:*

a to talk about the general present
b to talk about a present habit, something that happens repeatedly at regular intervals
c to talk about a natural law or something that is always true

Match the following examples of the present simple with the uses above:
1 *Do* you often *fall* asleep in front of the TV?
2 He *comes* from Brazil.
3 The pupil of the eye *closes* in bright light.
4 She *is* a computer programmer.
5 I *eat* fruit every day for lunch.
6 I *don't drink* much coffee.
7 Cakes and sweets *make* you fat.

2 *You use the present progressive:*

a to talk about something that is happening at the moment you are speaking
b to talk about an activity that is current but not necessarily happening at the moment you are speaking
c to talk about changes and developments in progress

Match the following examples of the present progressive with the uses above:
1 Sssh! We'*re trying* to sleep.
2 I'm afraid I'*m getting* fat.
3 He *isn't looking* for a new job.
4 Unfortunately, where I'*m working* at the moment I'm on the sixth floor.
5 What *are* you *doing* with that cigarette?
6 People *are becoming* more and more interested in physical fitness.

3 *Some verbs are not usually used in the progressive form of the verb:*

Sue *seems fitter* than José Augusto.
I *know* sugary, salty and fatty foods aren't good for me.
This cough medicine *tastes horrible!*

Verbs not usually used in the progressive form are:
Verbs of liking and disliking: e.g. *like, hate,* ....
Verbs of thinking: e.g. *think, mean, know,* ....
Verbs of perception: e.g. *taste, smell,* ....
Verbs of appearance: e.g. *seem, look,* ....
Verbs of possession: e.g. *have, belong to,* ....

Can you think of more examples in each category?

4 *When you use the present simple tense to describe a habit, you often use it with an adverb of frequency:*

always usually often sometimes occasionally hardly ever rarely seldom never

Look at the following examples. Where does an adverb of frequency usually go?
Do you usually *take the lift?*
We *don't* often *have* them in Santos.
My mother usually *fries things and* hardly ever *grills.*

5 *Put the verbs in the correct tense: present simple or present progressive.*

1 He (smoke) a lot but he (try) to cut down.
2 'Why you (stare) at that fat man?'
   'I (not mean) to be rude. I (think) I (know) him.'
3 'That (smell) good. What you (cook)?'
   'I (grill) some steak. I usually (fry) it but I (know) grilling is healthier.'
4 'What you (do)?'
   'I (look) at your old school photographs. In this one you (play) football. You (look) terrible! You (have) mud all over you, and your nose (bleed).'
5 Mrs Pound (not work) this week. She (look after) her grandson while her daughter (be) in hospital.
6 She (go) to exercise classes three times a week. She (get) slimmer and her health (improve).

Writing *Personal health and fitness*

1 *Both accounts on page 57 have the same paragraph plan. What is the topic of each paragraph? Choose the correct answer.*

Paragraph 1	Paragraph 2	Paragraph 3
walking	fatty foods	bad habits
taking exercise	eating fruit	lifestyle
doing gymnastics	diet	leisure activities

2 *The sentence which summarises the topic of each paragraph is called the topic sentence. It is often the first sentence of the paragraph.*

1 Underline the three topic sentences in each account.
2 How does each writer continue after the topic sentences? Does he or she:
   a give a few examples about the topic?
   b write down everything he or she can think of about the topic?
   c introduce ideas on a different topic?

3 *Write a similar account about yourself, using your answers to the questionnaire on page 56. Use the same paragraph plan as Sue and José Augusto. Begin each paragraph with a topic sentence, then develop the topic with two or three examples.*

2 What's the cure?

Vocabulary *Doctors and dentists*

Which word is the odd one out? Why?

1 joint   ankle   knee   elbow
2 lung   muscle   skin   cure
3 bruise   break   sprain   dose
4 pill   bandage   plaster   crutch
5 symptoms   surgeon   diagnosis   treatment
6 ambulance   filling   brace   drill
7 injection   X-ray   operation   blood

Listening 📼 *Taking exercise*

1 *One of the ways you can get medical information in Britain is by phoning a number in the HEALTHCALL directory. This is recorded information provided by the telephone company. You are going to hear the recorded tape for EXERCISE.*

Section 1

1 Section 1 of the tape mentions five parts of the body. What do you think these parts will be? Quickly write down your ideas. Listen to the tape and see if you were right.

2 Here is a summary of Section 1 of the tape. The information is not all correct. Listen to the tape again and make any necessary corrections.

Exercise is good because it:
 a helps you to keep slim
 b stimulates circulation
 c encourages deep breathing
 d is good for the heart, lungs, muscles, skin and joints

Exercise:
 is any vigorous physical activity
 stops you feeling breathless and sweaty

Recommended amount to be done each day:
 at least 1 hour

Section 2

3 Before you listen to Section 2, guess what the speaker will talk about next. Choose one of the following:
 a Information about the heart and lungs
 b Advice about starting an exercise programme carefully
 c Forms of exercise suitable for different people
Listen and check.

4 Listen to Section 2 again and complete these notes:

Everyone who starts a new programme of exercise should ....
People over 40 ....
Consult your doctor first if you are:
      a ....
or   b ....
or   c ....

Section 3

5 The speaker now considers other related ideas. Which of these do you think she will mention?
 a exercise and losing weight
 b enjoying your exercise
 c exercise and heart attacks
 d exercise and sleep
Listen and check.

6 Listen to Section 3 again and check the information in these notes. Make any necessary corrections.

Points to remember
 a Narrow range of possible forms of exercise
 b Exercise can't harm healthy people
 c Aim at two or three 60-minute sessions per week
 d Choose something you enjoy
 e Get fit quickly
 f Exercise helps you sleep better

2 *Do you think recorded advice like this is a good way of getting medical information? What are the advantages and disadvantages?*

Vocabulary *Symptoms*

What symptoms do you have when you have these illnesses?

an allergy   a cold   flu   food poisoning

Match each of these illnesses with one of the four sets of symptoms here.

1 You've got a temperature and a headache. Your stomach hurts and you're being sick.

2 You're sneezing. Your eyes are itching and watery. You've got a rash.

3 You're sneezing. You've got a sore throat, a runny nose and a cough.

4 You've got a temperature and a headache. You feel cold, but you're sweating. Your back, arms and legs are aching.

Speaking *Advice*

1 *Everyone enjoys giving advice to other people, but the suggestions are not always very good. Here are some pieces of advice about treating the illnesses above. Which pieces of advice are appropriate for each illness? Do you think it is good advice?*

Why don't you go and see a doctor?

Try drinking ginger tea.

Make sure you have plenty of warm drinks.

It's best not to eat anything for a couple of days.

You'd better take your temperature every hour.

Have you tried consulting an acupuncturist?

You really ought to stay away from other people.

You should go to bed for a week.

If I were you, I'd buy a large box of tissues and carry on as usual.

You could live in a dust-free, pollen-free bubble!

I suggest you eat small amounts of plain food.

If you find out what you're allergic to, you'll be able to avoid it.

What about drinking hot lemon juice and honey?

Which is the most *formal* piece of advice here? Which is the *strongest*? Which are more like *suggestions* than strong advice?

2 *Do this in groups of three. Student A (see page 190) has broken his or her leg. Student B (see page 191) and Student C (see page 192) give advice about the best way to carry on everyday life in this situation.*

3 Physically different

Speaking *Disability*

1 *What methods of helping the disabled can you see in the photos? How do they work? Can you think of any others?*

2 *Do you know, or can you imagine, what differences there are between the everyday lives of someone who is disabled and someone who isn't?*

Reading *My left foot*

1 *In what way do you think Christy Brown, the writer of the following passage, was disabled? How did he manage to paint pictures? How easy do you think it was for him?*

Then mother managed to buy me some more paints and brushes, along with one or two drawing books and a pencil. This, of course, broadened my range of expression and allowed me to have a greater choice of subject. After the first few weeks of uncertainty and awkwardness, I settled down contentedly with my new pastime. I painted every day upstairs in the back bedroom, completely by myself.

I was changing. I didn't know it then, but I had found a way to be happy again and to forget some of the things that had made me unhappy. Above all I learned to forget myself. I didn't miss going out with my brothers now, for I had something to keep my mind active, something to make each day, a thing to look forward to.

I would sit crouched on the floor for hours, holding the brush between my toes, my right leg curled up under my left, my arms held tightly at my sides, the hands clenched. All my paints and brushes were around me, and I would get mother or father to pin the drawing paper to the floor with tacks to keep it steady. It looked a very queer awkward position, with my head almost between my knees and my back as crooked as a corkscrew. But I painted all my best pictures this way, with the wooden floor as my only easel.

Slowly I began to lose my early depression. I had a feeling of pure joy while I painted, a feeling I had never experienced before and which seemed almost to lift me above myself. It was only when I wasn't painting that I became depressed and cross with everyone at home.

2 **Find the words or phrases in the third paragraph of the passage which mean:**

1 leaning forward, with his legs under him and his back bent
2 folded
3 with the fingers pulled in tightly
4 short nails
5 strange
6 not graceful
7 not straight
8 instrument for pulling a cork out of a bottle
9 wooden frame for holding a painting while it's being painted

3 **Choose the best answer (A–D) for questions 1–5.**

1 Where does the passage come from?
  A a letter describing the writer's family life
  B an article recommending the teaching of painting to children
  C a book telling the story of the writer's life
  D a book explaining how to start painting

2 What does the writer say about his new pastime?
  A He only had the most basic equipment.
  B He drew his pictures before painting them.
  C He couldn't paint what he wanted to.
  D He needed some time to get used to it.

3 What happened to the writer as a result of taking up painting?
  A He rediscovered feelings of happiness.
  B He stopped going out with his brothers.
  C He was able to express his unhappiness.
  D He decided he liked being on his own.

4 The writer got his parents to pin drawing paper to the floor so that
  A he could put his paints and brushes on it.
  B the floor would be protected from paint.
  C the paper didn't move when he was painting.
  D he could copy the pattern of the floor.

5 Why did the writer paint sitting on the floor?
  A He could carry on painting for hours.
  B It was the easiest way for him to paint.
  C There was no table or chair in the room.
  D He had his best ideas in this position.

4 **Why do you think the writer became depressed and cross when he wasn't painting? Would you have felt the same?**

Grammar *Adjectives ending in -ing and -ed*

1 **Some pairs of adjectives are formed from verbs:**

Christy's disability was depressing: *it made him* depressed.
His unhappiness was worrying: *his mother was* worried.
He found painting exciting: *he was* excited *about it.*

Which group of adjectives below describes the effect something creates? Which group describes how you feel about that effect?

2 **Complete these sentences with the correct adjective formed from the verb in brackets.**

1 I thought 'Children of a Lesser God' was one of the most .... films I've ever seen. (MOVE)
2 She was .... when the doctor told her the test results were negative. (RELIEVE)
3 After his holiday he looked very .... (RELAX)
4 Why does a lot of medicine taste so ....? (DISGUST)
5 You looked .... when they told you how much the treatment would cost. (SURPRISE)
6 He never takes exercise because he finds it extremely .... (BORE)

The television programme was	annoying. boring. disappointing. frightening. interesting.	I was	annoyed. bored. disappointed. frightened. interested.

Speaking 🔊 *Expressing opinion*

'Able-bodied children can learn a lot from being educated with disabled children.'

1 Listen to Barbara, Reg and Cherry expressing their opinions on this subject. What is each person's opinion?
2 Listen again and make a note of the language the speakers use to:
   – express their opinions
   – give reasons for these opinions
   – support their reasons with examples
3 Prepare to take part in a discussion on the same topic or one of the others given here. Note down some ideas – if possible some ideas *for* and some *against*.
4 Discuss the topic(s) in small groups. What conclusions do you reach? Who had the most convincing arguments?

> People today pay too much attention to the health of their bodies and not enough to the health of their minds.

> Medical science is now so advanced that it can cure almost every illness.

> If everyone gave up smoking tomorrow, the number of hospital patients would be halved.

> What's the point of worrying about your weight? Some people are naturally slim and some are naturally fat.

Pronunciation 🔊 *Individual sounds*

The following sentences contain all the different sounds in the English language. Listen to the tape and repeat the sentences.

1 Coughs and sneezes spread diseases.
2 Warm hands, cold heart.
3 The way to a man's heart is through his stomach.
4 A sore throat, a hoarse voice and a runny nose? Could be flu.
5 Five cracked ribs, a fractured hip, a broken leg and a sprained ankle. Ouch!
6 How about an injection in your jaw?
7 Take care, nurse. My shoulder hurts, and I've got earache.
8 They'd rather use crutches than a wheelchair.
9 Unusual double vision.

Make a note of the sounds which caused you particular difficulty and remember to practise them regularly.

The way to a man's heart ...

Coughs and sneezes ...

4

Exam skill *Rewriting sentences*

Question 2 in Paper 3 tests your knowledge of English grammar and sentence structure. You have to rewrite ten sentences so that the new sentence means exactly the same as the sentence printed before it.

EXAMPLE: Where's the optician's?
ANSWER: Could you tell me ..... *where the* .... *optician's is* ..... ?

1 Here are three points to remember when you do this question:

1 Ask yourself: 'What is each sentence testing?' This will help you to remember the appropriate grammar rule.

What do you think each of the examples (**a–d**) is testing? Choose the correct answer from the box.

| adverbs advice comparatives |
| conditional sentences making deductions |
| passive the present superlatives |

a I'd like to join a private health club but I haven't got enough money.
If ....

b Sue is healthier than José Augusto.
José Augusto ....

c I think you should have a check-up.
What about .... ?

d I'm sure your aerobics teacher isn't properly qualified.
Your aerobics teacher ....

2 Change as little as possible of the original sentence. Make sure that your version has exactly the same meaning.

What is wrong with these versions of **b** and **d** above?

b José Augusto is much less fit than Sue.
d Your aerobics teacher must be properly qualified.

3 Make sure that your version is both grammatically correct and that it makes sense.

What is wrong with these versions of **a** and **c** above?

a If I liked to join a private health club, I wouldn't have enough money.
c What about checking up?

2 Now practise with these ten sentences. They all test grammar points you have worked on in Units 1–5.

1 Is the common cold caused by a virus or by bacteria?
Could you tell me...

2 It may rain, but don't worry. I'll fetch you from the station.
Don't worry – if...

3 I'm sure it's difficult living without running water in the house.
It ....

4 I don't think he saw the road sign.
He...

5 Summers in Athens are hotter than in London.
Summers in London ....

6 Silver is half the price of gold here.
Gold costs...

7 The female mosquito spreads malaria.
Malaria...

8 In the photo I can see a woman digging in the garden.
In the photo there...

9 Not many people go to that island because it's so expensive.
If that island...

10 It was exciting to hear the competition results.
I was...

Test exercises

1 *Complete this passage. Use only **one** word in each gap.*

ARE YOU A LARK OR AN OWL?

Do you read the newspaper (**1**) .... you have breakfast? If you
do then you (**2**) .... be a 'lark', or morning type of
person. 'Owls', or evening types, tend not to spend much time over breakfast. They
(**3**) .... little appetite then, and, (**4**) .... they are
usually late risers, they are short (**5**) .... time anyway. Around half of
(**6**) .... adult population are either morning (**7**) ....
evening types; the rest fall somewhere (**8**) .... the middle.
(**9**) .... can be up to a twelve hour difference in the time of day
when the (**10**) .... types reach the point when they are most alert
and mentally at their (**11**) .... Larks tend (**12**) ....
reach this point in the late morning, while owls (**13**) .... it around
10 pm. For reasons (**14**) .... are unknown, evening types tend to
be more adaptable (**15**) .... morning types. For example, evening
types can (**16**) .... cope much better with shift work and jet lag,
and (**17**) .... is easier for an evening type to become a morning type
than the other way (**18**) .... Are we born (**19**) ....
these differences, or are they just formed (**20**) .... habit? We don't
really know.

2 *Complete each of the following sentences so that it means exactly the same as
the sentence before it.*

1 I visit my grandmother on Tuesdays and Fridays.
   I visit my grandmother twice...
2 Drunk driving causes many accidents.
   Many accidents..
3 Why don't you stay in bed for a few days?
   If I ....
4 I'm sure you've got flu.
   You ....
5 Take these pills three times a day and you'll soon feel better.
   If ....
6 Fruit and vegetables are better for your health than cakes and sweets.
   Cakes and sweets are not..
7 The nurse may be taking his pulse, but I can't see very well.
   It looks ....
8 The new doctor is going to give me a thorough health check.
   I..
9 Before you buy a boat you ought to learn to swim.
   Before you buy a boat you had ....
10 I prefer having an injection to feeling the dentist's drill.
   I'd rather ....

3 *Choose the word or phrase (A–D) which best completes each sentence.*

1 I can't give up cigarettes completely, but at least I'm cutting .... the number I smoke a day.

A down   B off   C out   D up

2 I suggest you .... that foot X-rayed.

A have   B having   C to have   D will have

3 Do I need a .... to get antibiotics from the chemist?

A dose   B prescription   C receipt   D recipe

4 The singer cancelled the show because of his .... throat.

A hurt   B ill   C sick   D sore

5 Doctors .... have time for any outside interests.

A ever   B now and then   C occasionally   D seldom

6 The chemist was .... by an explosion in her laboratory.

A damaged   B harmed   C injured   D spoiled

7 It was so hot in the conference room that I almost .... out.

A carried   B passed   C stood   D threw

8 How much exercise do you .... a week?

A go   B make   C take   D work

9 .... the weekends I do as little as possible so that I'm refreshed by Monday morning.

A At   B By   C For   D In

10 He needs sleeping pills because he's so .... by his work that he can't sleep.

A disappointed   B exhausted   C nervous   D relieved

6 UNIT SIX
A place called home

1 Neighbourhoods

Speaking *Home surroundings*

How many of these things can you do in your neighbourhood?

- play dominoes in the street
- go to primary school
- buy bread
- go to the dentist
- go swimming
- find a job
- go to university
- buy antique furniture
- exchange foreign money

In your town/city, where do the | rich people poor people | live?

Where is the | entertainment business industrial | area?

Listening 🖭 *Clive comes home*

1 *A popular type of soap opera concerns the lives of a group of people all living in the same street or area. Is there one like that on your TV or radio?*

Look at this programme listing for an episode of a radio soap opera.

> **RADIO PRD**
>
> **7.45pm**   **Streets apart**
> *Episode 93*
> Clive comes home at last,
> but Silvia is still worried.
> Bret hides his surprise.
> Where is Nancy?

What could be the relationships between these people? Listen and find out.

2 *The characters say these things:*

How thin you've grown!
You still look just like a film star.
I don't suppose you read about it where you were.
Where have you left your suitcase?
I've already eaten, thank you, mother.
He's obviously as impetuous as ever.

But they really mean much more than they actually say. What do you think the speakers are really thinking?

Grammar *Present perfect*

1 HAVE/HAS + PAST PARTICIPLE
You haven't changed a bit.

You use the present perfect tense when you want to show a relationship between past time and present time.

Match each description of the use of the present perfect with one of the example sentences below:

a to talk about an action which started in the past and is still continuing

b to talk about a very recent past action, for which no definite time reference is given

c to talk about an action which is part of a person's experience, and for which no definite time reference is given

d to talk about a past action which has had a result which can be seen in the present

e to show that one action must be completed before another can happen

1 *You've only just arrived.*
2 *As I've waited ten years, I can wait another ten minutes.*
3 *I'll show you after you've had something to eat.*
4 *How thin you've grown!*
5 *Have you ever seen 'Neighbours'?*

2 You often use the present perfect with some of these time adverbials. Which ones?

ago   all my life   already   ever   just   last week
lately   for two hours   never   next week   now
since 1945   so far   recently   yesterday   yet

3 Complete this letter by putting each verb in brackets in the correct tense (present simple, present perfect or past simple):

Dear Donna,
I have some wonderful news for you. Clive
(1) .... (return) at last. He
(2) .... (be) with us for five days now.
He looks very different, but he **(3)** ....
(suffer) a lot, so it is not surprising. He
(4) .... (become) much thinner and he
(5) .... (lose) the good looks he
(6) .... (have) when he was a little
boy. I **(7)** .... (buy) him some smart
new clothes and I **(8)** .... (cook) all his
favourite meals, but so far he **(9)** ....
(refuse) to accept anything I give him. He says he
(10) .... (feel) more comfortable
in jeans and that he **(11)** ....
(lose) his taste for rich foods. At least now he
(12) .... (not quarrel) with his father as
much as he used to.
    The thing that really upsets me is that he **(13)** ....
(not forget) that dreadful girl who **(14)** ....
(be) such a bad influence on him in the old days. On his
first day home he **(15)** .... (go) to look
for her. Her family **(16)** ....
(move) away from this neighbourhood some years ago, but
they still **(17)** .... (live) somewhere in
the city. Fortunately, he **(18)** .... (not
find) any trace of her yet.
    You and he **(19)** .... (get) on so
well together when you **(20)** .... (be)
children. Would you like to come and stay for a few days? I
am sure you could help him forget the past.
    Give my love to your parents.
    With love from

Aunt Silvia

Speaking *Episode 94*

In groups of three or four, improvise Episode 94 in this soap opera: THE MEETING WITH NANCY. One student is Clive, another Nancy, and the other student(s) should invent their own character(s).

Try and use these words and phrases:

Present perfect adverbials	*'Neighbourhood' words*	*Reunion expressions*
since I left home	run-down	It's been a long time since ...
during the last three years	built-up	Have you missed ... ?
all my life	gossip	Do you remember when ... ?
recently	suburb	I'll never forget ...
never	amenity	Whatever happened to ... ?

Discuss the outline of your episode, then act it out.

Give him an inch . . .

Property

● **What was once a tiny alleyway next to a house is now a 4ft by 21ft fully equipped flat with all mod cons. HUGH PEARMAN looks at the small world of 'linear living' where not an inch of space is wasted.**

IT'S NOT much, but it's home. Francis Chan, a structural engineer, lives in Hampstead, north London, in a flat that's just 4ft wide by 21ft long. He loves it.

Tiny though it is, this is no converted broom cupboard. Peter Baynes, Chan's architect, has achieved a brilliant piece of design, according to architectural experts. And all the comforts of conventional luxury homes are built in.

The Chan mini-mansion – "You could call it linear living," he comments – occupies what was once an alleyway down the side of a big Victorian house. Not an inch of space is wasted.

When you step in through the front door, you're standing in the shower, on Britain's only self-cleansing doormat. A door opens on to an equally tiny lavatory with washbasin. Two steps further in comes the kitchen, complete with full-sized cooker and fridge, microwave and washer/drier. A worktop folds down from the wall.

Another step and you're into the dining/office area. Four people can squeeze in here for dinner, says Chan as he swings the table-top into place. He even has a fold-down drawing-board for when he's working at home. The bed is hidden beneath a lid right at the back. "I don't even have to make the bed," Chan comments. "I just put the lid down."

Storage is ingeniously tucked in all along the flat – Chan's business suits hang neatly on the wall over the bed. Daylight comes in through rooflights. Central heating consists of one electric convector – with the meter outside so that bulky meter readers don't have to shoulder their way in. It feels like a very small boat and Chan admits he toyed with the idea of naming it the "boat-house".

Chan bought the big house next door – divided into three flats – three years ago. He and Baynes started to restore it but Chan ran short of money, which put paid to his plan to live in the ground floor flat himself.

His idea to build a mini-office to replace the existing lean-to shed in the alley was rapidly modified. It became his home instead.

"Peter spent more time designing this tiny flat than he did on the whole of the rest of the house," recalled Chan. "It cost around £4,700 to build last year. Now it's been valued at £30,000. It proves that good design doesn't need to cost more. It just needs a lot of care."

Chan's microscopic home has been taken up by the influential Architect's Journal. Its editor, Peter Carolin, recently appointed Professor of Architecture at Cambridge University, said: "This is an excellent solution to a very unusual problem. It's very modest and completely appropriate – it's even witty. Francis Chan must be a very tidy man and Baynes must be very talented. It's the kind of solution a really good architect can come up with."

Chan hails originally from Hong Kong where, he says, "flats are 15 times bigger". In Britain his home does not quite beat the celebrated Knightsbridge broom cupboard, an 11ft by 6ft one-bed flat.

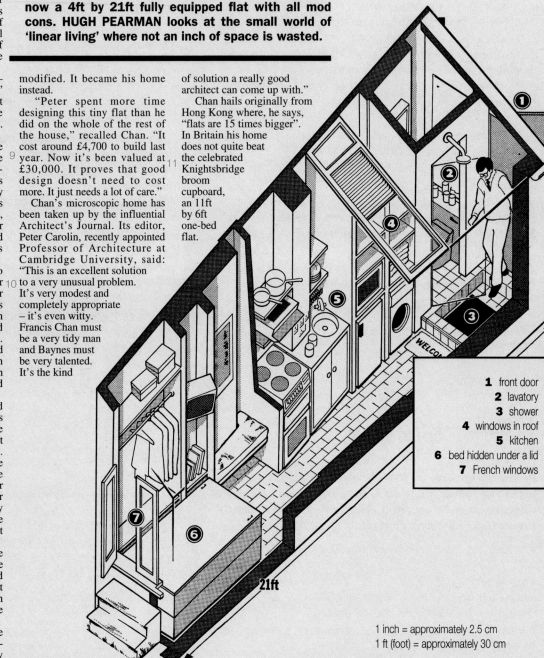

1 front door
2 lavatory
3 shower
4 windows in roof
5 kitchen
6 bed hidden under a lid
7 French windows

21ft

1 inch = approximately 2.5 cm
1 ft (foot) = approximately 30 cm

Reading *Give him an inch*

1 **Find the answers to these questions about Francis Chan's home by quickly reading the text opposite.**

1 How big is the flat?
2 Where is it positioned?
3 Where's the shower?
4 How many people can be invited to dinner at the same time?
5 Where's the bed?
6 Why did Francis Chan decide to live in a home like this?
7 How much did the flat cost to build?
8 What does the editor of the 'Architect's Journal' think of the flat?

2 **Discuss your answers to these questions.**

1 Imagine you lived in Francis Chan's flat. What would be its advantages and disadvantages?
2 'All the comforts of conventional luxury homes are built in' to his house. What do you consider are *essential* items (e.g. a washbasin) in a house, and what are *luxury* items (e.g. a microwave)? Make two lists with about ten items in each.
3 Look at your list of essential items. If you had to save money, decide in what order you would sell or stop using them.

Word formation *Compounds and adjectives*

1 COMPOUND ADJECTIVES
Adjectives which are made with combinations of two (or sometimes more) words are called compound adjectives:

good-looking   old-fashioned   three-day

1 Find examples in the text of compound adjectives which are made with:
   a a present participle (paragraph 4)
   b a word that ends in *-ed* (paragraph 4)
   c a phrasal verb (paragraph 5)
   d a numeral (paragraph 11)

2 Turn each phrase into a compound adjective + noun:
   EXAMPLE: a garden which is 10 metres long → *a ten-metre garden*
   a a television which has broken down
   b a friendship which has lasted a long time
   c a cake which was made at home
   d a test which takes two hours to do
   e a book which costs half as much as usual

2 COMPOUND NOUNS
Nouns which are made with combinations of two or more words are called compound nouns:

teapot   washing-up   bubble bath

1 In paragraphs 4, 5 and 6 find at least two examples each of compound nouns which are:
   a one word
   b with a hyphen (-)
   c two words

2 What compound nouns do the following definitions refer to?
   EXAMPLE: an alarm which warns you about a burglar → *a burglar alarm*
   a a pan used to fry food
   b something used to open tins
   c a room where people eat meals
   d your sister's husband
   e a container where you throw waste paper

3 ADJECTIVE FORMATION

Many adjectives can be formed by adding a suffix to a noun or verb. This word formation table contains some words from the text.

1 Complete the table with the related nouns, verbs and adjectives, using your dictionary, if necessary.

Noun	Verb	Adjective
luxury	–	
comfort		
	–	conventional
	waste	
care		
	live	
	–	witty
		electric

2 In the completed table there are examples of eight different adjective suffixes. Sometimes you need to make a change to the verb or noun before adding the suffix (e.g. wit – wit*ty*, luxury – luxur*ious*). Think of more examples of adjectives which have the suffixes in the table.

3 Give the adjectives which can be formed from these nouns and verbs.

a poison	**i** heart	**q** neighbour
b energy	**j** vary	**r** blood
c terror	**k** sense	**s** economy
d hope	**l** pain	**t** friend
e danger	**m** fog	**u** emotion
f hunger	**n** break	**v** courage
g day	**o** smoke	
h nation	**p** education	

Directed writing *A burglar's point of view*

Look carefully at these three houses and then complete Bugsy the Burglar's letter.

Dear Boss,
I've been to look at the three houses in Victory Street, as you asked me. Two of the houses would be easy to burgle, but I'm not sure about the third.

Number .... would be the easiest to get into because
....
....
....
....
....
....

I don't think number .... would give us many problems either, for the following reasons. ....
....
....
....
....
....
....

But we'd better not try and burgle number .... because
....
....
....
....
....
....

I'll phone you at the usual time to hear what the plan is.
Yours, *Bugsy B.*

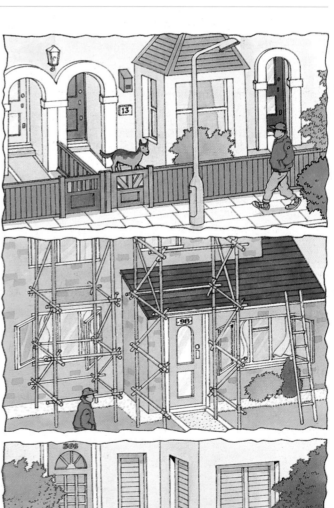

3 Interiors

Listening 📼 *A beautiful memory*

1 *What was the first home you ever lived in? Was it like either of these homes? Would you have been happy to live in these homes as a child?*

2 *Listen to Sue talking about a house she remembers from her childhood.*

1 Whose house is she describing?
2 Which part of the house sounds the nicest to you?
3 Who is living there now?

3 *Listen again and mark if each statement (1–8) is True or False.*

		True	False
1	When the speaker was a child, she thought the house was very large.	☐	☐
2	She couldn't understand why they didn't use the drawing room every day.	☐	☐
3	She liked the living room best.	☐	☐
4	She liked the kitchen because it was warm and smelled nice.	☐	☐
5	Her grandmother used to get cross with her for not helping to pick the vegetables and fruit.	☐	☐
6	The interior of the house is the same now as it was when the speaker was young.	☐	☐
7	When she returned, she felt unhappy at the size of the house.	☐	☐
8	She realised it is not a good idea to revisit the past.	☐	☐

4 *Have you ever been in a similar situation? How did/would you feel?*

Grammar *The past (1)*

1 PAST SIMPLE
The regular past form is made by adding -ed to the infinitive:

paint → painted

Irregular past forms must be learnt by heart:

go → went   know → knew   rise → rose etc.

The past simple indicates an action which happened, or a state which existed, at a time in the past. The time reference is given or understood from the context:
I went back to it a few years ago.
The name of the house was Crosslands.

Some examples of adverbials used to refer to past time are:
yesterday   last year   in 1987   a week ago
at the end of the last century   earlier this month
when I was a child

2 PAST HABITS
You can express past habits with the past simple and an adverbial such as 'always' or 'twice a week':

My grandmother baked bread twice a week.

You can also use:
used to ⎫
would/'d ⎬ + infinitive
My grandmother used to make ice cream and we'd eat it in the kitchen.
These forms show that something happened regularly in the past, but that it no longer happens. 'Would' is more common in written than in spoken English.

3 PAST PROGRESSIVE
was/were + -ing *form*

It was snowing.

The past progressive indicates an action in progress at a particular time in the past. It suggests that the action was temporary and incomplete:
Her parents were working abroad at the time.

Often the past progressive action is 'interrupted' by another action; the past simple is used for the 'interrupting' action:
I was picking and eating the strawberries in the garden when my grandmother came to the window and told me to stop.

The past progressive also indicates background in a story:
All the furniture was wearing clothes.
It was snowing. Night was falling. Jamie walked to the window. He was waiting for someone ...

4 PAST PERFECT SIMPLE
had + past participle

The house had shrunk.

The past perfect indicates an action that happened, or a state that existed, at some time *before* another action or state in the past:
I went back to it a few years ago and I had the feeling the house had shrunk; it had become smaller.

5 **Read this extract from an account of a visit to an ancient Minoan palace. Put each verb in brackets in the appropriate past tense.**

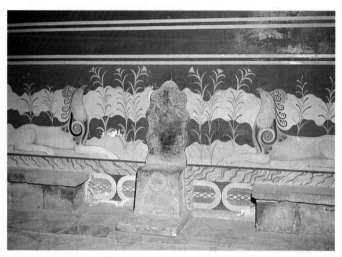

The Throne Room at Knossos, Crete, 15th century BC

I next (**1**) .... (come) to a low-ceilinged outer room. Here some students (**2**) .... (photograph) three huge jars which the archaeologists (**3**) .... (dig up) recently. I (**4**) .... (cross) this room, and (**5**) .... (enter) the Throne Room itself. It (**6**) .... (be) rectangular in shape, and surprisingly small. On the wall opposite, a Minoan artist (**7**) .... (paint) two magnificent griffins, lion-like animals with the heads of eagles. Between the griffins, the oldest throne in the world still (**8**) .... (stand), the throne of King Minos himself!

On each side of the Throne there (**9**) .... (be) low stone benches with room for up to 16 people. Here the King (**10**) .... (sit) with his advisers to discuss important affairs of state. In front of the Throne, broad steps (**11**) .... (lead) down to a deep basin set in the floor. Here people (**12**) .... (wash) themselves ceremonially.

I (**13**) .... (try) to imagine what life must have been like at that time when a crowd of noisy tourists (**14**) .... (come) in behind me. So I (**15**) .... (turn) and (**16**) .... (go) out again into the bright sunlight.

Writing *Description of a place*

Imagine the room in the picture has played an important part in your life. In your autobiography you want to describe your first impressions of the room.

1 GETTING IDEAS
Your description of the room is going to include:
- what you saw, including colours
- what you heard, smelled and touched
- your feelings

Look at the picture carefully for a few moments. You were there a long time ago, but you have never forgotten it. Is it a pleasant or unpleasant memory? Or are your feelings mixed?

Now write some brief notes about all the sights, colours, sounds, smells, textures and feelings that you 'remember'. Adjective and noun combinations are best.
For example: *old-fashioned furniture*
                        hard scratchy chair covering
                        strong smell of polish

Horace Pippin, 'Victorian Interior'

2 FINDING A FOCUS

1 Feelings
Do the adjectives you have written reflect your feelings about the room? For example, have you written 'heavy old-fashioned furniture' or 'elegant antique furniture'? Think of one word or short phrase which sums up your 'memories'. For example, for mainly unpleasant feelings the word could be 'uncomfortable'; for mainly pleasant feelings it could be 'safe'.

2 Path
Now organise the different parts of your description. Imagine your words following the path of a movie camera. For example, start with a general view and then move to take in selected details in close-up; or start with a detail and gradually build up a wider impression.

3 WRITING

1 Here are the beginnings of two possible descriptions of the room. Read them and decide in each case what the writer's focus is.

  a The first thing I noticed about the room was its warmth and light. A gently hissing oil lamp brought out the cheerful red and gold in the carpet ...

  b The first thing I noticed about the room was a stiffly arranged vase of flowers, and a strong hospital smell of disinfectant and polish ...

2 Finish writing one of the descriptions, making sure you maintain the original focus.

3 Compare your description with another student's. How has your partner maintained the focus? Compare both your descriptions with the ones on page 190.

4

Exam skill *Reading*

Your ability to understand written English is tested in Paper 1, Section B. There are three reading passages and a total of 15 multiple-choice items. The third 'passage' may in fact be a collection of short texts (see, for example, pages 24–5).

Timing

You have one hour to do Paper 1, which includes both Section A (see Unit 7 Lesson 4) and Section B. Do a practice paper before the exam to find out how much time you need to spend on each part of this paper.

Here are three steps which should help you do your best in Section B.

Step 1

For passages 1 and 2:
– carefully read the passage once to understand as much as you can.

For passage 3:
– look quickly over the passage(s) to get a general idea of the topic. Don't try to read every word.

Practise now with this passage: read it carefully to understand as much as you can. Use the strategy you practised in the reading activity on page 19 to help you with any unfamiliar words. You should be able to answer all the questions even if you don't understand every word.

Mary Knox-Johnston

London is famous for its ghosts, with thousands of reported sightings over the centuries. The paranormal is not choosy where it shows itself – theatres, pubs, churchyards, commercial buildings, council houses, even Vine Street Police Station, public toilets and the underground.

Says Tom Perrott, chairman of the members-only Ghost Club and a member of The Society for Psychical Research (SPR): "It's generally thought these things only happen in romantic moonlit ruins or ancient halls hung with rows of antlers, but experiences in modern buildings are equally frequent."

Clive Seymour is an investigator with The Association for the Scientific Study of Anomalous Phenomena (ASSAP). He says: "People claiming to have paranormal experiences are far more numerous than anyone would think. Most of them are level-headed, reasonable types."

A few miles from Thamesmead, on the edge of London, is the rambling Georgian home of Mary Knox-Johnston, descendant of Plantagenets and mother of celebrated round-the-world yachtsman Robin.

Mary Knox-Johnston, elegant and briskly courteous, is a no-nonsense person with peculiar tales to tell: "Soon after we moved here I was woken up one night by this incredible noise. There was obviously a terrific fight going on – shouting and clashing of swords. It seemed to be coming from the hall. I leaned over the banister, but I couldn't see anything."

Her housekeeper Doris Crawford, who lives in a flat within the house, had the same experience.

According to Mrs Knox-Johnston, there was a much older house on the land hers now occupies. "You can see the foundations from aerial photographs, and it's known to be the site of fighting during the Civil War in the 1640s."

One story tells of a Cavalier and his two sons who fled London making for the coast. They were caught and hanged by Roundheads at this very spot.

Another extraordinary incident happened a few years back. Mary left three pound notes lying flat on a padded chest on the landing. One disappeared. She and Doris looked everywhere for it. Eventually it was found tightly rolled up and standing on its end in the *downstairs* hall. No one else was in the house at the time.

"Money has always been funny here," says Mary. "My cleaner and I once saw six pound notes rise up off the table. Instinctively I banged my hand down on them but now I wish I'd just stood and watched."

Other incidents include apparitions – one which sat heavily on the bed; another of a child as real as a living person; others more ethereal. There are unaccountable smells of oranges and cigars. Dusters, laid down for a moment by Doris, vanish and reappear in another room. Two car accidents happened in exactly the same place outside the house – the steering wheel "taken over".

"My husband didn't experience anything at all here," said Mrs Knox-Johnston, "and neither have any of my sons. They all pull my leg about the whole thing."

Some people, says Tom Perrott, are naturally psychically sensitive, though they may not realise it. Others are not.

Practise this now with these multiple-choice questions (1–5).

1 Where, according to the article, do paranormal experiences take place?
 A in places connected with death
 B in historical places
 C in deserted places
 D in all sorts of places

2 Clive Seymour thinks that the majority of people who have paranormal experiences are
 A imaginative.
 B sensible.
 C mentally disturbed.
 D religious.

3 What was extraordinary about Mrs Knox-Johnston's story of the fight?
 A She could hear the noise but see nothing.
 B The hall filled with smells of cigars and oranges.
 C She saw men in old-fashioned clothes in the hall.
 D It happened regularly but only at night.

4 What was extraordinary about the story of the three pound notes?
 A They rose into the air by themselves.
 B An extra one was found with the other three.
 C One was found in a different position.
 D One was never found again.

5 What does the case of Mrs Knox-Johnston suggest about the paranormal?
 A Everyone is equally able to experience it.
 B Certain people are more likely to experience it.
 C Disbelieving people are unlikely to experience it.
 D Women experience it more than men.

Choose the correct answer for questions 1–5.

Test exercises

1 *Complete this passage. Use only **one** word in each gap.*

My garden at Compton Acres is less (**1**) .... 70 years old. That is still young in comparison with many of Britain's great (**2**) .... However, several important features had been allowed to fall into a (**3**) .... bad condition by the (**4**) .... I bought the property in 1986. My first task has been to repair (**5**) .... features.

It (**6**) .... become difficult to reach the places in the garden with the best views because so (**7**) .... paths were in such poor condition. The Italian formal garden, for example, has always (**8**) .... many visitors, and as a result (**9**) .... paths were in a terrible state. But hundreds of metres of paths (**10**) .... recently been repaired.

We have also done a (**11**) .... of work on many of the garden's wooden buildings. A major job was (**12**) .... completely rebuild the roof (**13**) .... the Japanese summer house. We also (**14**) .... the greenhouses to a more practical location.

Work (**15**) .... this is essential before you can get on (**16**) .... the real business of gardening. I am not sure (**17**) .... the visitors realise how much work of this (**18**) .... is necessary. But I (**19**) .... thoroughly enjoying the job of returning the garden to (**20**) .... former glory.

2 *Complete each of the following sentences so that it means exactly the same as the sentence before it.*

1 I've never been to Scotland before.
This ....

2 My neighbour came to live here ten years ago.
My neighbour's ....

3 I don't advise you to rent a flat in that part of town.
You'd...

4 I think the best thing you can do is stay in a cheap hotel.
If I...

5 The cost of living in Tokyo is much higher than in Madrid.
The cost of living in Madrid ....

6 It's ages since I last saw the McDonald twins.
I have...

7 The old town hall has been pulled down.
They...

8 This is the first time I've lived in such a friendly neighbourhood.
I haven't ....

9 The children were wearing their new school uniforms.
The children had...

10 In the past Gerald drove to work, but he doesn't any more.
Gerald used ....

3 *Choose the word or phrase (A–D) which best completes each sentence.*

1 I'm going to sell this old sofa – it takes .... too much space.
    A after   B down   C off   D up

2 If you feel cold during the night, there's a spare .... in the wardrobe.
    A blanket   B mat   C pillow   D sheet

3 Do you mind if I open the window? It's terribly .... in here.
    A smoked   B smokeless   C smoking   D smoky

4 The old palace was sold because the government could no longer afford to
    .... it.
    A maintain   B provide   C shelter   D support

5 He loves being an architect – he finds the work interesting and ....
    A variable   B varied   C various   D varying

6 When they were .... out the cupboard in the spare bedroom they found
    a dead mouse at the back.
    A coming   B clearing   C letting   D going

7 I've .... my keys at home – how am I going to get back into the flat?
    A forgotten   B kept   C left   D lost

8 Many library-goers take books off the shelves and don't .... them to their
    proper places.
    A remove   B renew   C replace   D return

9 For the Carnival party they .... wonderful costumes from a special shop.
    A hired   B lent   C let   D rented

10 She's such .... child – always singing and dancing.
    A an alive   B a live   C a lively   D a living

On the move

1 On the road

Vocabulary *Cars*

1 *Compare and contrast the two cars shown here in terms of:*

- comfort
- convenience
- efficiency
- reliability
- safety
- speed

Use these words to help you:

accelerate	battery	bonnet	boot	brake

accelerate   battery   bonnet   boot   brake
bumper   change gear   crash   fuel consumption
go fast   headlights   indicator   overtake
park   petrol   seat belt   spare tyre
steering wheel   suspension   windscreen

2 *Which of the cars would you use if you:*

- wanted to impress your friends?
- wanted to go to the beach for the day?
- had to drive across Europe?
- needed a car for your work?

3 *Which car available today would you recommend for:*

- a college student living at home?
- a couple with four young children?
- a famous model?
- a photojournalist?

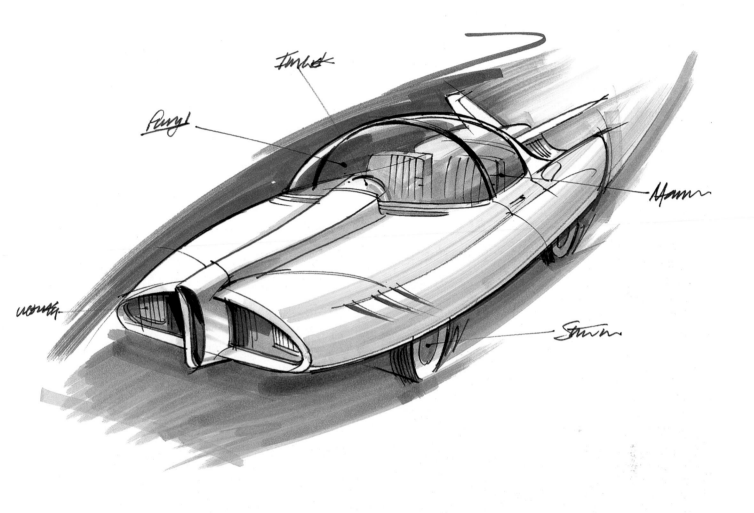

Listening 🔊 *Motoring*

1 *Listen to these five short radio items (1–5). Write the number of each item in the correct boxes in the chart to record both:*

– what type of item it is (TYPE)
– what it is about (CONTENT)

TYPE
Traffic report   ☐ ☐
Advertisement   ☐ ☐
News story   ☐ ☐

CONTENT
M11 traffic to Cambridge can expect delays   ☐
Special Renault deals this month   ☐
Crash blocks A604   ☐
New research is planned for Britain   ☐
Special deals on spare parts   ☐

2 *Listen to item 5 again and fill each gap in these notes about the story with one, or at most two, words:*

– Collision between (1) .... heavy goods vehicles and a van on the A604 at Godwinchester
– Heavy goods vehicles: a tanker carrying agricultural (2) .... and a 38-ton lorry loaded with (3) ....
– Driver of the (4) .... taken to hospital for a (5) ....
– (6) .... seriously injured

1 *Look at all the words in large print. What do you think the article is going to be about?*

2 *Read the article and see if you were right.*

Frank Symondson: 'Women are bad for business users.'

Ada Smith: 'They have to carry children.'

Ian Lewis: 'They are terrible.'

Lynne Christian: 'Women are safer.'

Simon Welsh: 'If you're a bad driver ...'

As a new government report sinks those jokes about women drivers, STEPHEN HILL takes to the streets to find out what local people think

Ladies first for safety

WOMEN drivers are the safest people on the road, says a government report.

Researcher Dr Jeremy Broughton analysed every road accident in Britain for one year and the results contradict all men who have ever uttered the immortal phrase: "Women drivers!!!"

The report shows that a male motorist's risk of death at the wheel is one in 300 whereas a woman's is one in 850.

A man's chance of injury in a car crash between the ages of 17 and 70, the average driving lifetime, is one in 25 and a woman's is one in 40.

And although a third of women drivers will be injured in accidents during their time on the road almost half of all male drivers will meet the same fate.

But Dr Broughton's findings have come under fire from local men. Tradition, it seems, dies hard.

"No way are women safer drivers," said Ealing Post Office worker Ian Lewis. "I drive a van and they are terrible."

"They pull out in front of other cars and slow down all the traffic," said fellow Ealing Post Office worker Paul Bedworth.

However, the women thought differently: "Women are much safer because they're much more cautious," said Chiswick resident Lynne Christian. "They are slower," she added, "But that's why they're better and safer."

Ealing's Simon Welsh felt that the sex of the driver was irrelevant: "If you're a bad driver, you're a bad driver," he said. "It doesn't matter whether you are a man or a woman. Then again, there's been no trouble with the girls I've known."

Ada Smith of Harrow reckons that the load a woman carries in the car makes a difference: "They have to carry the children," she explained. And she added their drinking habits made them safer road users. "They don't drink as much as men. Men are always being stopped for drinking and driving."

But Kilburn lorry driver Frank Symondson told a different story: "Women are bad for business road users," he said. "When I'm doing deliveries and there's a woman trying to reverse into a parking space up ahead, all the traffic is slowed up and I'm late. They don't know how to control a car," he added.

Men, it seems, feel they are in control of any situation behind the wheel, whereas women feel that the female cautious and less aggressive approach to driving is safer.

But perhaps Carol Williams from Harrow best summed up the situation: "They are both as bad as each other," she said.

New study says women safer drivers

3 *Answer these questions.*

1 What do men mean when they say 'Women drivers!!!' (paragraph 2)?

2 Fill in the table of statistics about car safety.

Chance of:	Men	Women
a Death when a driver		
b Injury when a driver		
c Injury in a car crash between 17–70		

3 What are the opinions of the seven people interviewed in the article? Fill each gap with the correct figure.

a .... women felt that women were safer drivers than men.

b .... men thought that women were worse drivers than men.

c .... people considered that the sex of the driver was unimportant.

4 *How do you feel about the results of this survey? How do you react to the opinions expressed in this article?*

Grammar *Reported statements*

1 **You can report what someone says directly:**

"Women are much safer because they're much more cautious," said Chiswick resident Lynne Christian.
or indirectly:
Ada Smith reckons that the load a woman carries in the car makes a difference.
Simon Welsh felt that the sex of the driver was irrelevant.

These two sentences are examples of reported statements. The reporting verb ('reckons', 'felt') is followed by 'that' and a clause.

When you change direct statements to reported statements, various changes have to be made to what is reported:

1 PUNCTUATION CHANGES
Inverted commas (" ") are used to mark the beginning and end of direct statements only:
"They are slower," she added.
The report shows that a male motorist's risk of death at the wheel is one in 300.

2 PRONOUN CHANGES
First and second person pronouns change to third person:
"I drive a van and they are terrible," said Ian Lewis.
Ian Lewis said that he drove a van and that they were terrible.

3 'POINTER WORD' CHANGES
'Pointer words' are words referring to specific times and places, e.g. 'this', 'now', 'here', 'tomorrow'.

Direct	Reported
now	at that time / then
this (e.g. morning)	that (e.g. morning)
today	that day
yesterday	the day before
tomorrow	the day after
next (e.g. week)	the following (e.g. week)
last (e.g. year)	the (e.g. year) before
here	there
ahead	ahead of (him)
come	go

4 VERB TENSE CHANGES
When the reporting verb is in the past (e.g. 'said', 'added', 'explained'), changes usually have to be made to the verb(s) in the 'that' clause:
Ian Lewis said that he drove a van and that they were terrible.

Direct	Reported
am/is, are, have/has	was, were, had
present, simple or progressive	past, simple or progressive
present perfect	past perfect
past, simple or progressive	past perfect, simple or progressive
can	could
may	might
must	had to
will	would

Note

1 Past perfect verbs in direct speech remain unchanged in reported speech.
2 Other modal verbs – 'could', 'might', 'ought to', 'should', 'would' – do not normally change. 'Must' can also remain unchanged.

2 *Change these direct statements into reported statements.*

1 "Women are much safer because they're much more cautious," said Lynne Christian.
Lynne Christian said that ....
....

2 "Women pull out in front of other cars and slow down all the traffic," said Paul Bedworth.
Paul Bedworth said that ....
....

3 "Women have to carry the children," Ada Smith explained.
Ada Smith explained that ....

4 "It doesn't matter whether you are a man or a woman," replied Simon Welsh. "But there's been no trouble with the girls I've known."
Simon Welsh replied that ....
....
....

5 "When I'm doing deliveries and there's a woman trying to reverse into a parking space up ahead, all the traffic is slowed up and I'm late. They don't know how to control a car," complained Frank Symondson.
Frank Symondson complained that ....
....
....

6 "I had an accident yesterday. I was slowing down at a zebra crossing and a lorry hit me in the back!"
She said ....
....

7 "I can't drive. My mother won't teach me but my sister may give me lessons next summer."
She told ....
....

" – fill her up!"

*"Well, Mr Nedkins, I'm afraid you haven't passed the test. But if you'd care to wait
a moment or two, I'll fill in this form showing the points on which you failed."*

2 Airmail

Speaking *Airport*

Look at the picture and decide who is saying these things:

1 'I know it's silly, but I'm too scared to go up.'
2 'But the travel agent said I didn't need a visa.'
3 'I don't know how that got into my suitcase.'
4 'My body says it's bedtime, but my watch disagrees.'
5 'What happens if we miss our connecting flight?'
6 'What a wonderful suntan!'
7 'Non-smoking window seat, please.'
8 'Do you need such a large bottle?'
9 'It's brown with a red strap.'

How do you think each conversation continues?

Writing *A letter to a friend*

1 *What kind of letter is this? Read it to find out the sender's reason for writing.*

26 Glendale Road
Chester CH4 7HB

3 May 1994

Dear Marco,

Thank you for your letter. I was pleased to hear about your exam results. Congratulations!

I have some exciting news for you. I'm not frightened of aeroplanes any more! I told you about the first time I tried to go on a plane, didn't I? I had a panic attack and had to be taken off screaming. It was so dreadful that I never wanted to try it again.

Then last month I went to an 'air anxiety' seminar. There they explained exactly how planes manage to stay in the sky, taught us some breathing exercises to do when we felt panicky, and put us in a flight simulator. It was horribly bumpy and noisy!

Next we visited the airport just to get used to planes taking off and landing. After that we actually flew to Paris. I didn't enjoy it, but I didn't scream either.

I will soon be ready for the long flight to Brazil. Does your invitation still stand?

Give my best wishes to all your family. Please write to me again soon.

With love from
Jill

2 *Look at the letter and complete these notes about the layout and organisation of a letter to a friend.*

1 Your address should go in ....
2 The .... comes underneath this. Remember the names of months always have a .... letter.
3 The correct punctuation after the salutation (Dear + your friend's name) is ....
4 You should start your letter with a general friendly beginning, such as ....
....
5 In the next paragraph you should give ....
6 You should organise what you want to say to your friend in ....
7 If you add one or two general closing sentences, it will sound ....
8 You should .... your letter with an expression such as .... or 'With best wishes from'.
9 The last thing you write is ....

3 *Here are some things you might write in a letter to a friend. Sort them into two groups: beginnings and endings.*

a I'm sorry I haven't written for a long time.
b I'm looking forward to seeing you soon.
c Take care of yourself.
d It's ages since I last heard from you – I hope you and your family are all well.
e Have a wonderful time and be sure to write and tell me all about it.
f I passed our old school yesterday and I couldn't help thinking of you.

4 *After a friendly beginning you should give your reason for writing. For example, Jill's reason for writing to Marco is to give him some news. Match each of the following reasons for writing with the appropriate sentences.*

EXAMPLE: 1–c

1	to give news	**a**	I'm having a party next Saturday. I wonder if you would like to come, and stay the whole weekend?
2	to invite	**b**	I want to thank you for the really wonderful weekend I spent with you. I will never forget all your kind hospitality.
3	to accept an invitation	**c**	You'll never guess what happened to me the other day.
4	to refuse an invitation	**d**	I can see you're in a difficult situation. This is what I think you should do.
5	to thank	**e**	I'm afraid I'm in a bit of trouble and I don't know who to turn to. I wonder if you could possibly help me?
6	to apologise	**f**	Thank you very much for your kind invitation. I should love to come.
7	to ask a favour	**g**	Thank you very much for your kind invitation. I'm very sorry that I won't be able to come because ...
8	to give advice	**h**	I don't know how to tell you this. You remember that book you lent me? Well, I'm afraid it had a slight accident. I'm terribly sorry.

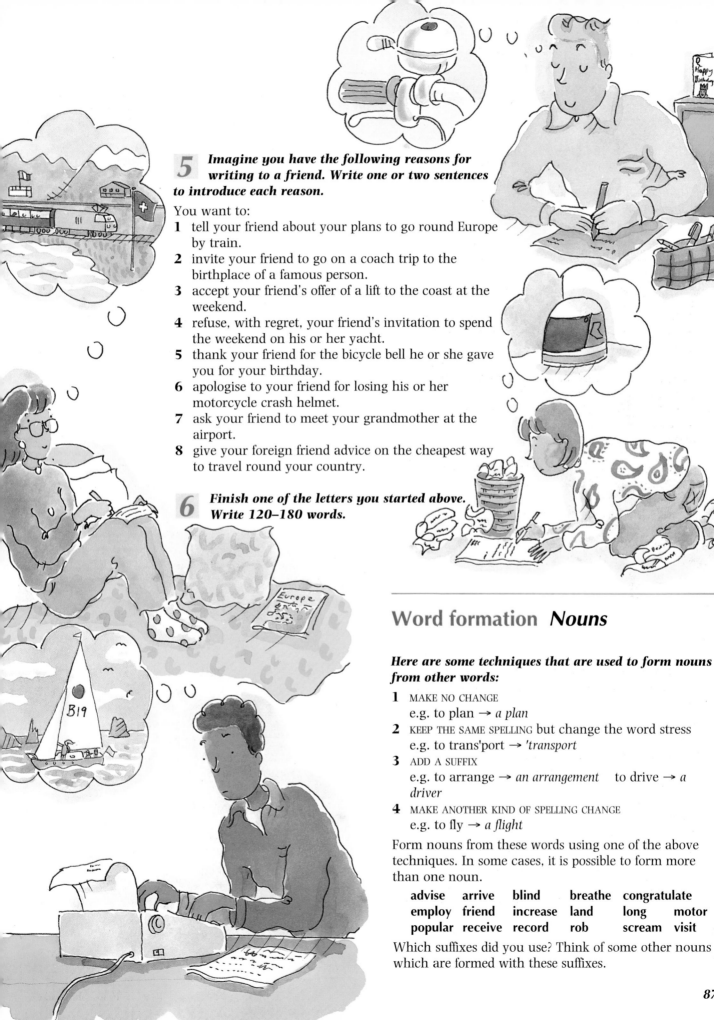

5 *Imagine you have the following reasons for writing to a friend. Write one or two sentences to introduce each reason.*

You want to:
1 tell your friend about your plans to go round Europe by train.
2 invite your friend to go on a coach trip to the birthplace of a famous person.
3 accept your friend's offer of a lift to the coast at the weekend.
4 refuse, with regret, your friend's invitation to spend the weekend on his or her yacht.
5 thank your friend for the bicycle bell he or she gave you for your birthday.
6 apologise to your friend for losing his or her motorcycle crash helmet.
7 ask your friend to meet your grandmother at the airport.
8 give your foreign friend advice on the cheapest way to travel round your country.

6 *Finish one of the letters you started above. Write 120–180 words.*

Word formation *Nouns*

Here are some techniques that are used to form nouns from other words:

1 MAKE NO CHANGE
e.g. to plan → *a plan*
2 KEEP THE SAME SPELLING but change the word stress
e.g. to trans'port → *'transport*
3 ADD A SUFFIX
e.g. to arrange → *an arrangement*   to drive → *a driver*
4 MAKE ANOTHER KIND OF SPELLING CHANGE
e.g. to fly → *a flight*

Form nouns from these words using one of the above techniques. In some cases, it is possible to form more than one noun.

advise	arrive	blind	breathe	congratulate
employ	friend	increase	land	long motor
popular	receive	record	rob	scream visit

Which suffixes did you use? Think of some other nouns which are formed with these suffixes.

3 Exotic holidays

Speaking *Discussing a photo*

1 What can you see in each photo? Where do you think it might be? Would you like to be there now?
2 What sort of things would you be able to do in each place?
3 What makes a holiday 'exotic' for you? If you could have an exotic holiday anywhere in the world, where would you go and what would you do?

Listening 🔊 *A good holiday?*

1 **Listen to Peter talking about a holiday he's recently had with his family.**

1 Does he seem to have had a good time?
2 Which aspects of the holiday does he mention?

2 **Listen again and mark if each statement is True or False.**

	True	False
1 They chose a holiday which would be good for the children.	☐	☐
2 The main reason for choosing the hotel was its children's pool.	☐	☐
3 The hotel served mainly local food.	☐	☐
4 This was the speaker's first time in this part of the world.	☐	☐
5 He thought the price of the holiday was reasonable.	☐	☐
6 They didn't have to pay the cost of the flight.	☐	☐
7 The weather in Penang is the same all the year.	☐	☐
8 The speaker liked the climate in Penang.	☐	☐

3 **Would you have enjoyed a holiday in a place like this when you were a child? Did you always agree with your parents' choice of holiday?**

Country	Hepatitis A Polio Typhoid*	Malaria	Yellow Fever	Other
Bahamas	r		E	M
The Gambia	r	r	E, r	M
India	r	r	E	
Morocco	r	r, a		
Peru	r	r	E, r	
Thailand	r	r	E	

* = Immunisation against typhoid may be less important for short stays in first class conditions.
r = Immunisation or tablets recommended for protection against disease.
E = Immunisation essential if the traveller arrives from an infected country, i.e. where yellow fever is present.
M = Meningitis, depending on area visited and time of year.
a = Depends on area visited.

Grammar *Modal verbs (1)*

can	could	have to	may	might	must
need	ought to	shall	should	will	would

1 **You can use a modal verb when you want to express ideas like possibility and obligation, or when you want someone to behave in a particular way, for example, to follow your advice:**

They may *have two holidays this year.*
You must *pay a deposit when you make a reservation.*
You should *take your family to Penang.*

Modal verbs are followed by the infinitive without 'to', except for 'have *to*' and 'ought *to*'.

2 **Read these sentences, which refer to the speaker in the listening exercise, and underline the modal verbs.**

1 He has to travel round South East Asia for his job.
2 He won't go to big hotels.
3 In his hotel in Penang his children could run around without getting lost.
4 'You can swim in the big pool if I am with you,' he told his son.
5 Although it's hot in Penang, you needn't have air-conditioning.
6 The family will remember the holiday for a long time.
7 He may go back to Penang.
8 'Shall I lend you the hotel brochure?'
9 'Could you give it back to me when you've read it?'
10 'You should book several weeks in advance.'

Which of these ideas does each underlined modal verb express?
EXAMPLE: (**1**) has to – obligation

ability   advice   lack of necessity   obligation
offer   permission   possibility   probability
request   unwillingness

Are there other modals which express the same or similar ideas?
EXAMPLE: obligation – must

3 **Which of the places in the chart would you like to go to? Choose two or three, then tell your partner:**

– where you would like to go
– what health precautions you should take

EXAMPLE: 'I'd like to go to the Bahamas. You *needn't* take malaria tablets, and you *needn't* be immunised against typhoid if you are staying for a short time in a good hotel. But you *should* be immunised against hepatitis A and polio. You also *must* be immunised against yellow fever if you are coming from an infected country.'

Reading *Penang, Pearl of the Orient*

1 **Read quickly through this passage and choose the best answer (A–D) for 1–3 below.**

1 Where has this passage come from?
- A a diary
- B a magazine article
- C a travel brochure
- D a geography book

2 The main intention of the writer of the passage is to
- A write a favourable review of Penang.
- B look at the good and bad points of Penang.
- C write a personal account of a visit to Penang.
- D provide a detailed travel guide to Penang.

3 For which sort of reader is this passage written?
- A local people
- B Western tourists
- C historians
- D travel agents

2 **According to the passage, how true is each of the ten statements below? Mark each T (= True), F (= False) or DK (= Don't Know).**

1 Penang would not be a good place to take children. ☐

2 It would be suitable for a group of old people. ☐

3 People who like visiting ruins and museums should not go to Penang. ☐

4 People who want to avoid other tourists might find Penang unsuitable. ☐

5 People who like good food will have a good time in Penang. ☐

6 You won't get a sense of the real Malaysia if you go to Penang. ☐

7 People who enjoy shopping could have a good time here. ☐

8 You have to be careful of beach crime in Penang. ☐

9 It may be too hot for people used to cooler North European temperatures. ☐

10 You need to take a jersey or jacket to wear at night. ☐

3 **If you were making a 30-second TV advertisement for holidays in Penang, which aspects would you film?**

Lying just off the north-west coast of the Malaysian Peninsula, its shores lapped by the warm waters of the Straits of Malacca, Penang, the Pearl of the Orient, is an island of bright beauty – the premier holiday resort of Malaysia. Exotic, exciting, mysterious and splendidly charismatic, its appeal is instant.

So much to enjoy

Tall coconut palms fringe its beaches of fine white sand. Its climate is tropical – hot and humid, with the temperature seldom dropping below 20 degrees centigrade even at night and usually rising to 30 degrees centigrade during the day. And its hospitable people are among the friendliest in the world.

Georgetown, the island's capital, is a delight – a sprawling, lively city, its atmosphere an intriguing combination of Chinese and Old Colonial. Trishaws are still a favourite form of transport here, and the shopping streets, with their colourful bazaars and multitude of wares,

never fail to fascinate. The waterfront has been the hub of life ever since Captain Francis Light of the East India Company acquired Penang from the local sultan to be Britain's first trading station on the Malay Peninsula. He encouraged the then tiny local population of fishermen and pirates to clear the ground for settlement by firing silver coins from his ship's cannons into the jungle. The outlines of the original wooden stockade he built back in 1786 are marked now by the stone walls of Fort Cornwallis, a national monument. A park lies within the walls, with several cannons on display, including the one called Seri Rambai, in whose barrel childless women place flowers in expectation of miraculous fertility.

The food on the island is mouthwatering, with strong Chinese and Indian influences apparent. I had a memorable lunch at the Prosperous Restaurant in Georgetown – spare ribs,

crab, prawns and chicken dishes all served with delicious spicy sauces. And the tropical fruit is superb – red, spiny-skinned rambutan with a centre like a lychee, purple mangosteen (whose sweet-sour flavour, a cross between a strawberry and a grape, was Queen Victoria's special passion), papaya, custard apple, starfruit and the evil-smelling durian that the hotels forbid you to bring inside.

Along the north coast of the island runs the fabulous stretch of sandy beach known as Batu Ferringhi, Foreigner's Rock, where most of the resort hotels lie. Golden Sands, with its incredible landscaped pool beside the sea, and the Rasa Sayang, with its authentic Malaysian ambience and air of sheer luxury, are two of the best-loved, standing right beside the white sands and backed by dense jungle. A stay at the Rasa Sayang is my idea of holiday heaven.

4

Exam skill *Vocabulary (1)*

One place where your knowledge of vocabulary is tested is in Paper 1, Section A. You will have to complete 25 vocabulary multiple-choice sentences. Try these ten typical examples:

1 The baby .... a lot but he can't walk yet – he's only eight months old.
A crawls   B creeps   C steps   D trips

2 The manager is away in Japan .... business: she'll be back next week.
A at   B by   C in   D on

3 I'm sorry I'm late. The traffic was very ....
A dangerous   B heavy   C much
D serious

4 The light turned to green, the guard blew his whistle and the train .... the station.
A drew out of   B got away from   C set out
D took off

5 If we went that way, I'm sure we .... get there quicker.
A can   B must   C need   D would

6 The increase in car use is .... the government's failure to support public transport.
A due to   B in addition to   C in spite of
D on behalf of

7 To get to the island, you .... the ferry from the harbour.
A make   B ride   C take   D travel

8 His attempt to cycle across the Sahara was .... from the start: he's lucky he's still alive.
A hopeful   B hoping   C hopeless
D unhopeful

9 When the famous film star got on the plane the chief .... showed her to her seat.
A guard   B porter   C receptionist
D steward

10 He's a great .... – his parties are famous for interesting people and wonderful food.
A guest   B host   C stranger   D visitor

The sentences test various aspects of your vocabulary knowledge. Find the one(s) above which test(s) your knowledge of:
1 the differences in meaning between similar words
2 words which usually go together
3 linking words and preposition phrases
4 phrasal verbs
5 the meaning of different prefixes and suffixes

This part of the exam also tests your knowledge of the rules of grammar. Which item tests this?

Note: In the exam the sentences will cover a wide range of topics (unlike the vocabulary tests at the end of each unit in this book, which mainly test what you have just learned).

Timing

A simple division of time for Paper 1 is into four 15-minute parts, three for the three reading passages and one for Section A. But you should work out the division of time which suits you best.

Now try some more multiple-choice vocabulary items:

11 She missed the start of the show because her taxi was .... up in the traffic.
A broken   B held   C picked   D stood

12 The weather was so nice I decided to go to work .... foot.
A at   B by   C in   D on

13 Some streets are so dangerous that postmen won't .... the post there any more.
A deliver   B fetch   C provide   D send

14 The burglar moved so quietly that no one heard ....
A anything   B everything   C nothing
D something

15 In Venice the quickest way to get around is to take a boat along the ....
A canals   B channels   C tracks   D trails

16 Look! Some .... has been left behind on the platform.
A handbag   B luggage   C suitcase
D wallet

17 We watched the plane .... down the runway, lift off and climb into the clouds.
A accelerate   B land   C overtake
D reverse

18 The taxi driver sounded .... about arriving at the airport on time.
A doubted   B doubtful   C doubtless
D undoubted

19 Our car is already full – is there any .... in yours for a rucksack and a small suitcase?
A place   B room   C seat   D vacancy

20 When they .... at the party, they found most people had already left.
A arrived   B entered   C got   D reached

Test exercises

1 *A police officer is being interviewed on the radio about an incident on the motorway. Complete the conversation.*

INTERVIEWER: I believe there was quite a lot of excitement on the motorway today. Can you (1)..?

POLICE OFFICER: It all started when a lorry which was carrying surgical needles began to lose part of its load.

INTERVIEWER: You mean needles were falling off the back of a lorry as it drove up the motorway? Wasn't (2)..?

POLICE OFFICER: Well, it could have been worse. Fortunately, there wasn't a serious accident, but the breakdown services and the tyre companies have done a lot of good business today!

INTERVIEWER: How many (3)..?

POLICE OFFICER: We've counted up to 70 so far, and we're still counting. Some vehicles had punctures in all four tyres!

INTERVIEWER: Did (4)..?

POLICE OFFICER: No, he didn't. That's why he didn't stop. I was sent to follow his lorry up the motorway.

INTERVIEWER: Did (5)..?

POLICE OFFICER: No. My tyres were punctured too, and the lorry driver innocently carried on!

INTERVIEWER: What's the situation now? Can (6)................................?

POLICE OFFICER: Not yet. We've closed a six-mile stretch while we sweep the motorway clear of needles.

INTERVIEWER: Have (7)..?

POLICE OFFICER: Yes. All motorists who were travelling on that stretch of motorway this afternoon should check their tyres to make sure they haven't got a slow puncture.

2 *Complete each of the following sentences so that it means exactly the same as the sentence before it.*

1 It is possible that the departure will be delayed until tomorrow.
The departure ....

2 It is essential that every passenger has a boarding card.
Every passenger ....

3 'I have nothing to declare,' the actress told the customs officer.
The actress told the customs officer that ....

4 'When I retire I'm going to sail round the world!' he said.
He announced that ....

5 The police officer told the children to lock their bikes when they left them unattended.
'You ....

6 Going by plane is much more expensive than taking the train.
Taking the train ....

7 He succeeded in putting his tent up in the dark.
He managed ....

8 The steamer seems to be turning round and coming back.
It looks as if ....

9 Flying in a helicopter wasn't very frightening.
Flying in a helicopter didn't ....

10 I don't often take a taxi.
I hardly ....

3   *The word in capitals at the end of each of the following sentences can be used to form a word that fits suitably in the blank space. Fill each blank in this way.*

EXAMPLE: His sister is a ...*famous*... writer.   FAME

1 She works as a .... in a big office.   TYPE
2 They speak .... in Brazil.   PORTUGAL
3 What's the .... of the Statue of Liberty?   HIGH
4 The .... of space is expensive.   EXPLORE
5 It was a valuable vase, but now it is cracked it is ....   WORTH
6 Many pop singers suffer from ....   DEAF
7 .... sports players win bigger prizes than amateurs.   PROFESSION
8 She is an .... talented musician.   EXCEPTION
9 He is old, but he is not ....   FOOL
10 I think this dispute can be settled ....   PEACE

4   *Choose the word or phrase (A–D) which best completes each sentence.*

1 A good way for old people to visit foreign countries is .... coach.
   A by   B in   C on   D with

2 .... Dr Yaffé, people can learn to overcome their fear of flying.
   A According to   B As far as   C By means of   D Except for

3 One advantage of driving an automatic car is that you don't have to keep changing ....
   A accelerator   B brake   C gear   D tyre

4 All her family came to the airport to .... her off on her trip to Australia.
   A call   B get   C see   D take

5 .... the main tourist resorts, you'll find less crowded beaches and cheaper hotels.
   A Ahead of   B Away from   C Because of   D Owing to

6 The safety regulations say there .... be a life jacket for every passenger.
   A can   B might   C should   D would

7 In the old days it was common to see a farmer driving a horse and ....
   A cart   B tractor   C truck   D van

8 The recent customs operation against drug traffickers was highly ....
   A succeed   B success   C successful   D successfully

9 The airline company admitted that .... error was the cause of the crash.
   A conductor   B driver   C pilot   D rider

10 One-day .... to Oxford and Stratford are very popular with tourists visiting London.
   A excursions   B expeditions   C travels   D voyages

11 Is there a place .... we can eat cheaply near here?
   A that   B there   C where   D which

8 What's in the news?

1 From our own correspondent

Speaking *Stop press*

1 Would you read this story or just turn the page? Do you think it is 'News'?

THESE sensational pictures are the first real evidence of an amazing aerial UFO encounter in London skies.

2 What do you most/least want to read about in a paper?
3 How regularly do you read a paper? Which one(s) do you read? Why?
4 How much of what you read do you believe?
5 Have you ever been involved in anything that has been reported in a paper? If so, what happened?

Reading *The news*

Look quickly through the openings of these news items, taken either from a teleprinter or a newspaper. Write the number of each item (1–5) in the correct place on the table.

	Number
Crime	
Human interest	
Politics	
The weather	

1

...DETECTIVES ARE ON THEIR WAY TO FRANCE TO QUESTION MAN WHO IS WANTED IN CONNECTION WITH DISAPPEARANCE OF MISSING SCHOOLGIRL.

2

Five drugs smugglers were convicted at a London court yesterday in the wake of one of the most ingenious attempts to transport cocaine ever seen by Customs investigators.

3

...CANADIAN CONSERVATIVE PARTY HAS BEEN RE-ELECTED WITH A MAJORITY OF MORE THAN 40 SEATS.

4

The Victoria Cross awarded to George Hamilton, a pilot who shot down a Zeppelin, sold for £90,000 at Christie's London yesterday, nearly £40,000 more than its estimate.

5

Heavy snow in south-east England last night brought warnings from the police that people in the area should stay indoors unless journeys were essential.

Which item would you like to know more about?

Listening 🎞 *The news*

1 **Listen to a news broadcast covering the five items (1–5) and answer the question on each.**

1 How long has the suspected murderer been missing?
2 Where were the drug smugglers arrested?
3 Is the Canadian Conservative Party's new majority larger or smaller than before?
4 Where and when was the Zeppelin shot down?
5 What weather is forecast for London this morning?

2 **Before listening to the news broadcast again, do this vocabulary activity:**

- form groups of three students
- take one box (**A–C**) each and make sure you understand all the words in your box
- discuss in which news item (**1–5**) you think each word or phrase comes

A

airship   controversial   extradition warrant
fund   gang   landslide   suspected   warm up

B

anti-inflation measures   drop (n.)   frosty
hitchhiking   intercepted   leukaemia
pleading   treatment

C

bombed   charity auction   couriers
magistrate   manhunt   minus 4
parliamentary   term in office

3 **Listen to the news items again and mark if each summary sentence (1–5 below) is True or False. Correct any mistakes you find.**

	True	False
1 The body of the missing schoolgirl has been found.	☐	☐
2 Five drugs smugglers have been sent to jail for smuggling cocaine inside cassettes.	☐	☐
3 The Conservative vote was 9% lower than in the previous election.	☐	☐
4 A war medal has been sold to raise money for a charity for old people.	☐	☐
5 The temperature in London is expected to stay below zero all day.	☐	☐

Grammar *The past (2)*

1 *Past simple or present perfect? What is the name of each tense being described here?*

a It is used to express an action which happened in the recent past, when no time reference is given.

b It is used to express an action which happened in the past, when a definite time reference is given.

Which of the two tenses is being used in each example below? Why?

1 Lieutenant Hamilton shot down the airship in 1916.
2 The bravery of a flying ace has raised £90,000 for sick children.
3 He came quietly when stopped and asked for his papers.

2 *In which of the sentences below is it impossible to add 'last night'? Why?*

1 The Conservative Party has been re-elected.
2 Customs men found more than £2½ million worth of drugs.
3 Heavy snow brought warnings from the police.

3 *Which of these time adverbials can you use with each sentence below?*

recently   last night   just   at 11 o'clock
an hour earlier   already   30 minutes ago
while hitchhiking

1 He was captured in France.
2 Five members of a drugs gang have been jailed for a total of 72 years.

Where in the sentence can you put the time adverbial?

4 *Put the verbs in brackets in the correct tense: past simple or present perfect.*

SIGHT AFTER THIRTY YEARS OF DARKNESS

A man whose sight (**1**) .... (return) miraculously to him after 31 years is looking at a world that is stranger and more wonderful than he ever (**2**) .... (imagine).

Mr J. F. Fish, a well-to-do businessman, (**3**) .... (be) on honeymoon when he (**4**) .... (strike) by a falling tree. The injury (**5**) .... (blind) him by paralysing the optic nerves. For three decades he (**6**) .... (visit) specialists who (**7**) .... (try) without success to restore his sight. This week, while sitting at home listening to his wife read to him, vision suddenly (**8**) .... (return) to his left eye. It (**9**) .... (be) cloudy, but strong enough to enable him to recognise objects.

'A wonderful thing (**10**) .... (happen)!' he exclaimed. 'I can see you again.'

Mrs Fish (**11**) .... (not believe) him, but when her husband (**12**) .... (be) able to identify objects in the room, she (**13**) .... (faint) with joy.

Despite the handicap of lost sight, Mr Fish (**14**) .... (have) a successful career as a teacher and businessman. It is hoped that the restoration of his sight will be lasting.

Pronunciation 🔲 *Weak forms*

1 *All the words in small type have the same vowel sound. What is it?*

Five members of a drugs gang who sliced open LP records to smuggle cocaine into Britain have been jailed for a total of 72 years.

Heavy snow brought warnings from the police that people should stay indoors.

Listen to the tape and check.

2 *Certain words, such as the examples in small type above, are usually pronounced in their weak forms.*

What is the rule for the use of weak forms? Make the rule by filling each gap (**1–4**) with the correct word from the box.

full   modal   pronounced   stressed

'Grammar' words (e.g. articles, personal pronouns, prepositions, auxiliary and (**1**) .... verbs) are usually unstressed in the sentence; so these words are (**2**) .... in their weak form.

When they are (**3**) .... in the sentence (e.g. 'Which John Smith do you mean?' – '**The** John Smith.') they are pronounced in their (**4**) .... form.

3 *Prepare to read this news item aloud. Put brackets ( ) round the words you will pronounce in their weak forms.*

Five drugs smugglers were convicted at a London court yesterday in the wake of the most ingenious attempts to transport cocaine ever seen by Customs investigators.

Practise reading the item. Check your pronunciation against the example on tape.

2 News into history

Speaking *Historic moments*

1 *Here are some news photos of historic moments. Do you know what happened? What details can you give about each one?*

a

President Kennedy is shot in the head as he drives through Dallas, Texas (22 Nov 1963).

b

British Prime Minister John Major helps light one of a chain of 1,300 beacons signalling the arrival of the world's biggest single consumer market (12 midnight 1 Jan 1993).

c

Neil Armstrong, the first man on the moon, is reflected in the visor of his companion Edwin 'Buzz' Aldrin (21 July 1969).

d

Boris Yeltsin climbs on a tank outside the Russian Parliament and declares the coup against President Gorbachev illegal (20 August 1991).

e

Nelson Mandela and his wife, Winnie, salute supporters after his release from prison (11 Feb 1990).

f

Souvenir hunters chip away at the Berlin Wall (autumn 1989).

2 *How important historically do you think these moments were? Which would you most like to have witnessed?*

Listening 🔊 *Assassination!*

_1_ **Listen to part of a radio programme about historic news items, then answer these questions:**

1 When, where and how did President John F. Kennedy die?

2 Who was Lee Harvey Oswald? What happened to him?

_2_ **Listen again. Choose the best answer (A, B, C or D) for questions 1–4.**

1 From this programme we learn that President Kennedy
   A came from a famous political family.
   B was the youngest president of the USA.
   C was a keen sports player.
   D had a son and a daughter.

2 We also learn that the President was in Dallas because he
   A was on a private holiday.
   B was on his way to meet his wife.
   C lived there.
   D was making an official visit.

3 What do we learn about the President's death?
   A He died instantly.
   B He died the day after he was shot.
   C No one knows who killed him.
   D He was shot twice by one person.

4 What do we learn about Lee Harvey Oswald?
   A He denied killing the President.
   B He was shot when he was arrested.
   C He was found guilty of killing the President.
   D He was employed by the Mafia.

_3_ **There have been many theories about the assassination of President Kennedy. Do you think the truth will ever be known?**

---

1 A large city in the South of the USA. During the American Civil War (1861–65), Atlanta was a major supply centre for the Southern army. It was taken by Northern troops on 1 September 1864 and most of the city was burned.

2 A nickname for the troops from the Northern States.

3 The large farm where Scarlett grew up. She moved away when she married, but her husband was soon killed in the Civil War. At the time of this passage she is living in Atlanta at her aunt's house.

Reading *Turning point*

_1_ **This passage is about a historic moment in the past, and its effect on ordinary lives. Read it quickly for the general idea, then choose one answer (A, B, C or D) for questions 1–2.**

1 Where has the passage been taken from?
   A an autobiography   C a novel
   B a history book   D a play

2 What historical event is taking place?
   A the Second World War
   B the North American Civil War
   C the arrival of the Spanish in South America
   D the arrival of the English in North America

(The city of Atlanta[1] is on fire. Scarlett is preparing to escape. She has sent a message to Rhett begging him to bring her a horse.)

'Good evening,' he said, in his drawling voice, as he removed his hat with a sweeping gesture. 'Fine weather we're having. I hear you're going to take a trip.'

'If you make any jokes, I shall never speak to you again,' she said with quivering voice.

'Don't tell me you are frightened!' He pretended to be surprised and smiled in a way that made her long to push him backwards down the steep steps.

'Yes, I am! I'm frightened to death, and if you had the sense God gave a goat, you'd be frightened too. But we haven't got time to talk. We must get out of here.'

'At your service, Madam. But just where were you figuring on going? I made the trip out here for curiosity, just to see where you were intending to go. You can't go north or east or south or west. The Yankees[2] are all around. There's just one road out of town which the Yankees haven't got yet and the army is retreating by that road. And that road won't be open long. General Steve Lee's cavalry is fighting a rearguard action at Rough and Ready to hold it open long enough for the army to get away. If you follow the army down the McDonough road, they'll take the horse away from you and, while it's not much of a horse, I did go to a lot of trouble stealing it. Just where are you going?'

She stood shaking, listening to his words, hardly hearing them. But, at his question, she suddenly knew where she was going, knew that all this miserable day she had known where she was going. The only place.

'I'm going home,' she said.

'Home? You mean to Tara[3]?'

'Yes, yes! To Tara! Oh, Rhett, we must hurry!'

He looked at her as if she had lost her mind.

'Tara? God Almighty, Scarlett! Don't you know they fought all day at Jonesboro? Fought for ten miles up and down the road from Rough and Ready even into the streets of Jonesboro? The Yankees may be all over Tara by now, all over the County. Nobody knows where they are but they're in that neighbourhood. You can't go home! You can't go right through the Yankee army!'

'I will go home!' she cried. 'I will! I will!'

---

2 Do the following activities on background, plot and character.

1 The events in the passage are set against the background of the American Civil War. What do you know about this? Can you answer any of these questions?
   a Who was fighting whom?
   b Why was the war fought?
   c Who won?

2 Answer these questions using information in the passage:
   a Why are Scarlett and Rhett in such danger?
   b Why has the day been miserable for Scarlett?
   c What do we learn about the characters of Scarlett and Rhett?
   d What sort of relationship exists between them?

3 Consider these questions.

1 If you were going to make a book cover for the novel based on this scene, what would you show? Would you use photos or a design? What theme(s) would your cover suggest?

2 Do you enjoy historical stories? What historical novels or films have you read or seen? Were they based on the history of your country, or that of another country?

3 Is there anything happening today which is similar to the situation described in the passage? Could any of the events in today's news turn out to be of historic importance?

Grammar *Conditional sentences (3)*

1 Sometimes we want to talk about things that did not happen in the past. We want to imagine how things might have been different.

1 When both the clauses refer to the *past*, what verb form do we use in the *main clause*, and in the *if-clause*?

2 When the main clause refers to the *present* what verb form do we use?

3 Sometimes we are not certain what would have happened in a different situation. In this case, what can we use instead of 'would'?

2 Think of some important moments in your country's history, for example:

- an important battle
- the death of a famous person
- a great discovery
- the results of the last election

Talk about how things might have been different if the event hadn't happened.

3 Think of some important events in your own life, for example:

- passing an exam
- making a special friend
- visiting an exciting place
- getting a job
- escaping an accident

Talk about what would have happened, and how you would have felt, if things had turned out differently.

3 How could it happen here?

a

Vocabulary *Disaster*

*Match these words for different types of disaster with
the pictures.*

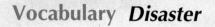

avalanche	drought	earthquake	fire	flood
hurricane	nuclear explosion		plane crash	
shipwreck	volcanic eruption			

b

d

e

f

g

h

i

j

*Are these disasters usually man-made or natural?
Can they be predicted or prevented? What needs to be
done after one has happened? Have any of these
disasters been in the news recently?*

Grammar *Time relationships*

1 *Here is some information about an earthquake in Armenia. Match the first part of each sentence (a–g) with the correct second part (1–7).*

a The earthquake struck at 11.41 am
b Snow fell during the next few days,
c At first it was thought 55,000 people had died,
d As soon as news of the tragedy had been broadcast,
e A plane carrying relief supplies crashed
f Restoration of the affected area began
g A senior government official promised the town would be completely rebuilt

1 when trying to land.
2 as the people of Spitak, Armenia, were busy with their morning work.
3 by the end of the following year.
4 two weeks after the earthquake.
5 but later the figure was put at 25,000.
6 which made rescue operations difficult.
7 aid worth millions of dollars began to pour in.

Underline the time references in each sentence.

2 *Fill the gaps in the following news story with one of these time expressions. Use each expression once:*

after	afterwards	before	initially
meanwhile	soon	until	while

Chernobyl's Nuclear Reactor No. 4 blew up at 1.24 am on April 26, 1986. (**1**) .... that night none of the local villagers had dreamt there was any danger from the power plant, and even (**2**) .... the explosion they did not realise how serious the situation was. 'We decided to carry on as normal,' says Petr Remezenko. '(**3**) .... we regretted that decision.' (**4**) .... a cloud of radioactive dust was spreading over Scandinavia and central and eastern Europe, the Remezenko family were digging potatoes in their garden, almost in the shadow of the blazing reactor. However, the authorities (**5**) .... started to evacuate the entire area within a radius of 30 km of the plant. Families were asked to take in evacuees (**6**) .... permanent accommodation could be found for them. (**7**) .... , urgent plans were made to build replacement homes. The number of people who died as a result of the accident was (**8**) .... very small, but who knows what the long-term effects on present and future generations will be?

3 *Answer the following questions, using the time expressions in exercises* 1 *and* 2 *as examples.*

1 What are the grammatical differences between 'during', 'while' and 'meanwhile'?
2 When do you use 'soon', and when do you use 'as soon as'?
3 When can you use 'after' and when should you use 'afterwards'?
4 What does 'by' mean in 'by the end of the following year'?
5 When do you use the past perfect tense in a time clause?
6 When do you use the past progressive tense in a time clause?

Writing *Telling a story*

1 *Listen to the story of how Colin Blake was caught in a fire in an underground station.*

2 *The story is written in five paragraphs. Each paragraph has one focus:*

1 setting the scene
2 the underground station
3 the fire
4 help
5 the ending

Listen to the story again and make notes of some key words in each paragraph. Do not try to write down every word.

3 *Write the whole story. You do not have to use exactly the same words as the original, but your version should:*

– have the same paragraph organisation
– tell the story clearly and logically
– be grammatically correct

4 *Compare your version with that of other students. If necessary, make corrections.*

5 *Look at the original text on page 190. Underline:*

1 the use of reported speech
2 the use of direct speech
3 the expressions of time
4 the expressions of place
5 the words which give details about the kind of fire it was
6 the words which link each paragraph to the one before

4

Exam skill *Set books*

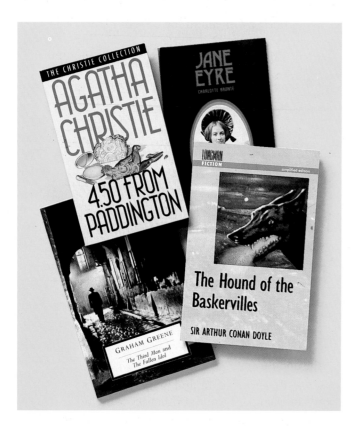

The set books are an optional part of the First Certificate exam. Each year there are three set books to choose from. The set book is likely to be a simplified reader, but it may also be unsimplified. It may be a novel, a biography, a collection of short stories or a play. If you like, you may answer on a set book in the Composition Paper and also in the interview.

Composition Paper

You will be able to write one composition based on a set book. Any composition should follow the rules of composition writing. See Unit 14 Lesson 4 for a summary.

Interview

The interview will follow the same pattern as other interviews (see Unit 13 Lesson 4) but all the examiner's questions will be based on the set book. You will have to talk about:
- pictures related to the book or its theme
- the significance of some short extracts taken from the book
- some discussion topics related to the book

Points for study

You do not have to show a literary appreciation of the book you have read, but you should be able to:

PLOT
- tell the whole story
- describe the main events in the story and say why they are important
- indicate significant objects and say what part they play in the story
- say how you react to the ending of the story

CHARACTERS
- describe the characters
- describe the relationship between them
- describe the position of the narrator of the story, if there is one

BACKGROUND
- describe the background and say what you learn about life in that country or region, among those kinds of people, at that time

IDEAS
- talk about the significance of the title
- discuss some of the book's main ideas
- discuss whether the book has any 'message'
- discuss the significance of any words or phrases which are repeated throughout the book
- say, if the story was written a long time ago, what relevance it has for a modern reader
- discuss the suitability of the book's cover and any illustrations it has

PERSONAL REACTION
- explain your reaction to the book
- describe how any aspect of the book relates to your own life and experiences

For a collection of short stories you should be able to do all of the above for each story, and:
- pick out some common themes in the stories
- say which stories you like most

PRACTICE

Do some of these exercises. Base your answers on a set book, or any book that you have read recently, either in English or in your own language.

1 Composition (120–180 words)

1 Describe two or three significant events in the book, and say why they are important to the outcome of the story.
2 Write about a sensational event in the book as if you were writing a news story for a popular newspaper the day after it happened.
3 Compare and contrast two characters in the book.
4 Choose two characters from the book and explain why you would or would not like to go on holiday with them.
5 You have just arrived in the town or village where some events of the book take place. Write a description of your surroundings as part of a letter to your family.

2 Interview

1 Explain the significance of the cover illustration and of three other pictures from the book. Suggest an alternative cover design. If the book is not illustrated, suggest four appropriate subjects from different places in the book. Give your reasons.
2 Find three pictures (for example, from a newspaper) which illustrate the theme of the book. Explain the connection between your pictures and the ideas in the book.
3 Choose four extracts (3–5 sentences each) from different places in the book. Explain what is important or interesting about the characters, places, events or ideas which are mentioned.
4 Choose three objects mentioned in the book. Explain the part they play in the story. Describe the part that similar objects have played in your life.
5 Imagine that a very successful film has been made of the book. You have been asked to plan a sequel to this film. Discuss what ideas and characters from the original book and film will be used in the sequel, and what developments and new ideas there will be.

Test exercises

1 Complete this passage. Use only **one** word in each gap.

NON-STOP NEWS

Kate Adie, the chief foreign correspondent of a television news company talks about her job.

The limitations of broadcasting were brought home to me (**1**) .... I was reporting recently on a crisis on the other side of the world. (**2**) .... days we are faced with doing non-stop broadcasting. Even (**3**) .... a television channel does not (**4**) .... to have non-stop news output, (**5**) .... the one I work for, it has non-stop news input. Twenty-four (**6**) .... coverage is complicated by any time difference. In my recent assignment we were eight hours ahead (**7**) .... the time in London. The (**8**) .... team, about 25 people, gathered (**9**) .... at 7.30 am to discuss things and get the camera crews out on the streets. (**10**) .... lunchtime we were editing, and by mid-afternoon we were doing live two-way reports (**11**) .... Breakfast Time News. By the evening the lunchtime news (**12**) .... being done, and by midnight we were into the Six O'Clock News, with another live two-way report for the Nine O'Clock News at five in the (**13**) .... The problem with such (**14**) .... twenty-four hour operation, (**15**) .... from the lack of sleep, is that you end up broadcasting rather (**16**) .... reporting. People say, 'What was it (**17**) .... out there?' And I say, 'How do I know?' I (**18**) .... have spent more time on the streets if I (**19**) .... not had to prepare so (**20**) .... bulletins.

2 *Complete each of the following sentences so that it means exactly the same as the sentence before it.*

1 He has been a television cameraman for five years.
   He first ....

2 The fishermen went out to sea because a storm wasn't forecast.
   If ....

3 It is often easier to prevent a disease than to cure it.
   It is often less ....

4 The astronaut caught a cold, so she wasn't allowed to go on the space
   flight.
   If ....

5 The President read the report before he made a decision.
   The President didn't ....

6 The police took photographs of the scene, and then they looked for
   fingerprints.
   After ....

7 People won't read the article because it doesn't have an interesting
   headline.
   If ....

8 I won't vote for him because he has been involved in a financial scandal.
   If ....

9 The rescuers couldn't get to the injured people until the hurricane was
   over.
   It wasn't until ....

10 'Inflation will be down to 3% by the end of next year,' the minister said.
   The minister promised that ....

3 *Complete these sentences with a phrasal verb that includes the word* **get**.

EXAMPLE: Stop chatting and ...*get*... ...*on*... ...*with*... your work.

1 She doesn't smile any more because losing her job has really ....
   her ....

2 You won't .... as a journalist unless you
   can make people talk to you.

3 She .... doing the
   housework by saying she had a headache.

4 I must .... checking the
   sales figures before the annual conference.

5 It took him three months to .... his
   operation.

4 *Complete these sentences with a phrasal verb that includes the word* **up**.

EXAMPLES: First ....*cut*........ up the onions and then fry them gently.
          I never ....*get*........ up early on Sunday morning.

1 How much money would it cost to .... up a hairdressing
   business?

2 After his wife left him he .... up their three children by himself.

3 Christie made a bad start in the race but he soon .... up
   .... the leaders.

4 All the teenagers swam across the lake except one who had to
   .... up because she was exhausted.

5 I'll ask the Editor not to publish the story if you come with me and
   .... me up.

9

UNIT NINE
Making your way

1 Right foot forward

Speaking *Jobs*

1 *What do these jobs have in common?*

cashier	interpreter	receptionist
shop assistant	steward(ess)	tour guide

2 *Explain which job(s) you would:*
- enjoy doing
- find demanding
- be unsuited to

Vocabulary *Work*

1 *Make seven groups of three words with similar meanings. Take one word from each column.*

A	B	C
agency	appoint	commission
crew	bonus	firm
dismiss	break (n.)	hire
fee	company	lay off
leave (n.)	sack (v.)	salary
take on	team	time off
tip	wages	union

EXAMPLE: *Tip, bonus* and *commission* are all types of money you receive for work.

2 *Explain the differences between the three words. These may be to do with:*

- **Meaning**

  EXAMPLE:

  A *tip* is a small extra payment which a customer who has already paid for the meal gives to the waiter.

  A *bonus* is an extra payment which an employee occasionally receives (e.g. at the end of the year).

  A *commission* is a payment which a salesperson receives for every sale made.

  OR
- **Use**

  EXAMPLE:

  Take on is more informal than *appoint* and *hire*.

Listening 📼 *First job*

1 **What is the most important factor in a first job: training, good wages, interesting work, or something else?**

2 **Listen to part of a radio programme in which two young people (Matt and Tina) talk about their jobs. Complete the chart which summarises what they say. Write one or two words in each space.**

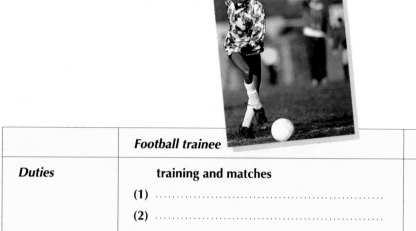

	Football trainee	Bicycle courier
Duties	training and matches (1) .... (2)	(7) ....
Wages	(3) .... two pairs of boots	(8) ....
Qualifications	(4) .... (5)	(9) .... reliability (10) ....
Disadvantages	low wages (6) .... not much time off	bicycle theft (11) .... (12) ....

3 **How would you summarise Matt's and Tina's attitudes to their jobs? Would you like to do either of these jobs?**

Grammar *Reported questions*

1 **This is how the radio interviewer reported her questions. What did she actually say?**

I asked Matt if he spent all his time on the football field. I asked Tina what a bicycle courier did. I asked them both how much they got paid, and whether their jobs had any disadvantages.

1 How does a reported yes/no question begin?
2 How does a reported question-word question begin?
3 What changes do you make when you change a direct question into a reported question?

2 **Matt and Tina also had some questions for the interviewer. Report what they asked her.**

1 'Do you enjoy your job?' Tina asked.
2 'How did you get your first job in radio?' she asked.
3 'Do you think I could apply for a job here?' Tina wondered.
4 'Who is the most interesting person you have interviewed on this programme?' Matt asked.
5 'What famous people will you be meeting next week?' he asked.
6 'Can you choose the guests who appear on your show?' Matt wondered.

UNIT 9 **Making your way**

Speaking 🔊 *Asking politely*

1 **Which of these questions seems more polite?**

'What does that mean, being a football trainee?'
'Could you tell us what that means, being a football trainee?'

Listen to these five pairs of sentences. In each case, who do you think the person is speaking to? How can you tell? Think about:
– the language used
– the pitch of the speaker's voice (i.e. is it normal, higher than normal, or lower than normal?)

2 **What general rules about asking politely in English can you work out from these examples? Make the rule by filling gaps 1–4 with the correct word from the box.**

long   raise   friendly   strangers

When asking questions or making requests politely (e.g. when speaking to (**1**) .... or superiors), English speakers tend to use longer sentences (e.g. indirect questions) and to (**2**) .... the pitch of their voice.

When speaking to people they know well, or to strangers they want to seem (**3**) .... with, they don't use such (**4**) .... sentences and they don't raise their pitch so much.

3 **Practise asking politely in this role play. Work with your partner: take a role each and follow your instructions.**

Job applicant
You are looking for a job. Choose one from these advertisements and tell the Interviewer which you have chosen. Look at *Role card A* on page 190.

Interviewer
Look at *Role card B* on page 191.

When you have finished, swap roles and do another role play.

Bank clerks

Vacancy for school-leavers with some Maths and English (we have a busy money-changing counter).

Training provided, good job prospects guaranteed for the right applicants.

Contact The Manager, National Bank, Victory Square (Tel. 0796-43127).

Hotel receptionist

Required for busy tourist hotel by the sea. Popular with US tour groups. Pleasant manner, smart dress and ability to speak good English essential.

Apply to The Manager, Hotel Bellevue (0394-21974) for more details.

Waiter/Waitress

Staff required in friendly family-run restaurant. Experience preferred though not essential. English necessary as we are popular with tourists. To start immediately.

Contact The Family Kitchen (0278-43496).

Assistant

Assistant required at airport shop.
We sell a variety of typical local products in the International Departure Lounge.
Professional appearance and good command of English important.

Call the Manager on 081-727-9488.

2 The pound in your pocket

Speaking *Money and me*

How well do you manage money?

Find out by:
- filling in the questionnaire for yourself.
- checking your score on pages 190–1.
- comparing your answers with those of your classmates.

	YES	NO
1 'I know how much money I have at this moment (in my pocket, in the bank, in savings).'	☐	☐
2 'I have no idea how much of my money goes on essential outgoings (e.g. food, home, travel).'	☐	☐
3 'I always know how much I spend a month on luxuries.'	☐	☐
4 'I sometimes go into the red at the end of the month.'	☐	☐
5 'I don't have any insurance on my possessions. Don't ask what would happen in the case of fire or theft.'	☐	☐
6 'I regularly put money aside for the future.'	☐	☐

Reading *Monthly budget*

1 Look quickly at this article to find out who:

1 spends the most money.
2 doesn't save any money.
3 pays for the use of a car.

1 Jason Codner, 17, is an administrative assistant with Thomson Holidays. His duties include filing, dealing with customer enquiries, using the office computer system and doing some basic accounting. 'It's great being treated like an adult,' he says. 'I have the right amount of responsibility and I'm doing something worthwhile.'

Jason took his job straight from school. 'It was weird suddenly having lots of money but I started saving straight away. I could easily afford £60 each month and still have plenty for going out.'

Jason's firm arranged an interest-free loan to buy a yearly season ticket and deducted the money direct from his salary. He spends most of his money on clothes and going out. Jason hopes to be promoted quickly. 'I've done a little accounting so I might consider doing that full time. I'm considering returning to college.'

Jason's monthly budget

Income (after deductions)	£470
Outgoings	
To parents for keep	£70
Season ticket	£35
Lunches	£75
Clothes	£85
Records/entertainment	£145
Savings	£60
Total	**£470**

2 When **Kirsty Ince** left school last year after 'A' levels, she was offered a job as a trainee manager with Kendals in Manchester.

Now, at 19, she is half-way through her two-year training course and has a day each week at college studying marketing, merchandising, personnel training and law. The rest of the time she works in different departments, doing paperwork, checking stock and sorting out price tags.

'I love the work. There's always something interesting happening, like when I dressed up as a clown for a Christmas parade,' she says. 'But it's quite demanding working long hours and fitting in college projects. I miss the long school holidays.'

A big perk is the staff discount which is useful when Kirsty occasionally treats herself to clothes. She has had to buy a navy suit for work but doesn't mind a bit. 'I can save my own clothes for going out,' she says.

Kirsty's monthly budget

Income (after deductions)	£410
Outgoings	
To parent for keep	£50
Train fares to work	£40
Car insurance/petrol	£85
Lunches at work	£30
Extras (toiletries, magazines, etc.)	£25
Clothes/going out	£110
Savings for holiday	£70
Total	**£410**

Simon Young, 18, from Birmingham, decided before taking nine GCSEs he'd had enough of studying and wanted a job'.

He was nervous at his interview for a clerk's position with an insurance company. 'I should have found out about the structure of the company. Fortunately I knew they sponsored sport and we talked about that.'

After getting the job, Simon learned he had passed only two GCSEs, but was kept on. As office junior, Simon began by filing and running errands. Since a promotion he deals with district offices, querying car insurance proposals.

He's on the same grade as people joining the company after 'A' levels and is studying part time for a B.TEC National in Business and Finance.

'I'm doing what I wanted,' said Simon. 'It worked out for me but I'd advise anyone else to go for at least four GCSEs.'

Simon's monthly budget

Income (after deductions)	£360
Outgoings	
To parents for keep	£48
Car loan repayment (third share, with mum and sister)	£40
Petrol (uses car for work)	£30
Holidays	£12
Clothes and entertainment	£205
Savings	£25
Total	**£360**

Lisa Hazlegreaves, 18, is a dental assistant. 'It is difficult to adjust to working after leaving school. Yes, you have more money, but you have to earn it and that is hard! I miss my friends quite a bit too.

'I earn £165 a month but I don't cope very well financially. For the last three months I've been overdrawn, so I pay bank charges on top of my overdraft repayments, but then I need some more money to pay my way for the next month. What I really need is a pay rise! I would like to save some money each month but it's just impossible.

'My job involves all types of dental work except examining people's teeth. I mix all the fillings, clean, do clerical work, make sure all the equipment is present and in good working order, the list is endless.

'It is nice to go home and have no homework, so you have time to enjoy yourself.'

Lisa's monthly budget

Income (after deductions)	£165
Outgoings	
To parent for keep	£48
Bus pass	£24
Lunch	£24
Going out/entertainment	£30
Clothes/make-up/toiletries	£22
Records	£12
Sundries	£5
Total	**£165**

2 *Choose the best answer (A, B, C or D) for questions 1–4.*

1 Who spends the least on travel each month?
A 1
B 2
C 3
D 4

2 Who has problems managing his or her money?
A 1
B 2
C 3
D 4

3 Who is supporting him or herself while doing further training?
A 1
B 2
C 3
D 4

4 Who have received help with some essential outgoings from their employers?
A 1 and 2
B 2 and 3
C 3 and 4
D 4 and 1

3 *Which person:*

1 spends the most on essential outgoings?
2 spends the most on non-essential outgoings?

4 *Which person:*

• do you think is most fairly paid?
• do you feel most similar to?

Vocabulary *Money*

1 *Make five pairs of opposites from these words or phrases:*

credit	debit	deposit	export	import
loss	pay in	profit	take out	withdraw

2 *Which word is the odd one out? Why?*

1 cash   coin   note   prize
2 cheque   credit card   fine   money order
3 bargain   discount   fare   reduction
4 bill   inflation   invoice   receipt
5 broke   comfortable   rich   well-off
6 badly-off   bankrupt   penniless   wealthy
7 allowance   grant   interest   scholarship
8 invaluable   priceless   worthless   valuable
9 bribe   charge   duty   income
10 cost   expense   pension   price

Listening 📼 *What shall we get her?*

1 *If you have money to spend on non-essential things, what sort of things do you buy for yourself? Do you like buying things for other people? Do you like window-shopping?*

2 *Listen to this conversation between George and Mildred and choose the best answer (A, B, C or D) for questions 1–3.*

1 Where is this scene taking place?
  A in a café
  B in a gift shop
  C in a hotel lobby
  D in a post office

2 What are the speakers doing?
  A just looking around
  B comparing prices
  C buying holiday souvenirs
  D organising for goods to be sent

3 What is the relationship between the speakers?
  A two good friends
  B brother and sister
  C boss and secretary
  D husband and wife

3 Listen again and choose the best answer (A, B, C or D) for questions 1–4.

1 What did they buy for Phyllis?

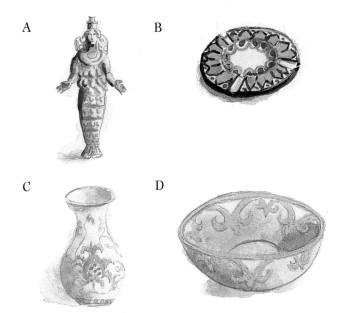

A   B

C   D

2 What did they buy for Simon?

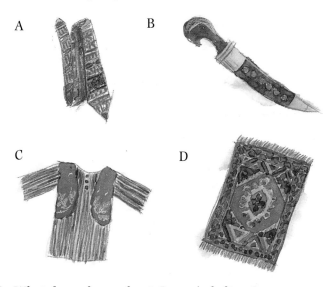

A   B

C   D

3 What do we learn about George's feelings?
A He doesn't want to help Mildred.
B He doesn't like Mildred's relatives.
C He doesn't want to spoil Simon.
D He doesn't like to spend money.

4 What do we learn about Mildred's behaviour?
A She's not an organised person.
B She doesn't trust George's advice.
C She wants to change Simon's behaviour.
D She does what George tells her to do.

4 Discuss these questions:

What's the | best / most useless | souvenir you've ever | given? / received?

Grammar *It's time; would rather; have something done*

1 **'It's time' can be followed by an infinitive:**

It's time to open a bank account.
It's time for us to go.
You can also use 'It's time' + subject + past tense:
It's time he learnt to dress like the rest of the world.
It's time the government did something about homelessness.
The meaning is present or future, not past.

2 **You also use a past tense with a present or future meaning after 'would rather' + subject.**

You often use this construction when you are disagreeing with someone, or making a complaint:
I'd rather we got her something useful.
I'd rather you didn't play the music so loud.

3 **'Get' and 'have' are used with a passive meaning in the pattern:**

get/have + object + past participle
This pattern can be used in situations where you ask someone to do something for you:
See if you can get them wrapped nicely.
I'm sure we could have it sent.
You ought to get your brakes checked.

4 **Complete the second sentence so that it means exactly the same as the first.**

1 The local council should build a new shopping centre.
It's time the local council ....
2 The old market needs repairing.
They should get ....
3 Please don't spend all your pocket money on chocolate.
I'd rather you ....
4 The boss ought to give us a pay rise.
It's time the boss ....
5 Someone must check the office accounts.
We must have ....
6 We haven't paid this electricity bill yet.
It's time for ....
7 You never save any money!
I'd rather you ....

3 Wrong foot forward

Speaking *Crime and punishment*

Are these things crimes, or something else? Arrange them in order of seriousness. What punishment would be appropriate for each one?

- taking flowers or fruit from a garden
- writing your name on a wall, monument, etc.
- fighting in the street, or at a football match
- trespassing
- travelling on public transport without a ticket
- deliberately breaking windows or other vandalism
- playing truant
- taking a bicycle, motorbike or car for a joy-ride
- driving without a driving licence

Reading *What makes young people commit crimes?*

The first sentence of a paragraph tells you the topic of that paragraph. It is called the topic sentence (see page 58).

Here are the topic sentences of a composition called 'What makes young people commit crimes?' Which paragraph do you think each one belongs to? Write your answer in the table below.

a Secondly, social conditions such as poverty and drug addiction are important.

b Firstly, lack of discipline at home and at school could be the cause.

c In conclusion, there are many factors which have caused an increase in crime among young people.

d More and more people under the age of sixteen are involved in crime.

e Finally, the police may also be to blame.

Paragraph	Topic sentence	Other sentences
1		
2		
3		
4		
5		

Here are the remaining sentences in the composition. Which paragraph does each one belong to? Add each sentence to the table. (Some paragraphs have three sentences, others only two.)

f They often ignore minor crimes.

g At school also, teachers cannot control large classes.

h It is difficult to know which of them is the most responsible, or how the increase can be stopped.

i In other cities, such as New York, young drug addicts commit crimes so as to be able to buy drugs.

j Young people often grow up without any firm idea about the difference between right and wrong, because parents are too busy working to guide their children.

k Consequently, many young people feel they can get away with things like theft.

l There are many possible reasons for this.

m In some cities, London for example, there are groups of homeless teenagers who steal in order to eat.

Underline the words or phrases which helped you decide the correct order of each sentence in the composition.

Look at page 191 to check that you have got the order right.

Grammar *Reason, result and purpose*

1 REASON
You can show reason in one of these ways:

1 because/as/since + clause
Young people often grow up without any firm idea about the difference between right and wrong, because/as/ since *parents are too busy working to guide their children.*

2 because of + noun
The punishment was severe because of *the seriousness of the crime.*
'On account of', or 'owing to' followed by a noun may also be used. These are more formal expressions than 'because of':
He resigned from the government on account of / owing to *his disagreement with the Prime Minister.*

2 RESULT
You can show result in one of these ways:

1 so/such ... that + clause

so	+ adjective / adverb + much / many / little / few	+ that + clause
such a(n)	+ adjective + singular countable noun	
such	+ adjective + uncountable noun / plural countable noun	

The crime is so serious that *the local police cannot handle it.*
Some parents work so hard *during the day* that *they have no energy in the evening.*
They have so much *work,* so many *responsibilities,* so little *free time and* so few *holidays* that *they do not talk much to their children.*
It is such a serious crime that *the local police cannot handle it.*
It was such bad weather that *no one wanted to go out.*
Some parents are such busy people that *they can't guide their children.*

2 too ... to

too	+ adjective / adverb (+ for + ...)	+ to + infinitive
not	+ adjective / adverb + enough	

Some parents are too busy *working* to guide *their children.*
He spoke too quickly *for me* to understand.
Some criminals are not old enough to go *to prison.*

3 Consequently, So, Therefore, As a result
These connectors usually come at the beginning of the sentence, followed by a comma. They join ideas between two sentences:
The police often ignore minor crimes. Consequently, *many young people feel they can get away with things like theft.*
Some parents are very busy with their jobs. As a result, *they cannot guide their children.*

3 PURPOSE
You can show purpose in one of these ways:

1 to + infinitive
Do you eat to live, or live to eat?

so as to / in order to / so as not to / in order not to
These are more formal than the simple infinitive:
Some homeless teenagers steal in order to *eat.*
Some homeless teenagers steal so as not to *starve.*

2 so that / in order that + modal verb + verb
Young drug addicts commit crimes so that *they can buy drugs.*
The bank robbers wore masks so that *they couldn't be recognised.*
'In order that' is more formal than 'so that'.

3 in case
When you talk about taking a precaution (doing something because something bad may happen), you use 'in case'. The verb in the 'in case' clause is in the present tense, even though you are talking about the future:
The President wears a bullet-proof vest in case *someone shoots him.*

4 Complete the second sentence so that it means exactly the same as the first.

1 Holmes followed the man to find out his address.
Holmes followed the man so that ....

2 I am sending you out of class since you are violent, rude and lazy.
I am sending you out of class because of ....
....

3 He isn't tall enough to become a police officer.
He's too ....

4 Some police carry guns because they may need to defend themselves.
Some police carry guns in case ....

5 On account of your clear explanation I understand the situation.
Because you ....

6 The class is too large for that teacher to control.
That teacher has such ....

7 The bank uses a video camera so that robbers will be discouraged.
The bank uses a video camera to ....

8 If she wasn't so young, the judge would send her to prison.
The judge won't send her to prison as ....

9 At the traffic lights my brother was driving too fast to stop.
At the traffic lights my brother was driving so ....
....

10 Lock all the doors and windows in case there are burglars in the neighbourhood.
Lock all the doors and windows because ....
....

Writing *Opinion composition*

Football hooliganism is a big problem in some countries. You are going to write an opinion composition (120–180 words) on this topic:

What makes people behave violently at football matches?

1 GETTING IDEAS
Discuss the possible reasons for football violence and write your ideas in two columns. For example:

Reason	Result
Too much drink	Drunken, violent behaviour
Players behave violently	Fans copy their heroes

2 ORGANISATION
Your composition should have the same organisation as the composition 'What makes young people commit crimes?'

Paragraph 1: Introduction
Paragraph 2: Reasons
Paragraph 3: Reasons
Paragraph 4: Reasons
Paragraph 5: Conclusion

Group together the reasons that are related. For example, put together all the ideas that are connected with copying someone's behaviour. Find three groups of ideas.

Write a topic sentence for each paragraph. For example, a topic sentence for Paragraph 2 could be:
Firstly, young men like to copy the behaviour of people they admire.

3 WRITING
Write about two sentences to complete each paragraph. These sentences should explain the idea of the topic sentence. For example, Paragraph 2 could be:

Firstly, young men like to copy the behaviour of people they admire. As a result, they start fights when they see their football heroes fighting on the pitch. The fights become bloody because the young men often carry knives, like their film heroes.

Use words like 'firstly' and 'finally' to link your paragraphs together.

4 CHECKING
Read through your finished composition carefully.

Exam skill 📼 *Listening*

Your ability to understand spoken English is tested in Paper 4. This paper contains usually three (but possibly four) separate listening passages recorded on cassette. Instructions are printed on the question paper, and further instructions are recorded on the cassette.

The three (or four) passages have a variety of:

- contexts, e.g. conversations, material from the radio (reports, talks, interviews, advertisements), announcements, phone messages
- voices
- lengths

Timing

Each passage is played twice. You have a short time to look through the questions before you hear the passage for the first time. Then there is a short pause before the second hearing. After this there is another short pause for you to note your answers. The whole paper takes about 30 minutes. At the end of the paper you will be given time to transfer your answers on to a special mark sheet.

Now practise with these three listening passages.

Part 1

*Listen to this extract from a talk given by a policeman and policewoman. For each of questions **1–8** tick (✓) one box to show whether the statement is True or False.*

		True	False
1	Bicycles were introduced to save the police force money.	☐	☐
2	One disadvantage of using bikes in city centres is that they're slower than cars.	☐	☐
3	One advantage of using police cars is that everyone notices them.	☐	☐
4	It's important that police on bikes should not wear uniform.	☐	☐
5	The children laughed at the police on bikes because they knew who they were.	☐	☐
6	The children were very concerned with fashion.	☐	☐
7	The operation has been in progress for one year now.	☐	☐
8	Neighbouring police forces think the idea is a good one.	☐	☐

Part 2

*You will hear a radio weather forecast for a winter's day in London. For questions **9–11** tick (✓) one of the boxes A, B, C or D to show the correct answer.*

9 What sort of weather is forecast for the day?
A cold and cloudy ☐
B cold and dry ☐
C frosty and windy ☐
D foggy and damp ☐

10 What is the top temperature predicted for central London?
A 6°C ☐
B 4°C ☐
C 1°C ☐
D – 5°C ☐

11 How much sun is forecast?
A a lot, both in the morning and the afternoon ☐
B more in the morning than the afternoon ☐
C more in the afternoon than the morning ☐
D not much, either in the morning or the afternoon ☐

Part 3

12 *You will hear five radio advertisements. Write the number of each advertisement (1–5) in the correct box.*

Advertisement	Number
for a home insurance policy	☐
for an alarm system	☐
for a book	☐
for a newspaper	☐
for a TV serial	☐
for TV and video sets	☐
against drug-taking	☐
against cheating on public transport	☐

13 *Complete each sentence with information taken from the correct advertisement.*

1 In Advertisement 1 *Ambitions Achieved* is about what might have happened if .... had survived.

2 Advertisement 2 is for the last part of .... at ....

3 The man in Advertisement 3 had to pay .... because he didn't buy a ....

4 The man in Advertisement 4 might have been less lucky if he hadn't had an ....

5 The offer in Advertisement 5 is that, if you buy certain systems, you also get a .... rent free.

Test exercises

1 *Complete each of the following sentences so that it means exactly the same as the sentence before it.*

1 I think we should raise your salary.
It's time we ....

2 I don't like you knitting in the office.
I'd rather ....

3 The photocopier needs servicing.
We must ....

4 I'll take some sandwiches because I may have to work at lunchtime.
I'll take some sandwiches in case ....

5 When did he start working at the bank?
How long ....

6 The report is too long for her to type before 2 o'clock.
It is such ....

7 The accountant is so busy that he can't give us the figures today.
The accountant is too ....

8 I can recommend Miss Chapman since she is quick, intelligent and reliable.
I can recommend Miss Chapman because of ....

9 My brother went into advertising to earn a lot of money fast.
My brother went into advertising so that ....

10 'Why won't you let me speak to my lawyer?' said the young man.
The young man asked them ....

2 *The word in capitals at the end of each of the following sentences can be used to form a word that fits suitably in the blank space. Fill each blank in this way.*
EXAMPLE: Her brother is a .....*famous*..... writer.   FAME

1 It's too cold to wear a .... dress.   SLEEVE
2 Because of the manager's .... the workers always
arrived late.   WEAK
3 On her wedding day she was too .... to eat.   EXCITE
4 What is the .... of your television screen?   WIDE
5 All .... should report to the reception desk.   VISIT
6 He ran up six floors and .... gave me the news.   BREATH
7 Don't let the children play with those .... ornaments.   BREAK
8 .... will be served at the end of the meeting.   REFRESH
9 The waitress smiled .... as she wiped the table.   APOLOGY
10 There is a great .... that the union members will
vote for a strike.   PROBABLE

3 *Choose the word or phrase (A–D) which best completes each sentence.*

1 One advantage of Business Club membership is the range of hotel
accommodation available at ....

A a debt   B a discount   C an expense   D a profit

2 When she started work, she put .... some money every week so that she
could afford a holiday later.

A aside   B back   C off   D out

3 He .... $100 on a game of cards, won $1,000 and then spent the rest of
the night losing it.

A bargained   B bet   C bribed   D charged

4 She .... a living working as a magician at children's parties.

A earns   B gains   C has   D wins

5 .... the company has produced their new model: they've spent years developing it.

A At a loss   B At last   C At least   D At once

6 She received a .... for driving the wrong way down a one-way street.

A fare   B fee   C fine   D note

7 The millionaire was angry that the painting he had bought turned out to be .... copy.

A an invaluable   B a priceless   C a valuable   D a worthless

8 She was so pleased with her new haircut that she gave the hairdresser a large ....

A interest   B pension   C prize   D tip

9 When he heard the doorbell ring, he ran downstairs, two steps ....

A at a time   B at times   C in time   D on time

10 We .... him of cheating in the exam but couldn't prove it, so we did nothing.

A confessed   B denied   C suspected   D tried

11 She was accused .... stealing a pair of tights from a department store.

A for   B of   C to   D with

12 I heard the news of the landing on the Moon .... I was having lunch.

A during   B meanwhile   C whenever   D while

13 Have you heard the weather .... ? It's going to be hot and sunny.

A article   B column   C forecast   D headline

14 When some of the schoolchildren misbehaved in the museum the director complained to the teacher ....

A at work   B in charge   C in order   D off duty

15 Crime is a major problem in this city: last year it .... by ten per cent.

A expanded   B improved   C increased   D raised

16 The guide asked .... there were any other questions people would like to ask about the cathedral.

A that   B what   C when   D whether

17 To get .... for the new book, the publishers distributed hundreds of free copies to journalists.

A advertisement   B announcement   C news   D publicity

18 She's not in her office but if you .... on for a minute I'll try and find her.

A count   B hang   C keep   D pass

19 The company is developing a new .... of shampoo made from seaweed and beer.

A brand   B name   C product   D trademark

20 It's not my .... that they lost their way: I gave them clear directions.

A blame   B fault   C guilt   D mistake

10

UNIT TEN
Relationships

1 Friendship

Speaking *My best friend*

1 **What makes a best friend? How much do you agree or disagree with each of these points?**

A best friend is someone who:
- knows all your secrets
- you can go on holiday with
- lives near you
- you can tell your problems to
- is the same age as you
- you have known for a long time
- asks for your advice
- would turn to you for help

Add any other ideas of your own.

2 **Put these ideas in your own order of importance. Which three do you think are the most important?**

Reading *When your best friend suddenly isn't*

1 **Not all close friendships last for ever. Can you think of some reasons why not? Read the following extract from a magazine article to find two reasons.**

JULIE AND SARAH

live three doors apart from each other. Their mothers are best friends too so they've known each other all their lives. Lately Julie has been finding Sarah a pain. She used to think she was funny and outrageous, but now she seems just childish and stupid. She used to admire her way-out clothes and hairstyles – now she's embarrassed to be seen on the streets with her. Julie is definitely outgrowing Sarah, who's upset by this, but she hates herself for it. She feels guilty because they meant so much to each other in the past. But then she tells herself things might have been different if Sarah had changed as well.

SIMON AND NICK

have been friends for years. They met on their first day at primary school and have shared everything since. Now Simon has gone away to college and they don't see so much of each other. Simon still writes to Nick and makes a point of seeing him when he's home during the holidays, but Nick feels left out. Recently he's been spreading rumours about Simon behind his back. He won't talk about it to Simon. He just says 'What do you care what I say?'

2 **Discuss these questions:**

- Have you ever known situations like these?
- Which of the friends do you sympathise with?
- What advice would you give each of them?

3 *Now read what a psychologist said. Choose the best answer (A, B, C or D) for questions 1–4.*

JULIE AND SARAH

It's not just the friend who is being outgrown who feels bad. Julie has been developing and changing faster and along different paths to Sarah, but she feels tied to the past. She should change her relationship with Sarah – they can no longer be best friends. And it's no good thinking that things might have been different if ... No, Julie has to face facts as they are. But she needn't cut Sarah off completely: she can perhaps find another place for her in her life. However, some friendships which have been very close can't survive this kind of adjustment.

SIMON AND NICK

This is a sad case of one boy growing up and the other remaining childish. It can't have been easy for Nick: he is obviously jealous of Simon's new friends and feels left out, so he attacks Simon because he's hurt. But he's ruining what could have remained a good – if different – friendship. It's no one's fault that Simon has gone to college and made new friends. With a different attitude on Nick's part – and Simon has shown he wants to keep Nick as his friend – this needn't have happened.

1 The psychologist comments that
   A Julie feels worse than Sarah.
   B Sarah feels worse than Julie.
   C both friends feel bad.
   D neither friend feels bad.

2 What does the psychologist recommend Julie to do?
   A drop Sarah as a friend
   B wait for Sarah to change
   C try to keep things as they were
   D accept that things must change

3 According to the psychologist, why has Simon and Nick's friendship ended?
   A Simon had got tired of Nick.
   B Nick was upset when Simon went away.
   C Simon grew up too fast.
   D Nick decided he didn't like Simon.

4 The psychologist thinks that if Nick had behaved differently
   A he wouldn't have stayed friends with Simon.
   B he might have made a new group of friends.
   C Simon would have found it easier to be his friend.
   D Simon would have been more to blame for the situation.

4 *Do you agree with the psychologist's advice? How close was it to your own?*

Grammar *Modal verbs (2)*

1 *The past form of a modal verb varies according to meaning.*

1 ABILITY

To talk about the present you use 'can':
The psychologist can advise Julie.

To talk about the past you use 'could', 'was able to' or 'managed to':
My best friend was able to get on with all sorts of people and could make friends easily. She even managed to make fierce dogs lick her hand.

2 POSSIBILITY, PROBABILITY, CERTAINTY

To talk about the present or future you use 'may', 'might' or 'could' (possibility), 'will' (probability), or 'must' (certainty):

Jason's not very talkative. He may be shy, and I might make him nervous, or he could be trying to make me jealous.

He will speak to you soon. He keeps looking at you. He must want to say something.

To talk about the past you use:
modal + have + past participle

You use 'would have', 'might have' and 'could have' to talk about something that was possible in the past, although it didn't actually happen:
Things might have been different.
Nick is ruining what could have remained a good friendship.
Simon would have introduced him to some new ideas.

You use 'may have', 'might have' or 'could have' to say that it is possible something happened but you don't know whether it happened or not:
I don't know why she's late – she may have had an accident; she might have stopped to talk to a friend; she could have missed her train.

You use 'must have' and 'can't have' to express certainty about the past:
It can't have been easy for Nick.
He must have felt lonely when Simon went away.

3 OBLIGATION OR NECESSITY

To talk about the present you use 'ought to', 'should', 'must' and 'have to':
Julie has to face facts. She must find another place for Sarah in her life. But Sarah ought to change as well. She should try to grow up.

You use 'had to' to express past obligation:
Simon had to go away to college.

'Ought to have' and 'should have' are used when an obligation in the past is not completed, or when something has been done that shouldn't have been done:
I ought to have told the manager, but I didn't.
You shouldn't have lied to her. She is very angry.

'Didn't have to' and 'didn't need to' express lack of obligation or necessity in the past:
He didn't need to / didn't have to get a visa to go to Greece.

'Needn't have' expresses the idea that something unnecessary was done:
Simon and Nick aren't friends any more. This needn't have happened.

2 **What would you say in these situations? Use a past modal verb together with the verb in brackets.**

EXAMPLE: Criticise a friend for losing a cassette of yours *(be more careful)*: 'You *should have been more careful.*'

1 Comfort a friend whose boyfriend has missed a date *(forget)*:
'Don't worry: he ....'
2 Explain to your mother why you didn't bring a new friend to meet her *(not approve of)*:
'You ....'
3 Explain why you didn't spend any money at the disco *(not spend anything)*:
'My friend paid so I ....'
4 Contradict one friend's explanation of why another friend didn't turn up for an appointment *(not forget)*:
'But she ....: I reminded her about it yesterday.'
5 Complain about having worked unnecessarily all weekend on a composition *(miss the football match)*:
'I ....: the teacher has just given us another week to finish it.'
6 Criticise a friend who drove after drinking several beers *(not drive / have an accident)*:
'You ....: you ....,'

Vocabulary *Feelings*

1 **Find the words or phrases about feelings in the article on pages 118–19 which mean:**

– self-conscious and uncomfortable (paragraph 1)
– unhappy because of having done something wrong (paragraph 1)
– not included (paragraph 2)
– envious and possessive (paragraph 4)
– with injured feelings (paragraph 4)

2 **How do you think these people feel? Choose words from the box.**

annoyed	anxious	apologetic	ashamed
disappointed	embarrassed	grateful	guilty
hurt	jealous	left out	lonely	miserable
proud	relieved	sympathetic	

Grammar *Present perfect progressive*

1 *have/has + been + -ing form*

Julie has been finding Sarah a pain.
Julie has been developing and changing.
Nick has been spreading rumours about Simon.

You use the present perfect progressive to talk about actions which began in the past and which are still going on. There are many occasions when it would be possible to use either the present perfect simple or the present perfect progressive. But you use the progressive tense when you want to emphasise how long a recent event has been happening, and that it has not been completed.

2 *Complete this extract from a conversation by putting the verbs in brackets in the correct tense: present perfect progressive, present perfect simple or past simple.*

Debbie is talking with an old friend, Jody, who she hasn't seen for some time. Jody can see that Debbie has a problem she wants to talk about.

JODY: Tell me – something (1) .... (bother) you recently, hasn't it?

DEBBIE: Oh, yes. I've got this terrible problem. I (2) .... (worry) a lot about my friendship with Annette. She just (3) .... (meet) someone and (4) .... (decide) she wants to marry him. At first I (5) .... (be) happy for them both. But now I never see her. I think she's trying to get rid of me.

JODY: Oh dear. What makes you think that?

DEBBIE: Oh, many things. For instance, for the past few months we (6) .... (do) an evening course in jewellery design. Last week she (7) .... (say) she (8) .... (want) to give it up. She (9) .... (work) on this wonderful series of earrings – but now she wants to drop everything. I can't believe it. And when I (10) .... (ring) her last weekend to talk about it, she (11) .... (refuse) to come to the phone. I (12) .... (wait) for her to ring me back but she still (13) .... (not call). I don't know what to do.

3 *Have you had any of these feelings recently? Or have you made any of your friends feel something similar?*

2 All in the family

Listening ▭ *A new baby*

1 *What sort of changes does the arrival of a new baby cause in a family? Which of these are positive, and which can cause problems? If there are problems, how can they be overcome?*

2 *Listen to this conversation between Jane, a new mother, and the counsellor on a radio phone-in.*

1 What is the new mother's problem?
2 What do we learn about her relationships with the two fathers of her children?

3 *Listen again and choose the best answer (A, B, C or D) for questions 1–3.*

1 The son feels angry because he
  A wants to be the only child.
  B hates the father of the new baby.
  C is jealous of what the baby is getting.
  D feels sorry for his own father.

2 What do we learn about the boy's own father?
  A He was a kind and loving father.
  B He made life difficult for his son.
  C He chose to leave his wife.
  D He preferred his daughter to his son.

3 The son is directing his anger towards his mother because he feels
  A she shouldn't have had another baby.
  B she is not looking after the new baby properly.
  C he will never be able to love the new baby.
  D he can't express his anger towards his father.

4 *What advice would you give the new mother? What would you say to the son?*

Speaking ▭ *Conversation skills (1)*

1 *Discuss these questions about informal conversation in English:*

1 How do you invite someone to speak? How can you tell when it's your turn to speak?
2 How do you show the speaker that you're interested in what he or she is saying?
3 What can you say when you're organising your thoughts, or looking for a word?
4 What tricks do you know for holding on to your turn?

Listen to extracts 1–4 from the phone-in. What answers to the questions above can you find?

2 *Now practise these conversation skills. Form groups of three (Students A, B and C) to discuss these questions:*

1 Is it better to be the eldest or the youngest child, or one in the middle?
2 Is it better to be part of a small or a large family?
3 Is it better to have young or older parents?

Before you start the discussion, look at your role cards: A on page 190, B on page 191 and C on page 192. Do not show your instructions to your partners.

Grammar *The article*

1 **With some nouns you can use 'a/an' and 'the', with others you can only use 'the' or have no article at all.**

Look at the nouns in the paragraph below and then put a tick (✓) in the appropriate place in the table.

Jane has children, a son and a daughter, from a previous marriage. She has just had a baby with another partner. The older children, especially the son, feel anger and resentment towards the new baby. Jane doesn't know how to deal with the anger they feel.

Type of noun	a/an	the	no article
singular countable			
plural countable			
uncountable			

2 **Why do we not use an article in the expressions in column A, but use one in those in column B?**

A	B
Greece	The United States
advice	the advice of a counsellor
love	the love she gave her children
My wife's in hospital.	She's in the hospital down the road.
I met Jane Fonda.	You mean the Jane Fonda?
Dr Davies	She is a doctor.
	I must go to the doctor.
Pope Paul	He spoke to the Pope.
old people	the old
at night	in the morning
play football	play the piano

3 **Check that the article has been used correctly in these sentences. Make any necessary corrections.**

1 At school children study subjects like the mathematics and the history, and learn how to take their place in the society.
2 The young people can learn a lot from the old.
3 She wants to be actress like girl next door.
4 In the morning he plays the squash before he goes to the work.
5 New houses are within easy reach of shops, public transport and leisure centre just opened by mayor.
6 Twice a week there are lectures in the library on the life and culture of the British Isles.

"Independent child..."

Word formation *Verbs*

1 **Change these nouns and adjectives into verbs by putting the prefixes en- (or em-) at the beginning, or the suffixes -ify, -ise/ize, or -en at the end.**

EXAMPLES: danger → *endanger*   simple → *simplify*
modern → *modernise*   short → *shorten*

able	beauty	close	courage	deaf	legal
power	public	pure	ripe	symbol	tight
wide					

2 **Change these nouns into verbs by changing the sound /s/ to /z/, and /f/ to /v/. Sometimes you only have to change the pronunciation, and sometimes you have to change the spelling as well.**

EXAMPLES: advice → *advise*   half → *halve*

belief	emphasis	grief	house	shelf	use

3 **Make compound verbs by combining the nouns in the first column with the verbs in the second.**

EXAMPLE: baby + sit → *babysit*

baby	clean
brain	dream
chain	see
day	shop
sight	sit
spring	smoke
window	wash

What do the compound verbs mean?

3 Bridging the generation gap

Reading *A Japanese experiment*

1 *Read this text and find information in it which surprises, impresses or shocks you.*

Kotoen in the Edogawa district of Tokyo is a home for the elderly, so you might expect it to be a gloomy place. However, the people who live there are always bright and cheerful. The reason for this is the happy voices of the children who attend the Edogawa Nursery School located in the same building. The nursery school on the ground floor accommodates 80 pre-school children aged one and a half to five or six. Kotoen, on the first and second floors, is the home for about 100 senior citizens.

Although many of the elderly residents live in the home by choice, they still long for family life. Being in the same building allows them to visit the nursery school whenever they wish, while the children often go upstairs to play. In the morning, both old and young gather outside for exercises. Special times such as Christmas and sports days are always celebrated together.

"We find the children learn how to care for others by talking and being with their older co-residents," explained Maeda Takumi, the director of Kotoen. "As for the elderly, through their association with the children they become more alive and their health improves. Seeing these old people, many of whom we thought had forgotten how to laugh or even express their thoughts, holding the children and happily talking with them, brings home just how important an affectionate relationship between the very old and the very young can be."

The success of Kotoen has created a sensation in Japan and brought responses from all over the country. The declining number of children now being born each year has left unused space at many nursery schools. It has therefore been suggested that these surplus areas are utilised by the elderly. In this way, in spite of living in small nuclear households, children can experience the advantages of close contact with people of a much older generation.

2 Now answer these questions by choosing the best alternative, A, B, C or D.

1 What is unusual about Kotoen home for the elderly?
A Old people choose to go there.
B The residents look happy.
C The residents live in family groups.
D It is next door to a nursery school.

2 According to the home's director, the old people's health improves because they
A do a lot of exercise.
B are looked after by young people.
C have close contact with children.
D learn how to express themselves.

3 According to the text, children in Japan
A live in large families.
B go to school at one and a half.
C go to crowded nursery schools.
D celebrate Christmas.

Grammar *Contrast*

1 There are various ways in which you may show a contrast between two ideas.

1 Look at the first paragraph of the passage opposite. What word introduces a sentence which is a contrast to the sentence before it?
   Give some other examples of expressions which introduce a contrast to the previous sentence.
2 Look at the second paragraph. What word joins two contrasting ideas in the same sentence?
3 Look at the fourth paragraph. What words here express the same idea as 'although'? Do you use these two expressions in the same way?

2 Rewrite each sentence using the word(s) in brackets. Make all necessary changes.

1 Although they had only known each other for two weeks, they decided to get married. (however)
2 Although he behaved badly, she praised him. (in spite of)
3 Although he promised it would never happen again, she insisted on a divorce. (nevertheless)
4 Despite his charm and good looks she did not like him. (although)
5 She is well-qualified, but I don't want to work with her. (in spite of)
6 Although they always seem kind and straightforward, I don't trust them. (yet)
7 He didn't know his neighbours very well, but he invited them to his party. (although)

Writing *'For and against' composition*

You are going to write a 'for and against' composition on this topic:

What are the advantages and disadvantages of living in the same house as your grandmother?

1 GETTING IDEAS
Read this list of points that a student made before writing the composition above. Mark whether each point is an advantage or disadvantage.

1 She embarrasses me in front of my friends.
2 She tells fascinating stories about life 50 years ago.
3 She stands up for me in family arguments.
4 She sews on buttons and irons shirts.
5 She has disgusting habits like sniffing and making a mess when she eats.
6 When I am ill she brings me hot drinks and magazines.
7 She criticises my choice in clothes, music and television programmes.

2 ORGANISING
This is the student's paragraph plan:

Paragraph 1: Introduction
Paragraph 2: Disadvantages
Paragraph 3: Advantages
Paragraph 4: Conclusion

Here are the topic sentences for each paragraph. Which paragraph does each one belong to?
a In conclusion, I cannot imagine life without my grandmother.
b On the other hand, in spite of her annoying habits, she is a wonderful person to live with.
c I cannot speak about all grandmothers but just about my own.
d The main problem with living with my grandmother is the generation gap.

3 WRITING
Write the composition, using the points in the list in ☐1 and the same paragraph plan and topic sentences. Write about 180 words.

4 CHECKING
Check what you have written carefully. Compare your version with other students', then with the version on page 191.

Exam skill *Completion exercises*

The penultimate question (question 4 or 5) in the Use of English paper is a completion exercise. You have to complete either a letter or a dialogue.

1 LETTER

The sentences of the letter are presented like a telegram. This means all the verbs are shown in their base form, and many words such as 'a', 'the', 'of' and 'in' have been left out. Look at an example of this type of exercise.

Example question

Make all the changes and additions necessary to produce, from the following sets of words and phrases, sentences which together make a complete letter. Note carefully from the example what kind of alterations need to be made. Write each sentence in the space provided.

EXAMPLE: I be very surprised / receive / letter / you this morning.

ANSWER: I was very surprised to receive a letter from you this morning.

7 Sussex Square
Brighton
17 May 1994

Dear Silke,

1   I like / tell / exciting news.

....

2   You remember Kurt because you introduce / Geneva last summer.

....

3   We write / each other and have long telephone conversations since / time.

....

4   Last month he come / stay / me and / parents.

....

5   I tell him I be worried / we spend too much money / stamps / telephone calls.

....

6   So Kurt say / we save money / if we get married!

....

7   We fix / date / first Saturday / August.

....

8   I still not meet Kurt's family, / make me / bit nervous.

....

I hope you will be able to come to the wedding.
Love to you and your family,

Judy

To do this kind of exercise successfully you must:

1 Read all the sentences first to understand the sense of the complete letter.

2 Decide what tense to write each verb in. Sometimes this decision will be influenced by:
   - the sense of the whole letter. For example, what tense should the verb 'fix' be in (7)?
   - a time phrase in the sentence, for example, 'last summer' in (2).
   - a previous verb, for example 'say' in (6). Sometimes the second verb has to be an infinitive or -ing form, for example, 'tell' in (1).
   - the kind of clause the verb is in. For example, what kind of sentence is the one with 'save' and 'get' in (6)?

3 Decide what words need to be put in. The missing words may be:
   - prepositions, for example in (2) and (5).
   - words like 'a/an', 'the', 'this', 'that', 'some', 'any', 'my', 'his', etc., for example in (1), (3), (4), (7), (8).
   - pronouns, for example in (1) and (2).
   - relative pronouns, for example in (8).
   - words like 'when', 'until', 'if', 'although'.
   - modal verbs, for example with 'remember' in (2).

4 Read through your finished letter to make sure it makes sense and is correct.

Now do the example question.

2 DIALOGUE

You have to complete some sentences in an unfinished dialogue. The incomplete sentences are usually questions. Look at this example.

Example question

Tom and Gerry are discussing Tom's new neighbours. Fill in the parts of the dialogue, numbered (1) to (7), which have been left blank.

TOM: I spent the weekend helping my neighbours move to their new house.

GERRY: Is (1)..?

TOM: No. Just in the next street. I'll still be able to visit them easily.

GERRY: What about your new neighbours? Have (2)..........
....?

TOM: Not completely. Only about half of their furniture has arrived so far.

GERRY: So you (3) ....?

TOM: That's not quite true. I peeped out of the window when they first visited the house.

GERRY: What (4) ....?

TOM: Ordinary, but friendly.

GERRY: How many (5) ....?

TOM: The parents and, I think, three children.

GERRY: I wonder if they'll come to our school. How (6) ......
....?

TOM: I think the oldest girl is about sixteen. She's very pretty.

GERRY: That sounds like the ideal neighbour! When (7) ......
....?

TOM: I'm not letting you near her until I've had a chance to make friends first!

To do this kind of exercise successfully you must:

1 Read everything carefully so that you understand the whole dialogue.

2 Complete the dialogue so that the questions and answers make logical sense.

3 Use accurate English, including correct spelling.

4 Check what you have written. For example, here are three suggested answers for (1). Which one is the best, and why are the other two unsatisfactory?
   a Is it near here?
   b Is it far away?
   c Is it move far?

Now do the example question.

Test exercises

1 *Make changes and additions to these sets of words in order to write a complete letter.*

12 Ashdell Road
Leeds LS6 1BP
14 June 1994

Dear Valerie,

1 Yesterday I buy / ticket / station when I hear someone call / name.

....

2 It be our old friend Marilyn, / I not see since we leave school.

....

3 My train leave / five minutes so we not have much time / conversation.

....

4 I only know that she live / Australia / last five years.

....

5 You remember / fat she be / school and / old-fashioned clothes she wear?

....

6 She be extremely slim now and yesterday she wear / latest fashion.

....

7 I wonder / she marry.

....

8 She like us all / meet / Saturday after next, if you be free then.

....

I expect we'll hear all her news then.

Love from *Liz*

2 *Complete each of the following sentences so that it means exactly the same as the sentence before it.*

1 Whose pullover is this?
   Who does...

2 Although they quarrel noisily, the Flintstones are good neighbours.
   In spite ....

3 Jack and Jill started going out together three months ago.
   Jack and Jill have..

4 It wasn't necessary to write me a 'thank you' letter.
   You..

5 They were best friends at school but deadly enemies in later life.
   Although ....

6 I'm sure Derek wasn't invited to the party.
   Derek can't...

7 I'm going to take my violin because they might ask me to play.
   I'm going to take my violin in case ....

8 Although she felt jealous, she managed to hide her feelings.
   Despite..

9 Why didn't you tell me about your engagement?
   You should...

10 I think Joanna has forgotten my birthday.
   Joanna must...

3 *Choose the word or phrase (A–D) which best completes each sentence.*

1 Can you please stop whistling? I find it a bit ....

A bothering   B irritating   C offending   D shocking

2 Because Romeo and Juliet didn't want either of their families to know, they got married in ....

A common   B difficulties   C secret   D tears

3 He proposed to his girlfriend the day before he was called .... to fight in the war.

A for   B in   C on   D up

4 I really .... her: she's 80 and she still goes swimming every day.

A admire   B amaze   C approve   D astonish

5 I'm reading a report about .... teaching of reading to children whose parents have never learned to read.

A a successful   B any successful   C successful   D the successful

6 Now that my old neighbour can't walk very well he really .... people going to see him.

A appreciates   B attracts   C feels   D impresses

7 What's upset you? You're in a really bad .... today.

A character   B emotion   C mood   D sense

8 She spent .... day by the phone waiting for news of her friend's operation.

A an anxious   B a conscious   C an exhausted   D a suspicious

9 .... we've only just met, it feels as if we've known each other all our lives.

A Although   B Despite   C However   D Yet

10 When my parents moved house they got .... a lot of things they didn't want.

A along with   B out of   C rid of   D round to

11 After her divorce she lived .... in a small flat until she met her new husband.

A alone   B lonely   C selfish   D single

12 I never eat ice cream: my teeth are too .... to cold.

A sensational   B senseless   C sensible   D sensitive

11 UNIT ELEVEN
Free time

1 A good sport

Speaking *What's in a sport?*

1 ***There are many different kinds of sport. A sport can:***

- be competitive or non-competitive
- be challenging or undemanding
- be traditional or modern
- require special equipment or none at all
- be done for exercise or just for fun
- be done regularly or irregularly
- be played in only one kind of weather or all kinds

Compare the sports in the photos, using the ideas in the list above. What other ideas about sport come up during your discussion?

2 ***What sports do you like – those which are competitive or non-competitive, challenging or undemanding? Talk about your own preferences, using the list of ideas above.***

Reading *Making a connection*

Quickly read the four passages (A–D) and answer these questions about each one.

1 What is the passage about? Which of photos **1–4** opposite can it go with?

2 Can you guess where each passage might have come from (e.g. a conversation between two friends, a magazine article, etc.)?

3 How does each passage relate to the ideas you discussed in *What's in a sport*?

A

You start by kicking a ball against a wall on your own. Then a friend appears and you have a game of seeing how long you can keep the ball up. Then, one by one, other friends appear and you play, say, four against four.

B

The waves here are incredibly powerful and pretty scary. When you're catching them your mind goes numb – all you're thinking about is making the wave and not falling off. You need a lot of experience surfing here before you feel confident. It can be terrifying but I can't wait to tackle them again.

C

A Japanese martial art and sport, derived from traditional fighting systems. Introduced to Japan in the 1920s by Gichin Funakoshi. There are eight major styles recognised in the world today.

D

This is one of the great traditional games of France, above all in the south. Everywhere you will see people playing it intently, not only in little village squares but also beside smart promenades.

Speaking 🔊 *Agreeing and disagreeing (2)*

1 *You are going to listen to two people discussing four passages (A–D) which are also related to photos 1–4 opposite. Quickly read each passage and think about which photo(s) it could go with. You will have the opportunity to discuss this later.*

A

I think if you train through the winter, by the time the season comes you're sick of it and you don't train hard enough. I usually have a break of about five months through the winter and then get back into it slowly.

B

IT'S NOT ONLY A relaxing game, it's educational – it requires a lot of concentration, self-control, sportsmanship, precision and sharp sight.

C

Playtime habits of kids are changing. They're going for more and more indoor sports and electronic games like computers. And facilities are being sold off. So traditional outdoor games are threatened.

2 *Listen to short extracts from the discussion the two people had about the passages. In each case, does the second speaker agree or disagree with the first speaker?*

3 *Listen again to the four extracts. Note down how the speakers agree or disagree with each other.*

D

As you know, there are several ways to strike someone with your elbows. You can use them to drive the edge of your hand into an attacker's throat. Then you can force your elbow back into his solar plexus – like this.

What can you say when you	agree disagree	with someone who says	'I think ...' 'I don't think ...'	?

4 *Which passage goes best with which photo? Practise the language for agreeing and disagreeing above.*

Pronunciation 🎧 *Question tags*

1 *People can ask a question using a question tag for two reasons:*

1 They are unsure of the answer, and want to check if it's true.
2 They feel sure of the answer, and want someone to agree with them.

They show the difference by the way they move their voice on the question tag. Listen to the examples:

'So it might be about football, mightn't it?'
  (Voice goes up at the end = speaker unsure)

'So it can't be about football, can it?'
  (Voice goes down at the end = speaker sure)

2 *Listen to these questions using question tags. Mark if the voice goes up or down on the question tag.*

1 'Concentration' and 'self-control' – I think this could be about surfing, don't you?
2 Surfing's not a game, is it?
3 So it could be about karate, couldn't it?
4 I wouldn't call surfing a traditional sport, would you?
5 Now this is about karate, isn't it?

3 *Work with your partner to practise using question tags.*

1 Make five statements you want to check are true. Listen to the examples first:
    A: You swim a lot, don't you?
    B: Yes, I do.
    C: Badminton's the most popular sport in your country, isn't it?
    D: No, it isn't actually. Football is.

2 Make five statements you feel sure are true. Listen to the examples first:
    A: Football's our national sport, isn't it?
    B: Yes, it is.
    C: Chris Evert was the most successful woman tennis player ever, wasn't she?
    D: No, she wasn't actually. Martina Navratilova was.

Speaking *Sports school*

1 *You have been given $30,000 to set up a special sports school. Decide:*

- what range of courses you will offer
- what facilities you will have
- where your school will be
- what time of the year your school will be open
- what you will need to buy
- what top-name coaches you would like
- how much you can afford to offer them
- how long your courses will last
- how much you will charge for them

Below are some sample costs for facilities, etc. You can add to these lists as you wish, but must set your prices according to the examples here.

Facilities	
Swimming pool	$1,000 each
Gym	$1,000 each
Football pitch	$500 each
Tennis court	$500 each

Places to rent	
Mountain	$10,000 a year
Beach	$2,000 a year
Ravine	$1,000 a year
River	$1,000 a year
Field	$200 a year

Equipment	
Nautilus machines	$2,000
Canoe	$500
Surfboard	$100
Set of picks	$50
Racket	$50

Coaches	
Gabriella Sabatini	$ ....a day
Maradona	$ ....a day

2 *Complete this advertisement for your sports school.*

SPORTS SCHOOL

Your chance to play your favourite game with some of the great sporting personalities.
We offer a unique range of courses, from an intensive weekend to ....
Our school is set in a superb location: ....

Learn from the professionals
Top-name coaches have been recruited for the sports school. These include Football with .... , Tennis with ....
The costs range from $ .... for an intensive weekend course to $ ....
For more information ....

2 Hobbies and pastimes

Speaking *Passing the time*

What are the most popular hobbies in your country? Are your hobbies similar to those of other people your age, or do you have an unusual interest?

Complete these sentences. Use your own ideas as well as the words in the box.

In my country, the hobbies or pastimes which are:
- most popular with children are.............................
- most popular with young people are ....
- most popular with older people are ....
- most traditional are ....
- most up-to-date are ....

> card games   collecting things   computer games
> dance   fishing   gossip   making things   music
> painting   photography   sailing   yoga

Listening 📼 *Scuba diving*

1 **What do you know about scuba diving? Think of three adjectives which describe it.**

2 **Listen to Roger, a Canadian scuba diver, talking about his underwater experiences. As you listen, put a tick (✓) against each point that Roger mentions.**

1 Scuba divers have to learn:
- **a** ☐ how long they can safely stay under water
- **b** ☐ how quickly they can come up to the surface
- **c** ☐ how to hold their breath

2 To get a scuba diving certificate you must:
- **a** ☐ have a medical examination
- **b** ☐ study in a class
- **c** ☐ do a written examination
- **d** ☐ practise in a swimming pool
- **e** ☐ swim three kilometres under water
- **f** ☐ dive at least three times in the open sea or a lake

3 According to Roger, sharks are:
- **a** ☐ frightening
- **b** ☐ aggressive
- **c** ☐ strange
- **d** ☐ harmless

4 Under the sea near western Canada you can see:
- **a** ☐ soft coral
- **b** ☐ hard coral
- **c** ☐ colourful fish
- **d** ☐ giant octopus

5 Other things you can do under water:
- **a** ☐ take photographs
- **b** ☐ talk to people
- **c** ☐ paint pictures

3 **Do you want to revise the adjectives you chose to describe scuba diving?**

Writing   *A talk (1)*

1   ***Look at this text of a talk to a group of secondary school students about photography.***

The text is not complete. These three sentences (**a–c**) should be added to it. Read the text and decide what the right position for each sentence is.

a   But remember some simple rules.
b   When you're used to handling your camera, you could specialise in something exotic like underwater scenes.
c   You will also need something to keep your photos in.

PHOTOGRAPHY AS A HOBBY
I'm here to give you some advice about my hobby: photography. I'm sure many of you already use a camera. But you can only call it your hobby if you do it all year, not just on holiday.

It needn't be an expensive hobby. Cheap cameras can take wonderful pictures. Buying, developing and printing film can cost a lot, so be careful you don't overspend your budget. An old shoe box will do.

You don't need any special training to take successful photographs. Don't aim the camera into the sun; keep the sun behind you. Make sure your subject fills the picture, otherwise it will disappear into the background. Finally hold the camera steady, unless you want a blurred picture!

Not all your pictures will be brilliant, but they will be unique. Of course, you may prefer to stick to pictures of holidays and your friends in embarrassing positions!

2   ***Underline the features which show this is the text of a talk.***

3   ***Which of these points does the talk cover?***

self-introduction   equipment   time needed
problems   pleasures   technique   training
options   cost   skills needed

4   ***Write the text of a talk giving advice to a group of secondary school students about your hobby (120–180 words).***

–   Include some points listed in *3* above.
–   Organise the points into paragraphs.
–   Include some features you noted in *2* above.

Grammar   *be used to doing / used to do*

1   ***Match each example sentence (a–c) with its correct description (1–3):***

a   *She's used to handling a camera.*
b   *She takes a lot of photographs.*
c   *She used to take black and white photos in the 1960s.*

1   Something she does regularly in the present.
2   Something she did regularly in the past, but doesn't do any more.
3   Something (possibly a bit difficult or unpleasant) which she is familiar with because she has done it often.

What structure is used to express each idea?

2   ***Complete the sentences with either 'be used to' or 'used to' and the correct form of the verb in brackets.***

1   As a child I .... (collect) stamps.
2   I don't feel stiff after our game of tennis. I .... (do) a lot of exercise.
3   .... you .... (ski) more often before you broke your leg?
4   My brother .... (complain) about feeling cold when we went sailing. But now he .... (get) wet and he enjoys it.
5   Do you find driving in London different from driving in Rome? .... you .... (drive) on the left yet?
6   She didn't like the sea in Scotland because she .... (not/swim) in cold water.

Word formation *Prefixes*

1 *These prefixes have certain meanings.*

co-	dis-	in/im/il/ir-	inter-	mid-	mini-
mis-	non-	out-	over-	post-	pre- re-
self-	sub-	super-	trans-	un-	under-

New words can be made by putting the prefixes in front of other words, for example:
*co*operate *dis*agree *ir*regularly
*inter*national *mid*night *mini*-skirt
*mis*understand *non*-competitive *out*grow
*over*spend *post*graduate *pre*paid *re*write
self-study *sub*way *super*market *trans*atlantic
*un*demanding *under*water

Study the examples and then write each prefix, with an example, next to its meaning in the table below:

2 *Add one or more of the prefixes to these words to make new words. What do the new words mean?*

appearance conscious dated done dress
formed honestly legal made marriage
mature natural owned responsible
sensitive smoking summer

3 *What other words do you know with these prefixes?*

Meaning	Prefix	Example
opposite / not (*4 prefixes*)	in/im/il/ir-	irregularly
bad(ly) / wrong(ly)		
again		
together		
between	inter-	international
before		
middle		
across		
after		
small		
too much / above		
bigger than usual		
under (*2 prefixes*)		
do better, faster, *etc.*	out-	outgrow
to / for oneself		

3 Having a good time

Reading *Party politics*

1 *How often do you go to parties? Do you enjoy them? What type of party do you like best?*

2 *Read this extract from a novel. Which of the two young women would you rather talk to at a party?*

That evening, like every other evening, Mui Ee stayed at home. She was ironing her school uniform when the telephone rang.

"Woman." It was her best friend Sissy on the
5 line. "What are you doing tomorrow night?"

"Saturday night?"

"Yes. There's going to be a party. You must go."

"But Sissy, you know I don't go to parties."

"Come on Mui, you're a junior college student
10 now. Your parents should let you have a little freedom to go to parties."

"No, it's not my parents," admitted Mui Ee. "It's me. I don't like going to parties. It's ..."

"Come on, Mui," insisted Sissy, "How are you
15 ever going to make any friends if you don't socialise?"

Mui Ee replied, "But I – I've never ever been to a party. I mean, what I am I going to wear?"

"Didn't you read *The Textbook*?"

20 "What textbook?"

"*The Teenage Textbook*, woman. The one I gave you for your birthday. Look, you have to go. I've invited all our old gang, as well as Rosie, Jillian, May Chu, Linda, Toni, Sangeeta. There'll also be guys.
25 Seng Huat's coming, so are Wong Chong Di, Rick – do you know him? He used to have a crush on me. Also, I've asked Hari and Jason to help out. Come on Mui."

"Well, OK," Mui Ee said eventually. "I'll come."

30 "Great. I have to go now, Mui. I have to go call some other people. See you tomorrow in school. Bye-bye." Sissy rang off.

That night, Mui Ee sat in bed, wrapped up in her soft blue blanket, two big pillows propping her up
35 and her favourite pink bolster in her arms.

She pulled out *The Teenage Textbook* from the chest of drawers beside her bed and opened it to the lesson on parties. This is what it said:

3 *Choose the best answer (A, B, C or D) for questions 1–2 and explain why each of the other three answers is not right.*

1 What do we learn about Mui Ee?
  A Her parents are strict with her.
  B Her life isn't very exciting.
  C She prefers staying at home.
  D She has more friends than she needs.

2 We learn that Sissy
  A doesn't really like Mui Ee.
  B doesn't have many friends.
  C is lively and outgoing.
  D is Mui Ee's only friend.

Read on to find out what *The Teenage Textbook* is.

LESSON EIGHT: EVERYTHING YOU NEVER WANTED TO KNOW ABOUT PARTIES

Guest who?

A good teenager must realise that the secret to the success of any type of party depends on who's on the
45 guest list. *The Teenage Textbook* recommends that you invite the following types of people:

1 The Rich & Famous – Such guests will raise the tone of the party greatly. Teenagers will usually be sufficiently impressed by the following categories of
50 Rich & Famous guests: National Sportspeople, Famous Fashion Models, Offspring of Rich & Famous People, People Who Have Made Song Requests On Radio, People Who Can Drive Cars, etc.

2 The Life and Soul – Your party would be empty
55 without this guest. The 'Life and Soul' of every party takes the lead in making a fool of him or herself and sets everyone else at ease. Such a person should have a low IQ and an even lower sense of humour. If you cannot find a 'Life and Soul' simply hire a mobile disco
60 DJ who can usually be relied on to make a fool of himself for a small fee.

3 The Silent Majority – You will need a lot of these people to add 'bulk' to your guest list. Generally speaking, guests who make up the silent majority are
65 not able to make conversation or communicate verbally. They are also so plain and anonymous that their own mothers would have difficulty recognising them. Such people include students in charge of the library, teenagers with bad breath and people who win
70 Mr and Miss Personality contests.

4 The Trendies – Such teenagers are not rare. Dressed in fashionably feminine designer wear, bright, chunky jewellery and earrings, beautiful eye make-up, blood-red lip gloss … and the girls are even worse.

75 **5** The Wallflower – Have one or two of these lonely people around, and your other guests will feel much better about themselves. People who are ignored or avoided in real life make the best wallflowers. Therefore you should pick teenagers who are aspiring poets,
80 score more than 6 As at 'O' level or speak in words of more than two syllables.

---

4 *Do you think the writer intends the reader to take this extract seriously or to find it funny? What examples can you find to support your ideas?*

5 *Choose the best answer (A, B, C or D) for summary questions 1–2.*

1 *The Teenage Textbook* is written in the style of
A a school textbook.
B a teenage novel.
C a guide to successful living.
D an advertising leaflet.

2 The main intention of the writer in both extracts is to
A advise.
B amuse.
C criticise.
D inform.

6 *How well do the five categories of guest describe the guests at parties you have been to? Can you think of people who fit these categories? Who do you invite to your own parties?*

Grammar *The future (1)*

1 *There are various ways of talking about the future. The way that you choose depends on your intention and your feeling of certainty about the future.*

1 will + infinitive
You use this form to express a *prediction* about the future:
Such guests will raise the tone of the party greatly.
You won't go to so many parties when you're older.

You also use this form to express a *spontaneous decision* about the future:
"Well, OK," Mui Ee said eventually. "I'll come."

2 be going to + infinitive
You use this form to express an *intention* about the future:
What am I going to wear?
I'm going to wear my new shoes.

You also use this form to express a *certainty* about the future which is based on evidence now:
Rick's smiling at you – he's going to ask you to dance.
You're driving too fast! We're going to crash!

3 Present progressive
You use this form, with a time expression, to express a *fixed future arrangement*:
What are you doing tomorrow night?
Peter and Lynne are getting married in January.

4 Present simple
You use this form, with a time expression based on a *timetable* or *the calendar*, to express *a fixed future arrangement*:
The train arrives at 19.28.
The party starts at 8.30 pm.

5 be thinking of
You use this form when you have not made up your mind yet:
I'm thinking of wearing my new shoes, but they may hurt my feet.
I'm thinking of going to Crete for my holiday, but I may go somewhere cooler.

2 Complete these sentences using the verb in brackets and one of the forms in 1

1 We .... (not stay) at home on Friday night. We .... (go) to the cinema.
2 I'm sure this record .... (be) a smash hit. But my grandmother .... (not like) it!
3 'I .... (have) a party in the garden.'
'What about the noise? It .... (disturb) your neighbours.'
'Oh dear, you're right. I know – I .... (invite) them, too!'
4 What a tremendous pass! Now Evans has the ball and he .... (shoot)!
5 You .... (find) playing the violin difficult at the beginning. But it .... (get) easier, so don't give up!
6 Look at that poster! Tony's favourite band .... (play) here next month. I .... (get) him some tickets as a birthday present.
7 I .... (do) a karate course next term, but I haven't made up my mind yet.
8 The plane .... (leave) London at 13.15 and .... (arrive) in Sydney at 20.05 the next day.
9 You can use the car this evening. I .... (not drive) to the theatre. There .... (not be) anywhere to park. I .... (take) the bus.

Speaking *Giving a party*

Imagine you and a friend are going to give a theme party to celebrate:

- an engagement OR
- a success OR
- a national anniversary

Decide what you want to celebrate and choose an appropriate theme (e.g. a Black and White party, a Masked party, a Jungle party).

Discuss and make decisions about:
- where you will give the party
- how the place will be decorated
- when it will be
- who you will invite
- what food and drink you will provide
- what entertainment there will be
- what you will wear
- what surprise you will have for your guests

When you have made your decisions, share your ideas. Whose party sounds the most fun?

Listening *Cinema attendance*

1 How often do you go to the cinema? What about your family and friends?

2 Listen to this classroom talk about cinema attendance in three countries. Then fill boxes 1–4 on the graph with the correct word, boxes 5–6 with the correct year and boxes 7–9 with the correct numbers.

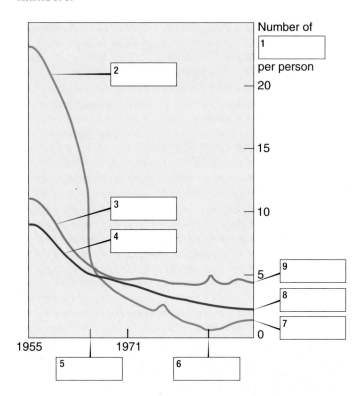

3 What is the present situation regarding cinema-going in your country?

"Excuse me, but that's my seat ..."

Exam skill *Interview (2)*

In the second part of the interview you have to talk about one (or possibly more) short passage(s) in the ways practised in Lesson 1.

This part should take about two minutes (individual interviews) or three minutes (group interviews).

INTERVIEW PRACTICE

Practise the first two parts of the interview.

First part

Describe what you can see in each photo. Say something about the people, the place and the activities.

Develop a conversation about a topic which interests you and which is related in some way to the photo. For example:

Photo **a** – Places where people meet socially in your country

Photo **b** – What pastimes you liked as a child and what you like now

Photo **c** – Sports you like playing and sports you like watching

a

b

Second part

Identify the topic of each passage. Match each passage to the correct photo. Say where you think each passage might have come from. Add any other comments you may have.

1

Let's face it, any hobby is an escape. A schoolboy gets home after a difficult day at school, but when he sets up his railway he's in a different world completely. It's the same for all of us – schoolboy, factory worker, businessman.

2

What do you think of people who say that football is a man's game?
They used to get on my nerves. Now, however, it's pretty obvious that they're wrong. Football is the fastest growing sport for women, with thousands of players and hundreds of clubs all over the country.

3

NO TWO PUBS ARE THE SAME. One may be refined, its neighbour rough; one noisy, the other quiet; one cosy and romantic, the next brightly lit and full of pensioners, carpenters, salesmen and dogs. At its best, the place and its customers combine to produce the greatest of English inventions.

c

Test exercises

1 *Complete this passage. Use only **one** word in each gap.*

Annie Oakley

American (1860–1926)

Annie Oakley was one of the best shots of all time. She was born in Ohio, where she
(**1**) .... wild animals and birds to help her family pay (**2**) ....
their debts. By the (**3**) .... she was 12 she could hit anything
(**4**) .... moved, though she did not learn to read (**5**) ....
her husband taught her.

In (**6**) .... teens she won a shooting match in Cincinnati against
(**7**) .... well-known Frank E. Butler. (**8**) ....
were later married (**9**) .... toured the circuses and music halls
before joining Buffalo Bill's Wild West Show in 1885. Audiences loved her and she
(**10**) .... soon a huge star.

Her skill was (**11**) .... She could hit a playing card at 10 metres
end on, or knock the ash (**12**) .... a cigarette held in her husband's
lips, or (**13**) .... else's – she (**14**) .... the same trick
in Berlin on Crown Prince William of Germany. She (**15**) ....
shoot the flames off a spinning wheel of candles, and even perform when lying
(**16**) .... the back of a galloping horse.

Annie Oakley was (**17**) .... injured in a train crash in 1901, but
recovered sufficiently to (**18**) .... touring. She (**19**) ....
remembered by millions today as the subject of (**20**) .... of the great
post-war Broadway musicals, Irving Berlin's 'Annie Get Your Gun'.

Annie Oakley, also known as 'The Girl of
the Western Plains' and 'Lady Sure Shot'

2 *Complete each of the following sentences so that it means exactly the same as
the sentence before it.*

1 We will cancel the picnic unless it stops raining by 11 o'clock.
  If ....

2 I have always played with a heavy tennis racket.
  I am ....

3 Frank once enjoyed boxing, but he doesn't now.
  Frank used ....

4 I may sell my stamp collection.
  I am ....

5 'What are you going to do tomorrow, Janet?' said Charles.
  Charles asked Janet ....

3 *The word in capitals at the end of each of the following sentences can be used to form a word that fits suitably in the blank space. Fill each blank in this way.*

EXAMPLE: Her brother is a .... *famous* .... writer.   FAME

1 As a doctor she wants to .... in child health.   SPECIAL
2 'Unless you find a new umpire, I'll drop out,' the tennis player shouted ....   PATIENCE
3 Taking drugs led to his .... from the Olympic Games.   QUALIFY
4 Although I .... with you, I'm afraid I can't help you.   SYMPATHY
5 Please .... that the electricity is switched off.   SURE
6 The stolen necklace has belonged to my family for 300 years, so it is ....   PLACE
7 He was able to .... the boy who had taken his bicycle.   IDENTITY
8 In spite of her .... for the job they decided to give her a chance.   SUIT
9 The ducks have to be .... before we can sell them.   FAT
10 I won't take my car to that .... mechanic again.   RELY

4 *Choose the word or phrase (A–D) which best completes each sentence.*

1 The football fans took it .... to be photographed with the captain of the team.
   A by all means   B by themselves   C in place   D in turns

2 Excuse me, is this seat .... ?
   A busy   B engaged   C full   D taken

3 If you've got any time .... this week, perhaps we could go bowling?
   A empty   B free   C limited   D vacant

4 I hadn't seen Patrick for ages, and then one day he suddenly turned .... at the gym.
   A down   B out   C over   D up

5 They were .... from holding the skiing competition by the bad weather.
   A forbidden   B hindered   C postponed   D prevented

6 The tennis champion is being .... for a shoulder injury.
   A cured   B healed   C mended   D treated

7 I was having such a good time at the party I didn't .... what time it was.
   A identify   B notice   C observe   D recognise

8 I'm not .... to going out late – I'm in bed by 10.30 every night.
   A use   B used   C usual   D usually

9 The father gently .... his child over his head and put her on his shoulders.
   A dragged   B picked   C stopped   D swung

10 We were making .... the port when the weather changed and a storm blew up.
   A for   B out   C up   D up for

12

Improving your mind

1 Brain power

Listening 📼 *Logic problems*

1 *You can get your body into shape by giving it some physical exercise. Similarly, you can get your mind working more efficiently by giving it some mental exercise, for example by trying to solve logic problems like this:*

In the Robinson family there are five brothers and each brother has one sister. If you count Mrs Robinson, how many women are there in the Robinson family?

Look at page 191 to check your answer.

2 *Listen to a psychologist giving you four more problems in logical thinking. Try and answer each problem as you hear it.*

The cocktail cherry

3 *Do you think this is a good type of mental exercise? Do you know any other similar logic problems?*

Reading *Fact or opinion?*

1 *Read this first sentence from a newspaper article. Decide whether the writer is presenting a fact or expressing an opinion, or a mixture of both.*

> Men's brains are physically bigger than women's but, like old-fashioned computers, less well equipped for communication with the rest of the world.

Which of the following adjectives could you apply to the sentence?

accurate   controversial   factual   false
incredible   prejudiced   provable

What do you expect the rest of the article to deal with?
– the results of recent research into the brains of men and women
– a discussion of all the ways in which men and women are different
– arguments showing ways in which women are superior to men

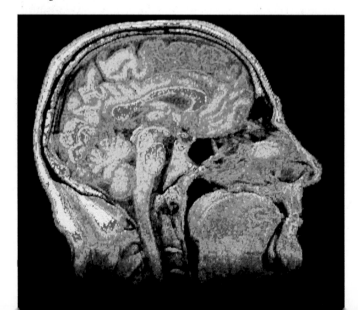

Read the rest of the article to see if you are right.

Research by US and Canadian scientists suggests that
5 the brains of men and women differ structurally in
ways that may explain differences in mental ability.
Men's brains are larger than women's, principally
because men are larger in all respects. But the isthmus
of the corpus callosum, which links the right and left
10 halves of the brain, is generally larger in women than
in men, according to a number of different studies
reported to the New York Academy of Sciences.

Since these fibres represent the main highway
within the brain, the researchers believe it may explain
15 why, on average, women have a superior ability with
words to men and why girls are less often dyslexic
than boys. Some researchers believe the physical
difference may also explain why men are generally
better at tasks involving spatial relationships, such as
20 engineering and reading maps. Speculating even
further, the sexing of brains (an infant science) may
account for the fact that there have been more women
poets and novelists than female painters or
sculptresses.

25 Such research has been discouraged by feminists for
a long time. They fear that it might be used to justify
male-female differences which they maintain are a
result of unfair social attitudes and conditioning.
Scientists admit that the physical differences between
30 male and female brains may have a less important
effect than education and experience. But at a recent
meeting of the New York Academy, the largest claims
for a physically significant difference between the
sexes, other than the obvious and well-researched ones,
35 were made by women. Sandra Witelson, a Canadian
neuropsychologist, said the differences in size already
mentioned may be "just the tip of the iceberg … The
physical structure of men's and women's brains may
be far more different than we suspect." But men were
40 doubtful about the importance of the finding that
women had a larger isthmus in their corpus callosum.
A male scientist said: "In the brain, bigger doesn't
always mean better."   *John Lichfield*

2 ***The writer is dealing with a controversial
subject. He is careful to show that:***

– he is reporting someone else's ideas, not giving his
own opinions
– he has no definite proof of the truth of some
statements
– there may be exceptions to some statements he
makes

The words in italics in this sentence show some of the
ways he does these things:

Some researchers believe the physical difference *may*
also explain why men are *generally* better at tasks
involving spatial relationships.

Underline other words and phrases in the text which
have the same function.

3 ***Choose the best answer (A–D) for questions 1–4.***

1 The isthmus of the corpus callosum is found
A only in women's brains.
B only in men's brains.
C only in large brains.
D in everyone's brain.

2 According to the text, how does the mental ability of
men and women differ?
A Women are better at using words.
B Women have fewer mental problems.
C Men are better at science.
D Men are better at art.

3 'it' (line 14) refers to
A the larger female isthmus.
B fibres.
C highway.
D brain.

4 Feminists have discouraged 'such research' (line 25)
because they fear it will
A show men are more intelligent than women.
B show women are more intelligent than men.
C prevent changes in social attitudes.
D cause changes in social attitudes.

Grammar *The -ing form of the verb*

1 **The -ing form is made by adding -ing to the infinitive:**

dream → *dreaming*

Look at the examples of the *-ing* form of the verb in this text:

While we are sleeping our mental life continues as dreaming. Some people say they look forward to solving their problems through dreams, while others say they only have frightening dreams in which they see horrible things happening. Mostly, however, we do not remember dreaming, so why do we do it? Research has shown that people who dream for short periods enjoy living and feel there is no point worrying about things. People who dream a lot have difficulty in dealing with stress. So perhaps dreaming is related to mental stress.

Find an example of an *-ing* form which:
- forms part of a progressive tense of a verb
- is an adjective
- is a noun and subject of a sentence
- follows a preposition
- follows a verb
- follows a verb plus an object

2 **Now complete these rules, using the examples from the text to help you.**

1 .... a preposition the verb is always in the *-ing* form.
2 Some ...., for example, 'remember', 'enjoy', are followed by the *-ing* form.
   Some more verbs which are followed by the *-ing* form are:
   admit   avoid   can't help   can't stand   continue deny   dislike   enjoy   finish   forget   hate   keep like   mind   prefer   remember   regret   stop
3 With some verbs, for example, 'see', it is possible to have the pattern: verb + ... + *-ing* form.
   Some more verbs which follow this pattern are:
   can't stand   dislike   feel   hate   hear   like   notice prevent   see   stop   watch
4 You use the *-ing* form after 'no ....', 'no use', 'no good' and 'worth/not worth'. For example:
   They feel there is no .... worrying about things.

3 **Complete these sentences by using the -ing form of each of these verbs once only.**

amuse	cook	do	go	grow up	have
leave	listen	make	play	stand	talk
tell	wash	watch	wave		

1 My old aunt can remember .... in the 1920s but she has forgotten .... to the doctor yesterday.
2 I admit .... to your phone conversation, but I deny .... anyone else about it.
3 I'm used to .... all the meals, but I object to .... all the dishes as well.
4 It's no use .... to the cinema because it's closed; there's no point .... chess with you because I always lose; there isn't a television programme which is worth .... – I hate .... nothing to do!
5 Do you mind .... the children this afternoon? They prefer .... model aeroplanes to .... jigsaw puzzles.
6 He watched the boat .... the harbour, and couldn't help .... in case Susan could see him .... on the cliff.

2 The happiest days of your life?

Vocabulary *Education*

Imagine you have to give a brief summary of your education to a friend from another country. Say something about:

- the places where you (have) studied
- what you were/are good at
- what you (have) enjoyed most about school
- anything you didn't/don't like about school

Use some of these words:

EXAMS AND QUALIFICATIONS
candidate   certificate   degree   diploma   fail
grade   mark   pass   result   take
LEVELS OF EDUCATION
nursery/primary/secondary school   academy
college   university
PLACES AT SCHOOL
canteen   gym   laboratory   library   playground
sports field   staff room   tennis court
SUBJECTS
art   biology   chemistry   computer studies
economics   geography   history   languages
literature   maths   music   physics
TEACHERS AND STUDENTS
head teacher   pupil   professor   undergraduate

Reading *School days*

1 *Look quickly through these three passages.*

Which one:
– gives information about a course? **1** ....
– tells an amusing story? **2** ....
– reports an interesting development? **3** ....

A-Team of golden oldies show how to make the grade

BRITAIN'S over-70s are pitting their wits against the younger generation in GCSE examinations and coming top of the class.

5 A survey released today by the Associated Examining Board shows that the intake of candidates for last summer's examinations included 130 aged over 70. Their results were on a par with their younger counterparts. Several candidates were over 80.

10 For some of the studious senior citizens, the exams were the first of their lives. Mr Harold Franklin, aged 74, of Leeds, chalked up his fourth GCSE – art, grade A – last June. He has been taking a GCSE each year since 15 he was 70 and has an A and two Bs in English language, sociology and social and economic history.

He left school in 1927 without any formal qualifications because his family needed his 20 wages. "I attended a council school during and immediately after the First World War. I lived among people who knew poverty, hardship and hunger at first hand. Jobs were scarce. There were not the educational 25 opportunities there are now. Senior citizens shouldn't be nervous of going back to school. I wish there were more people like me in my class."

Text B

Farewell to physics

FRENCH schoolgirl Marie Signac hated physics so much that she ritually burned her exercise book after taking her final exam in the subject. Unfortunately, she also destroyed her bedroom in the process. 5 Marie, 16, of Lyons, lost her clothes, furniture, television, stereo and computer, as well as the books she will need for English, the last of her five exams. Marie's mother said: "Physics certainly 10 wasn't her favourite subject and, after struggling with it for so long, she obviously thought the ritual burning was the right thing to do. She wanted to celebrate the fact that she would never 15 have to open a physics book again. Marie's very impulsive – I wish she would think before she acts." Says Marie: "I don't regret burning the book, but if only I'd had my bonfire in the garden!" 20

Text A

Local Studies Summer School – Lancaster

IN THE FOOTSTEPS OF THE ROMANTICS – EXPLORING THE LAKE DISTRICT
The school will assemble in time for tea on Sunday 19 July and will disperse after breakfast on Friday 24 July. It will be possible for participants to arrive on Saturday 18 July and to leave on Saturday 25 5 July, for an extra charge. The fee of £350.00 covers tuition, accommodation and food, but not transport. The following seminars are offered:
DEFENDING ENGLAND: Some Lake District Castles
LIFE AND LITERATURE IN THE LAKE DISTRICT
10 THE TERRIBLE MOUNTAINS: The Evolution of Lake District Tourism from the Eighteenth Century
MONASTERIES AND MANORS: Late Medieval and Tudor Houses
Applicants should select one of these and indicate their choice on the application form. A second choice, if any, may also be indicated.
15 Applicants will be directed to their second choice in the event of their first choice not recruiting sufficient students.

Text C

2 Choose the best answer (A, B, C or D) for questions 1–6.

1 What do the three passages have in common?
  A accommodation
  B exams
  C qualifications
  D students

2 What do Texts B and C have in common?
  A Both are about positive attitudes to education.
  B Both concern people who had no proper education at school.
  C Both are concerned with voluntary education.
  D Both mention the cost of education.

3 What do we learn about how Marie's mother felt?
  A She was angry with Marie for destroying her bedroom.
  B She was sorry that Marie had had to study a subject she disliked.
  C She understood why Marie had acted in this way.
  D She thought Marie was right to burn her book.

4 What do you think 'pitting their wits against' (Text B, lines 1–2) means?
  A competing with
  B cooperating with
  C making fun of
  D teaching

5 What do you think 'chalked up' (Text B, lines 12–13) means?
  A achieved
  B chose
  C entered
  D studied for

6 What do you think 'disperse' (Text C, line 3) means?
  A break up
  B carry on
  C check out
  D set off

3 Which of the three passages is written in the most formal language? Which of the following examples of formal language use can you find?

1 Use of passive, rather than active
2 Avoidance of contractions
3 Absence of colloquial language
4 More unusual, 'longer' words
5 Longer, more complex sentences
6 Reader not addressed directly as 'you'

Grammar *wish / if only*

1 You use 'I wish' and 'if only' to express a wish or regret:

If only I'd had my bonfire in the garden!
I wish there were more people like me in my class.
I wish she would think before she acts.

Which example expresses:
a a wish about the present?
b a wish about the past?
c a complaint about someone's behaviour?

What verb forms are used after 'I wish' and 'if only' to express the ideas in **a**, **b** and **c**?

2 What wishes or regrets do you have about your schooldays and other educational experiences and achievements?

EXAMPLES: I wish I didn't have to take an English exam. If only I hadn't put superglue on the biology teacher's chair!

3 Complete each of the following sentences so that it means exactly the same as the sentence before it.

1 They are sorry they missed the end of term party.
  They wish ....

2 I'm very bad at spelling, which is a disadvantage.
  If only ....

3 I don't like you arriving late for class.
  I wish ....

4 I regret not studying Russian when I had the chance.
  I wish ....

5 I'd like to be brainy, good-looking and rich!
  If only ....

6 Unfortunately our science teacher never takes us on trips to museums.
  I wish ....

7 The teacher is always asking me to recite poems in front of the class, which I hate.
  I wish ....

8 She regrets sending her son to a boarding school when he was 11.
  She wishes ....

Directed writing *Further education*

1 **Tony has just finished school, where he was a keen member of the Art and Drama societies. He wants to go to university to study something involving these subjects. His mother and his head teacher have different opinions about which course he should do.**

Look at the information contained in these extracts from a university prospectus, the head teacher's notes and some notes made by Tony's mother.

Bachelor of Arts (Honours) Theatre Design

About the course
A three-year course which includes all creative, technical and interpretative aspects of design in the theatre, including drama, dance and music.

Careers
Graduates become designers in theatre and television. Some go on to teacher training courses.

Entry requirements
Two GCE A level passes, preferably including Art.

Bachelor of Laws (LLB) (Honours)

About the course
A three-year degree course. The first two years cover basic legal subjects, the third offers a wide range of options for specialised study.

Careers
Most graduates enter the legal profession and the employment rate is very high.

Entry requirements
Three passes (at least grade C) at A level.

Bachelor of Education (Honours)

About the course
A four-year course designed to produce teachers at nursery, infant and junior level with all-round ability and a specific strength in their chosen subject.

Careers
Successful students will graduate as professional teachers with a major area of expertise.

Entry requirements
Two A level passes, including their chosen subject.

2 **Which of the courses do you think Tony should take? Why? Write your answers in the spaces provided.**

I think the best course for Tony to take would be ....
....
....
....

Art-A   History-C   sociable   ambitious

Results   Character

English-C   TONY NEWTON   hard-working

Recommendations for future

Teacher training?   NB Stress problems of making a career in world of Arts

TONY
ART fun fulfilling BUT what about money ?? can be done in spare time
LAW secure respectable well-paid good job possibilities

He could also ....
....
....
....

I wouldn't recommend him to ....
....
....
....
....

3 **How have you linked your ideas? Would any links be better if you used one of these phrases?**

Also, ...
In addition, ...
... not only ... but also ...
One reason is that ...
Another reason is ...
Secondly, ...

3 Great exhibitions

Speaking *Museums*

1 *Describe what you can see in these photos of museums. Which would you like to visit most? Which would not appeal to you?*

Henry VIII and his six wives, Madame Tussaud's, London

Limousine, Liberace's Museum, Las Vegas, Nevada, USA

Roman kitchen, Museum of London

Row of early twentieth century shops, Beamish Open Air Museum, north of England

2 *Do you think a museum should:*

- be serious or fun?
- be educative or entertaining?
- be big or small?
- be specific or wide-ranging?
- be quiet or noisy?
- be outdoors or indoors?
- be full of visitors or empty?
- be free or charge an entrance fee?
- have exhibits behind glass or exhibits you can touch and operate?

Choose the three most important things which, for you, make a good museum.

Writing 📼 *A talk (2)*

1 *In Unit 11 Lesson 2 you wrote the text of a talk in which you passed on some information to a group of people. You may also have to write a talk for a social occasion.*

In this talk you may be asked to do one of these things.

1 WELCOME   For example, welcome a group of foreign tourists to a local museum or building of historical interest.

2 INTRODUCE SOMEONE   For example, introduce a famous person who is going to speak about some aspect of life or culture in your country to a group of English-speaking students.

3 THANK   For example, your teacher is leaving to have a baby, and you thank her for her lessons on behalf of your classmates, and give her a present.

4 CONGRATULATE   For example, one of your classmates has got the highest marks in the whole world for an international exam. The school is giving a party in his or her honour and you have to make the speech of congratulation.

2 *Listen to someone welcoming tourists to a museum in Bogotá, Colombia. As you listen, make a note of:*

– how the speaker introduces herself
– how she welcomes the tourists
– what the museum exhibits
– the programme
– the highlight of the visit
– what the tourists mustn't do
– how the speaker finishes off
– other phrases that show she's speaking to a group

3 *Here are some examples of starting and finishing sentences for the other types of talk. Match them to the correct talk in* 1 *.*

STARTING

a I'd like to say, on behalf of the whole school, how proud we are of you, Alex.

b I'm very pleased to have the honour of presenting to you someone who is well-known in my country.

c Today is both a sad and a happy occasion.

FINISHING

d I know we'll all enjoy listening to what he has to say. Ladies and gentlemen, Mr Julio Iglesias!

e Thank you again. Please don't forget us, because we certainly won't forget you!

f Congratulations once again, Alex. We all wish you even greater successes in the future!

4 *Write one of the talks in* 1 *.*

– Include an appropriate beginning and ending sentence.
– Organise your ideas in paragraphs.
– Include some sentences to show you are speaking directly to a group.

Speaking 📼 *Conversation skills (2)*

1 *Listen to this conversation between the tour guide and a visitor in the Gold Museum, Bogotá about the object in the photo. What do you learn about the name of the object and the ceremony it represents?*

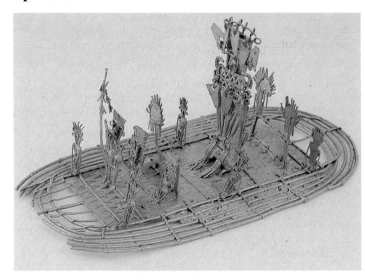

2 *What could you say if you wanted to:*

1 ask someone to repeat something?
2 ask someone how to say something in English?
3 check that you had understood what someone was saying?

How many expressions can you think of for each?

Listen to the conversation again. Which expressions from your lists did the speakers use? Did you hear any others?

3 *Practise the expressions by discussing an object with an interesting story which your partner has seen in a museum, or elsewhere.*

Pronunciation 📼 *Word linking*

1 *In written English each word is separated from the next, but in spoken English words are linked together by sound.*

Here are six of the most important ways of linking words together by sound. In each case:

– listen to the tape and say how the link is made.
– practise saying it.

1 Consonant to vowel
Examples: This‿is beautiful!
What's that‿in English?

2 Vowel (rounded lips) to vowel
Examples: So‿it is.
No‿it's not.

3 Vowel (stretched lips) to vowel
Examples: What's the‿English for ... ?
the‿ancient kingdom

4 'r' to vowel
Examples: Four‿of his chiefs
Or‿are you saying that ... ?

5 Consonant to 'h'
Examples: And then‿he went out.
People‿have been taking things.

6 Consonant to same consonant
Examples: of that‿time
the lake's‿still full

2 *Each phrase below contains an example of these ways of linking words together. Sort them into ways 1–6. Mark the links and practise saying them.*

of their own
they all sailed
they threw everything
say that again
the famous ceremony
you mean he actually had to

Now check your pronunciation against the examples on the tape.

Speaking *Our museum*

Plan a museum of your own. It should be unusual (e.g. for the blind, or for students or children only) and either in your home town or your school. Here are some possible subjects:

Home town – clothes worn in summer and winter / places where young people can go to eat on their own / different surfaces you walk on in the town / tops of buildings

School – contents of school bags / sounds and smells / clothes in fashion one year ago and those in fashion today

Decide, giving your reasons:
● what your museum will be about
● how big it will be
● how you will present your exhibits
● what admission fee you will charge, if any
● what services you will provide for your visitors

4

Exam skill *Vocabulary (2)*

In the Use of English paper there will be one or two exercises which test your vocabulary. These will either be word formation or word set exercises.

1 WORD FORMATION

In this kind of exercise you complete sentences by forming words. You form each word from one which is provided.

EXAMPLE: He said 'Good morning' in a most ..... *friendly* ..... way. FRIEND

EXAMPLE: My teacher ... *encouraged* ... me to take this exam. COURAGE

To do this exercise successfully you should:
- decide what kind of word is needed in the gap (noun, verb, adjective or adverb)
- decide what part of the word is needed, that is, a singular or plural noun, the correct tense or part of a verb
- check whether the sense suggests a negative prefix (e.g. *un-*, *dis-*) or suffix (e.g. *-less*)
- Check, if you add a suffix, whether any other spelling change is needed, e.g. beauty → beautiful

Do this exercise for practice.

1 'The Treasures of Tutankhamen' was the best .... I have ever seen. EXHIBIT
2 Experts say that .... do their best work when they are in their twenties. MATHEMATICS
3 It was a dull lecture, with nothing .... about it at all. MEMORY
4 I can't agree with your choice of career. I think you have chosen .... WISE
5 It .... me that we must now charge an entrance fee to our museum. SAD
6 You need weeks to see all the .... treasures in the British Museum. PRICE

2 WORD SETS

In this kind of exercise you also complete sentences. The words you use will all belong to some kind of set. The set may be, for example:
- words from the same topic area, e.g. education
- phrasal verbs with the same main verb, e.g. look
- phrases including the same preposition, e.g. in
- pairs of words with opposite meanings, e.g. pass/fail

In an exam it is always important to read the instructions carefully and study the example. In this kind of exercise it is doubly important, because there is a wide range of word sets that could be used.

Do these exercises for practice.

1 *Complete the following sentences with* **one** *word connected with education.*
   EXAMPLE: School finishes at 3 o'clock, but I still have to do two hours of ... *homework* ... every evening.
   a The school year is divided into three .... of 12 weeks each.
   b Twenty students in this class are registered as .... for the exam in June.
   c She left university with a first class .... in biochemistry.
   d As a postgraduate she did .... into the behaviour of rats.

2 *Complete these sentences with a phrasal verb that includes the word* **look**.
   EXAMPLE: How can I ..... *look* ..... *up* ..... this word in a dictionary if I don't know how to spell it?
   a After the exams the staff and students are all .... a relaxing holiday.
   b Thefts from art galleries throughout Europe are being .... by Interpol.
   c Can you .... the catalogue and tell me if there are any pictures by Bacon on show?
   d They .... their gym teacher because he was once in the Olympic team.

3 *Complete these sentences with a phrase that includes the word* **in**.
   EXAMPLE: When it fell, the vase broke .. *in* .. *pieces* .

a Put all the books .... on the library shelves, so people can find what they want.

b It's called the Tate Gallery .... of Sir Henry Tate who founded it.

c In theory anyone can learn how to swim, but ....many people fail to master it.

d Although they are different sciences, psychology and psychiatry have certain things ....

4 *Complete these sentences with a word that means the opposite of the word in capitals.*

EXAMPLE: If I PASS my driving test I can go home by car, but if I ....*fail*........I'll have to walk.

a He sometimes looks CRAZY, but he's really quite ....

b I like the contrast of ANCIENT works of art in a ....building.

c That old coin is valuable because it is RARE, but this one is ....so isn't worth much.

d It was hot in the classroom, so although the teacher was WIDE-AWAKE the students felt ....

Test exercises

1 *Make changes and additions to these sets of words in order to write a complete letter.*

Dear Student,

1 I write / make you / offer you cannot refuse.

....

2 Imagine be able / increase / brain power and improve / ability / study and pass exams!

....

3 Next month we launch / magazine / help you do this.

....

4 magazine contain exercises / be guaranteed / improve your mental ability.

....

5 magazine publish once / month and cost £1.75 / issue.

....

6 If you take out / year's subscription now we give you / discount / 25%.

....

7 In addition / generous offer we also give you / mystery free gift if you reply / 15 days.

....

8 We feel sure you want / take advantage / offer.

....

Please send your completed order form in the enclosed envelope (no stamp required).

Yours sincerely,

J. G. Goble

Marketing Director

2 *Complete these sentences with a phrasal verb that includes the word **go**.*
EXAMPLE: The firework ..*went*.. ....*off*....and we all jumped.

1 You're sure to win a prize if you ....that competition.

2 He ignored the interruption and ....with his story.

3 A gust of wind came through the open window and the candle ....

4 Does this lipstick .... my blouse?

5 There aren't any potatoes so you'll have to ....chips.

3 *Complete each of the following sentences so that it means exactly the same as the sentence before it.*

1 Do you think I could borrow your catalogue?
Would you mind ....

2 Paddy is pleased he is going to visit the Van Gogh museum.
Paddy is looking ....

3 Jane regrets leaving school at 15.
Jane wishes ....

4 I don't like you chewing gum in class.
I wish you ....

5 'You cheated in the exam, didn't you, Neil?' said the college principal.
The college principal accused ....

6 It isn't right to criticise me in public.
I object ....

7 I'd like to be a mathematical genius.
If only ....

8 There's no point in doing those intelligence tests.
Those intelligence tests aren't ....

9 They are sorry they didn't listen to the psychiatrist.
They regret ....

10 The teacher looked so funny I had to laugh.
The teacher looked so funny I couldn't help ....

4 *Choose the word or phrase (A–D) which best completes each sentence.*

1 The professor .... the question carefully before giving her reply.
A considered   B grasped   C realised   D reasoned

2 He can recite whole scenes of *Hamlet* by ....
A head   B heart   C memory   D mind

3 The head teacher could not attend the meeting, so her assistant stood .... her.
A by   B for   C in for   D up for

4 She doesn't feel like .... to a museum – she wants to go shopping.
A go   B goes   C going   D to go

5 Scientists are looking .... the differences in the structure of men's and women's brains.
A after   B into   C out   D up to

6 I wish you .... so much time working: why don't you come out with us occasionally?
A aren't spending   B couldn't spend   C don't spend   D wouldn't spend

7 The hijackers were .... the moment they left the plane.
A arrested   B excluded   C handled   D led

8 They've just announced the .... of the train from Moscow.
A admission   B arrival   C destination   D entry

9 When the lights went out it took us by .... and no one knew what to do.
A accident   B chance   C mistake   D surprise

10 The company is doing research into the design problems .... with computer viruses.
A associated   B collected   C compared   D sorted

11 The children are very excited .... going to the cinema tonight.
A about   B in   C of   D to

13 UNIT THIRTEEN
Science and technology

1 Computers

Vocabulary *Technology in daily life*

Which of the gadgets below do you use in your daily life? How do they make life easier? How can they go wrong? How can they be fixed? Can you do this yourself?

Use as many of the words as you can to talk about your experiences of modern technology.

GADGETS
**air conditioner   central heating   computer   fridge
hair drier   iron   microwave   mixer
photocopier   spin drier   stereo equipment
telephone answering machine   vacuum cleaner
video   washing machine**

ELECTRICITY
bulb   flex   fuse   plug   socket   switch

THINGS THAT GO WRONG
**burn   burst   crack   drip   fuse   leak
shrink   stick   stretch   tear   wear out**

MENDING
fix   loosen   repair   stick   tighten

TOOLS
drill   hammer   nail   screw   screwdriver

EXAMPLE: We use the washing machine every day in our house. Just think how long it would take to do all that washing by hand! Last week water leaked from the machine all over the floor. I don't know what the problem was – the plumber fixed it!

Listening 🎞️ *Easy to operate*

Listen to these four messages left on telephone answering machines. They are all about portable computers. Complete the notes that the listener to each message made.

Message 1

From: _____
He wants a portable computer which is:
1 _____
2 Usable anywhere
3 _____
Price limit: _____

Message 2

From: _____
Suggested make of computer: _____
Model number (a): _____ Price: £1,500
Model number (b): _____ Price: £ _____
Where to go: Technology Centre _____
_____ Twickenham

Message 3

From: _____
Phone number: _____
Date of complaint: 18th Feb.
Date of purchase: _____
Computer fault: Doesn't work.
Screen message: _____
The customer has tried switching on and off.
He definitely hasn't _____
He has looked in _____
Urgent because _____

Message 4

From: _____
Additional complaint: _____
He says he's going to write to: _____

Writing *A formal letter*

1 **After David had made his last phone call to the shop where he bought his computer, he wrote a letter to the shop's managing director. The letter deals with these five topics, each in a different paragraph. What should the order of the paragraphs be?**

- details of bad service
- request for action
- reason for writing
- details of fault
- details of purchase (date, make, model)

Check your answer with the skeleton letter.

2 **Complete the letter, using the information you noted in the telephone messages above.**

17 Clarence Road
London W14 9GP

. . . .
. . . .
. . . .
Twickenham TW3 9GH

Dear Sir,
    I am writing to complain about a faulty computer I bought in your shop, and also about your inadequate after-sales service. On Saturday 16 February . . . .
. . . .

    When I tried to operate my new computer at home . . . .
. . . .
. . . .

    I phoned your store . . . .
. . . .
. . . .

    I should be grateful if you could arrange either for a technician to come and put the fault right, or for a substitute computer to be delivered to me immediately.

Yours faithfully,

156

3 *This is a formal letter. Make sure you have not used any contractions, or any colloquial expressions which would be inappropriate.*

4 *If David had known that the name of the managing director of The Technology Centre was James Freeman, what changes would he have made to his letter?*

5 *Write another formal letter of complaint following the same layout and paragraph organisation as the letter above. Write about this situation (120–180 words):*

You recently bought either a computer game or a video tape as a present for a friend. The game or tape was wrongly labelled so your friend got a shock when he or she used it. The shopkeeper refuses to give you your money back. Write to the manufacturer.

Grammar *The infinitive*

1 *The infinitive is the base form of the verb. Sometimes the infinitive is used with 'to', and sometimes without 'to'.*

1 THE 'TO' INFINITIVE
You use the 'to' infinitive:

a to express purpose:
I'm leaving next week to start *work on the Mediterranean project.*
He went to the Technology Centre to buy *a computer.*

b to report orders, requests and advice:
He told me to look *in the instructions manual.*
He advised me to buy *the more expensive model.*

Some reporting verbs which can be followed by a 'to' infinitive are:
advise   ask   command   encourage   forbid
invite   order   persuade   tell   warn

c after certain verbs:
I intend to begin *in Spain and Morocco.*
He's planning to visit *all the Mediterranean countries.*

Some verbs which can be followed by a 'to' infinitive are:
afford   agree   appear   arrange   attempt
decide   expect   forget   hope   intend
learn   manage   offer   plan   promise
refuse   seem   want

d after certain verbs + object:
I'd like someone to phone *me back immediately.*
He wanted a technician to repair *the fault.*

Some verbs which can be followed by this pattern are:
allow   enable   expect   force   get   help
like   permit   prefer   remind   teach   want

e after certain adjectives:
It should also be fairly simple to operate.
It's unlikely to be cheap.

Some adjectives which are followed by a 'to' infinitive are:
difficult   easy   important   impossible
likely   pleased   possible   simple   unlikely
unusual   usual

2 THE INFINITIVE WITHOUT 'TO'
a The infinitive without 'to' is used after modal verbs:
I'd like someone to phone me back immediately.
It should *also* be *fairly simple to operate.*

b The infinitive without 'to' is used after 'let', 'make', 'would rather' (= prefer) and 'had better' (= should):
Could you let me have *your ideas as soon as possible?*
I can't make it work.
He'd rather have *a new computer than a refund.*
He'd better write *a letter of complaint.*

2 *Put the verbs in brackets into the correct form: the 'to' infinitive, the infinitive without 'to', or the -ing form.*

It used (1 be) a science-fiction fantasy that one day computers would (2 rule) the world. Some people thought it was impossible (3 prevent) these man-made devices from (4 become) more powerful than their creators, so they wanted (5 stop) more advanced computers (6 be) developed. Scientists were warned not (7 hand) over our destiny to machines. But computers can only (8 do) what we ask them (9 do). We can (10 get) them (11 complete) increasingly complicated operations, but, contrary to the science-fiction nightmare, computers can never (12 make) us (13 do) anything.

Today we expect computers (14 help) us (15 live) at the faster pace modern living demands. It is worth (16 mention) a few examples. Computers allow business people (17 keep) in touch with developments all over the world. They enable doctors (18 diagnose) illnesses more accurately. They let thousands of aircraft (19 fly) safely through our crowded skies without (20 bump) into other planes. In fact it is difficult (21 imagine) any area of life where computers do not play an important role.

2 In space

Listening 📼 *First step to the stars*

1 *Listen to this extract from a radio programme in which Mike Irving, an aeronautical engineer, and Flora Rivett, a writer of science-fiction and fantasy books, talk to the presenter, Jill Donnell.*

Find out the speakers' ideas about:
- how realistic the advertisement is.
- what sort of facilities will be available for space tourists.
- how much a space trip is likely to cost.

FARAWAY TRAVEL plc
offers
Round the world flights
TODAY
Flights to the Moon
TOMORROW

The Moon to Mars
THE DAY AFTER

Some scientists are confident that before long settlements like this will exist in orbit round Earth.

2

Listen again, choosing the correct answer (True or False) for questions 1–8. If you think a statement is False, correct it to make it True.

		True	False
1	The first holiday-makers will be able to stay on the Moon.	☐	☐
2	Space hotels will orbit the world once every one and a half hours.	☐	☐
3	The gravity inside a space hotel will be the same as on Earth.	☐	☐
4	Holiday-makers will not be able to play ball sports.	☐	☐
5	Holiday-makers will be able to do unusual things when they swim.	☐	☐
6	Holiday-makers will be able to fly without wings.	☐	☐
7	One way to make space travel cheaper is to use airplanes to put people into space.	☐	☐
8	In 20 years a trip in space will cost little more than a trip to Australia.	☐	☐

3

Would you like to visit a space hotel or settlement? What do you imagine life there will be like? Think about:

- being launched into space
- rotating round Earth
- doing the things you like to do regularly, such as going for a swim, having a coffee
- doing new and unusual things, such as flying

Grammar *The future (2)*

1

Future perfect	= will + have + past participle
Future progressive	= will + be + *-ing* form

We'll have made that development by the end of the decade.
In 20 years people will be having holidays in space.

Which tense is used for an action which:
- hasn't happened yet, but which will have happened before a particular time in the future?
- will be in progress at a particular time in the future?

2

You can also express an idea about the future like this:

be + | likely | + to + infinitive
       | sure |
       | bound |

Sport is likely to be an important ingredient.
It's sure to be important.
It's bound to be astronomically expensive.

In two of these examples the speaker thinks something will *certainly* happen, but in one the speaker only thinks it will *probably* happen. Which one?

You can also use 'about + to + infinitive' to talk about the future. What does 'about to' mean in this sentence?

I'm about to fly to Costa Rica.

3

In future time clauses *the verb is in a present tense (present simple, present progressive or present perfect); the verb in the main clause is in a future tense:*

Once you're in orbit, the engines will be switched off.
When the spaceliner has docked, you'll climb into the space hotel.
As soon as airplanes go into orbit, the price will come right down.

4

Look at what a scientist said about living in space. Fill in the gaps (1–10) including the words in brackets in a suitable form.

'In 50 years I think people (1) ....(live) in space. They (2) ....(more likely / live) in space settlements than on the planets. I'm sure we (3) ....(solve) the problems of sustaining life in space by the time my children have grown up. In 50 years space "farmers" (4) ....(grow) food in artificial space "fields". By then we (5) ....(find) a way to use solar energy for all our power needs. This will soon be essential, because we (6) ....(about / run out) of energy resources here on Earth. I know it (7) ....(bound / be) expensive at first, but once the technology (8) ....(develop) then the costs will fall. As for me, as soon as I (9) ....(have) the chance, I (10) ....(pack) my bags!'

Pronunciation 📼 *Exclamations*

1 *When people are surprised, they can show this by making an exclamation. An exclamation is marked by a bigger movement in the voice than usual: for a statement there is a big fall in the voice, and for a question a big rise.*

Listen to these examples from the programme. How does the voice move?

1 Amazing!
2 Wonderful!
3 Really?
4 What?

Practise saying them.

2 *Practise making the following exclamations.*

1 How interesting!
2 Fascinating!
3 Who?
4 It's incredible!
5 When?
6 Wow!

Check your pronunciation against the examples on the tape.

3 *Practise making exclamations by reacting to what your partner tells you about life in space. Then tell your partner something yourself.*

Student A should use the information in the red box, and Student B the information in the blue box.

Writing 📼 *Space diary*

The year is 2045: you are somewhere in outer space.

At some time during the day of 30 July you heard certain sounds. Listen to the sounds on the tape. What could they be? What were you doing when you heard each sound? What happened next? Was it an ordinary or an unusual day?

Write your diary entry for 30 July 2045 (120–180 words). Describe:
– the setting
– your companion(s)
– the events
– your feelings

Listen and react to what your partner tells you.

See if you can surprise your partner with these facts:
● The Moon is a quarter the size of Earth.
● Twelve astronauts have walked on the Moon.
● Because there is no wind or rain on the Moon, astronauts' footsteps will last for millions of years.
● When you look at Earth from space what you mostly see is clouds.

Listen and react to what your partner tells you.

See if you can surprise your partner with these facts:
● The Moon is over 4,700 million years old.
● Gravity on the Moon is a sixth of that on Earth.
● There is no air or water on the Moon.
● The Apollo 11 spacecraft had nearly two million working parts. A car has less than 3,000.

3 Mind over matter

Reading *Fire is fire*

1 *Here are some phrases from a newspaper article. What do you think it might be about?*

to prove	heat capacity
red-hot coals	embers
temperatures of 593°C	buckets of water
melt aluminium	the cake tin
laws of physics	poor conductors of heat

Quickly read the article to find out if you were right.

2 *Choose the best answer (A, B, C or D) for questions 1–5.*

1 What do you think the main aim of the writer is?
A to encourage people to try firewalking
B to promote the work of a particular university
C to report the results of an experiment
D to play a joke on the readers

2 'Firewalking is considered a sign of spiritual superiority.' How does the writer feel about this belief?
A sad that people have been misled
B scornful of the people who believe it
C hopeful that science will confirm it
D afraid that many people believe it

3 What should you do if you want to firewalk without burning your feet?
A wrap your feet in wet blankets before and after
B take your mind off what you're doing
C wait until the fire is cooler than 593°C
D walk quickly and lightly over the fire

4 Which of these phrases could be added after *the effects* (lines 102–3)?
A of the high heat capacity
B of cooling down
C of firewalking
D of the trick

5 What does *it* (line 124) refer to?
A firewalking
B mind over matter
C courage
D the first step

EARLIER this month, 120 sceptics gathered in Southampton to prove that anyone can walk over red-hot coals and come away with their feet intact. The "firewalk" was organised by Wessex Skeptics, one of a network of sceptics' groups around the country. Few people initially thought they would be able to walk on fire, but more than 100 of the sceptics, including university students, staff and friends, crossed the coals at temperatures of up to 593°C (1,100°F) – nearly hot enough to melt aluminium. None had had any "spiritual training" but all were able to walk home comfortably.

Firewalking is such a spectacular defiance of common sense that throughout history it has been touted as evidence of spiritual superiority. There are references to it in the Bible, and it has been reported in such divergent places as South Africa, Japan and Bali. In 1984 tens of thousands of Californians paid hundreds of dollars each for "fear seminars", at which firewalks were promoted as the cure for everything from drug addiction to insomnia.

In fact, firewalking has little to do with mind over matter and everything to do with the laws of physics concerning heat capacity and conductivity. To set up this month's event, the Wessex Skeptics raked the embers of a bonfire of storm-damaged oak and beech into a bed about 1 metre wide and 3½ metres long. Firewalkers were warned to walk briskly and avoid letting their toes sink into the embers. Wet blankets and buckets of water were positioned at the end of the walk, so they could cool their feet down quickly afterwards.

Physicist Robin Allen, a research fellow at Southampton University and president of the Wessex Skeptics, gave a prior talk on the physics involved.

A substance may be hot but will transfer that heat slowly. To take a commonplace example, think of a cake baking in a tin in an oven at 200°C. The air in the oven, the tin and, after a while, the cake, are at the same high temperature. If you put your hand in the oven, the air will feel hot but won't burn you in the time it takes to remove the cake. Similarly, you won't get burned touching the cake. But you *will* get burned if you touch the cake tin or the metal oven racks.

Metal holds large amounts of heat energy and transfers it quickly, whereas air and cake have low heat capacity and poor thermal conductivity. For firewalking, wood and its ash behave like the cake. In some parts of the world, porous rocks are used instead of embers – they are also poor conductors of heat. And, because feet have a high heat capacity, the embers actually cool down when walkers step on them. The trick is not to spend too long on the embers – the effects are cumulative.

It takes an average four or five steps to cross a 3½ metre bed of coals. At the recommended brisk pace, each foot is in contact with the embers for no more than a second or a second and a half, not long enough to cause burns. At the Wessex Skeptics firewalk, a few blisters did appear, but they were caused by embers sticking to walkers' feet. Experienced firewalkers recommend drying the feet carefully first to avoid this.

"The only mind over matter," says Mr Allen, "is finding the courage to take the first step." But don't try it at home. Fire is still fire – and still dangerous.

Wendy Grossman

3 *What do you feel about the contents of this article? Would you have dared to be one of Robin Allen's volunteer firewalkers?*

Grammar *Quantity*

1 **You use these expressions in front of a noun, or in front of an adjective + a noun:**

all another any both each either
every a few few a little little a lot of
lots of many most much neither
no other several some various

Few *people thought they would be able to walk on fire.*
They expected to get several *painful blisters.*

What kind of noun may each expression be used with?
Complete the diagram:

Used with
countable
nouns

many
....
....
....
....
....

Used with
both kinds
of noun

a lot of ....
....
....
....

Used with
uncountable
nouns

much
....
....
....

2 **These expressions may be used as pronouns:**

all another any both each either
a few few a little little a lot many
most much neither none others
several some

Firewalking has little *to do with mind over matter.*
A hundred people crossed the coals. None *had had any
'spiritual training' but* all *were able to walk home
comfortably.*

You can also use this pattern:
all/another etc. + of (+ the/this/my etc.) + noun/pronoun
all of the increase   some of her students
neither of them   most of us

3 **Answer these questions about the examples.**

1 *Each foot is in contact with the embers.*
Why can't you say *Every foot* here?
What happens if you say *Both feet*?
2 *Firewalking has little to do with mind over matter.*
Can you rephrase this using *much*?
How does using *a little* change the meaning?
3 *Few people thought they would be able to walk on fire.*
How does using *A few* instead of *Few* change the
meaning? What about *Several*?

4 **Use each of these words once to fill the gaps in
1–10:**

all another both each either every
few little much no none other
several

1 He was able to dip ....thumbs in the
boiling oil without burning himself.
2 My professor accepts this theory but most
.....................scientists don't.
3 She didn't hear ....of the two
explosions in the laboratory.
4 ....of the twins is hoping to become a
computer programmer.
5 ....student is expected to write a
report on his or her experiment.
6 One example of insulation is your coat;
.....................is licking your finger before you
touch a hot iron.
7 Our teacher loses ....opportunity to
demonstrate examples of physical laws.
8 ....of the firewalkers moved quickly
and ....burned their feet.
9 ....experimenters have tried to
photograph a ghost, but so far they have had
.....................success.
10 The report concludes sadly that ....
students have ....knowledge of
nuclear physics.

Speaking 🔲 *Conversation skills (3)*

1 **Listen to this discussion between a woman and a man about a scientific matter.**

1 What are they discussing?
2 What is the woman's point?
3 What does the man feel about it?

2 **Even when you are the listener in a conversation, you can take an active part in the interaction. You can do this by:**

1 Reacting with a comment like 'Really?' or 'I see'.
2 Paraphrasing the speaker's point.
3 Finishing the speaker's point for him or her.

Listen again to the conversation. What examples of **1–3** can you find?

3 **When do you think it could be useful to paraphrase the speaker's point? Tick the points you think are true.**

When the speaker:

1 is not making his or her point clearly. ☐
2 needs help for some reason. ☐
3 has been talking for too long. ☐
4 has said something you don't understand. ☐
5 is trying to avoid saying something unpleasant. ☐

4 **Practise being a listener who takes an active part in the interaction. Have a conversation about a topic your partner chooses from the list below.**

Dinosaurs
Fortune-telling
UFOs
Ghosts
Coincidences
The Loch Ness monster
Telepathy
The lost city of Atlantis
Astrology

Try to consider some simple scientific aspects of the topic (e.g. explanations and experiments).

4

Exam skill *Interview (3)*

In the third part of the interview you have to do an
activity. This will be connected in some way to the topic
of your conversation, but should approach the topic
from a new angle. You could be asked to:

- talk about your own experience
- give your opinions on a subject
- describe a person or place
- tell a story
- plan something
- put ideas in order, according to your own opinions
  or feelings

This part should take about four minutes (individual
interviews) or seven minutes (group interviews).

INTERVIEW PRACTICE

Practise all three parts of the interview. (Remember that
in the exam you will only have to do one activity in
each part.)

First part

Describe what you can see in the photos. Say
something about the people, the place and the activities.

Develop a conversation about a topic which interests
you and which is related in some way to the photos.

Second part

Match these passages to the photos. Say where you
think they have come from. Add any other comments
you may have.

1 Astronaut Robert A. R. Parker demonstrates
weightlessness in the zero gravity of the European
Spacelab, during its first flight on the space shuttle
Columbia (mission STS-9) from November 28 to
December 8 1983. At upper left is Dr Ulf Merbold, the
German specialist representing the European Space
Agency (ESA).

2 IF MORE girls are to do well in science at
school, then science should be feminised:
less about machines and more about the
effects of science on people's lives, and
teachers should not exaggerate the
dangers of handling laboratory
equipment, says a recent report.

3

**Games
from
Alternative
Software**

Jaws – for Spectrum, C64,
CPC, ST or Amiga. You are
Police Chief Brodie. With
your friend Hooper and
shark expert Quint you must
make the beaches of Amity
Island safe. Get rid of the
horror of the Great White
Shark. Lives and your job
depend upon it.

Third part

Do these activities.

1 Describe a science-fiction film or book that you have particularly enjoyed. Which was it closer to – fact or fantasy?

Do you think that modern scientific developments could produce monsters like Frankenstein?

2 Read the start of this newspaper article. How useful do you think the three subjects for research are?

Japan looks to the future

by John Harries in Tokyo

FLYING carpets, telepathy and techniques for communicating with plants are among the subjects for research that Japan should investigate to contribute to human happiness, says a Japanese government report.

The Japanese are also encouraging research into:
- household robots
- solar energy satellites

Put these five research subjects in your own order of usefulness.

What other scientific research do you think should be done to contribute to human happiness?

3 If you could travel back in time, which historical period would you go back to? Why? Which aspects of life in that period would you like to experience or investigate? If you could take one modern scientific development back with you, what would it be?

Remember

1 The interview will consist of a conversation between you and the interviewer round a topic chosen by the interviewer. You have already covered a wide range of typical topics in this book.

2 The interviewer has three photos, passages and activities for each topic. Which ones he or she chooses for you will depend on your own contribution to the conversation. Very different conversations can be developed using the same material.

Good candidate technique

1 Be as communicative as you can: don't be afraid to direct the conversation and ask questions where appropriate. Make the interviewer's job of getting language, reactions and ideas out of you as easy as possible.

2 If you have a pair or group interview, you should expect to talk much more to your partner(s) than to the interviewer.

3 Use as wide a range of correct language as you can to show what you can do well. But don't worry too much about making mistakes!

4 Greet and say goodbye to the interviewer politely. Be friendly, relaxed and positive.

Test exercises

1

*Complete this passage. Use only **one** word in each gap.*

ESCAPE FROM THE PRISONS OF THARQ

With a wildly beating heart, Valiant continued to run down the long dark tunnel. It was (**1**) ....time before he realised that the footsteps of (**2**) ....pursuers were falling further and (**3**) ....behind. After a while he was alone, (**4**) ....deep under the mountain city. This must (**5**) ....been the way the robbers came, he thought bitterly, dragging their priceless treasure with (**6**) ....

(**7**) ...., ahead of him, he made (**8**) ....a circle of pale light. His heart leaped: in the confusion of the attack he had (**9**) .... to escape from the prisons of Tharq, the evil War Lord of Borod! In a few seconds he was standing at the (**10**) .... of the tunnel looking (**11**) .... at the Martian night.

Below him (**12**) .... a deep valley, surrounded by huge cliffs. The surface of the valley was covered (**13**) .... enormous trees. Their leaves were (**14**) .... red and were thick with night flowers. In the black sky (**15**) ...., the two moons of Mars shone with a strange brightness.

But somewhere out there were the thieves of Kedam, the same (**16**) .... who had just kidnapped Princess Pulkem of Vaja, unwilling guest of (**17**) .... evil War Lord – the beautiful princess who in happier times (**18**) .... given him the jewel that he (**19**) .... round his neck and (**20**) .... now reflected the light of the two moons of Mars.

2

Complete each of the following sentences so that it means exactly the same as the sentence before it.

1 'I'd buy a Japanese computer, if I were you,' said Tom.
Tom advised ....

2 'Liz, could you wash the test tubes?' said Sue.
Sue asked ....

3 Their tenth wedding anniversary is on April 1st.
By April 1st they ....

4 She went to university because she was interested in studying chemistry.
She went to university to ....

5 'Shall I help you with the experiment, Professor?' said Ken.
Ken offered ....

6 I don't want you to photograph me in a bikini.
I don't want to ....

7 Most writers prefer using a word processor to a typewriter.
Most writers would rather ....

8 The people who have attended the revision class will have no trouble with the exam.
Nobody who ....

9 Robinson was the only physicist who didn't complete his research.
All ....

10 The laboratory technician will probably examine the rocks.
The laboratory technician is likely ....

3 *Choose the word or phrase (A–D) which best completes each sentence.*

1 The researcher carefully dried .... foot before walking quickly through the fire.

    A another   B both   C each   D every

2 The boat's .... – look at that pool of water!

    A bursting   B leaking   C stretching   D tearing

3 The company .... her pay for her uniform out of her own pocket.

    A allowed   B forced   C got   D made

4 The astronaut said that he lost weight in space because there was .... interesting to eat.

    A no   B none   C not   D nothing

5 I highly recommend this guide book – it's full of .... information.

    A used   B useful   C useless   D usual

6 I know him .... although we've never met – I often see him in the local market.

    A at first sight   B by sight   C in sight   D out of sight

7 The army .... to take over the country if the government did not do what it wanted.

    A convinced   B suggested   C threatened   D warned

8 The director of the Space Project has .... in protest at the cancellation of the research programme.

    A resigned   B restored   C retired   D revised

9 Most people .... an unhelpful colleague at work sooner or later.

    A come up against   B fall back on   C go down with

    D keep up with

10 When he described his .... woman to me, I wondered if he would ever find her.

    A exact   B ideal   C just   D right

14 UNIT FOURTEEN
The world around us

1 The environment

Vocabulary *Green issues*

Fill in this questionnaire. Compare your answers with those of your classmates.

POLLUTION

Put this list of eight different examples of pollution in your personal order of seriousness (i.e. 1 = worries me most, 8 = worries me least).

Traffic fumes ☐

Aircraft noise ☐

Litter ☐

Dirty rivers and beaches ☐

Nuclear waste ☐

Polluted drinking water ☐

Illegal rubbish dumping ☐

Use of pesticides and fertilisers ☐

Is there any other form of pollution that worries you?

(*Write it here*)...............................

WASTE

Here is a list of ways in which you can help reduce waste. Tick the box to show your position on each.

	I do already	I'd think about doing	I'm unlikely to do	Not possible
Use recycled paper	☐	☐	☐	☐
Write on both sides of paper	☐	☐	☐	☐
Reuse envelopes	☐	☐	☐	☐
Reuse plastic carrier bags	☐	☐	☐	☐
Buy food loose rather than pre-packed	☐	☐	☐	☐
Recycle household waste (e.g. glass, paper, tins)	☐	☐	☐	☐
Buy largest size packets (e.g. food, washing powder, etc.)	☐	☐	☐	☐
Use public transport whenever you can	☐	☐	☐	☐

Is there anything else that you do?

(*Write it here*)...............................

Listening 🔊 *The sea – sink or swim?*

1 Listen to this extract from a radio discussion in which Estelle Greenshaw, a photojournalist, and Dr Frank Spokewell, a representative from the oil industry, talk to the presenter, Stella Mercer.

1 What impression of the characters and opinions of the three speakers do you get?
2 What major environmental problems are they talking about?
3 Who do you feel most willing to believe?
4 Who do you think presents his or her points best?

2 Listen again and for questions 1–3 put a tick (✓) for every answer (a–e) that you think is correct.

1 What point(s) does Stella Mercer make in her introduction?
   a Water is vital for life on earth. ☐
   b Water pollution has always occurred. ☐
   c Water pollution has serious effects for mankind. ☐
   d The Mediterranean is one of the most polluted seas. ☐
   e It's easy not to worry about the pollution of the seas. ☐

2 What aim(s) are behind Estelle Greenshaw's photos?
   a to show the effect of humans on the sea ☐
   b to attack multinational industries ☐
   c to show how the sea can recover from man-made disasters ☐
   d to make people concerned about what is happening to the seas ☐
   e to raise money for an environmental protection agency ☐

3 What attitude(s) does Dr Spokewell show?
   a anger ☐
   b concern ☐
   c confidence ☐
   d disapproval ☐
   e optimism ☐

3 Are there any environmental problems in your area about which you could produce similar photos? What photos would you take?

70% of the surface of the Earth is covered by water

The River Rhine, said to contain over 2,000 chemicals

BEFORE: Killer whales in Prince William Sound

AFTER: 1,500 sea otters are thought to have died

Grammar *Passive of reporting verbs*

1 **Sometimes when you are reporting what people say or believe, you don't know, or don't want to say, who exactly the 'people' are. So you use an impersonal construction:**

People believe that hundreds of thousands of birds died.

The same idea can be expressed using the passive in two different ways:

a subject + passive of reporting verb + 'to' infinitive
Hundreds of thousands of birds are believed to have died.

b It + passive of reporting verb + that + clause
It is believed that hundreds of thousands of birds died.

Some other reporting verbs that can be used in this way are:

*calculate   claim   consider   discover   estimate
feel   hope   know   prove   report   say   show
think   understand*

2 **Finish each of the sentences so that it means exactly the same as the sentence before it.**

1 Someone has calculated that the water of the River Rhine contains over 2,000 chemicals.
It ....

2 People consider that one in three bathing beaches is unfit for swimming.
One in three bathing beaches ....

3 About 1,500 sea otters are thought to have been killed.
People ....

4 People say that fewer than 1,000 blue whales survive in the southern hemisphere.
Fewer ....

5 At least 130,000 dolphins are reported to be caught in the nets of tuna fishers every year.
It is reported ....

6 It is estimated that in the past 15 years about 10 million dolphins have been killed.
About 10 million dolphins ....

7 In ancient Greece people thought dolphins were men who had abandoned life on land.
In ancient Greece it ....

8 In ancient Rome it was believed that dolphins carried souls to heaven.
In ancient Rome dolphins ....

Pronunciation 🔲 *Adding something extra*

1 **When people want to add something extra to what they are saying, they show that it is extra by using a different pitch level.**

1 Listen to extracts 1–4 from the radio programme. In each extract the speaker adds:
- some examples OR
- an extra idea OR
- a comment which shows what he or she is feeling

Which does the speaker do in each extract? How does the speaker show this with his or her voice?

2 In a discussion, when might you want to add something extra to what you are saying? Tick the points below which you think are true.

a to give examples of your point ☐
b to make sure that someone understands you ☐
c to give yourself time to think ☐
d to keep someone else from interrupting ☐
e to alter something you have just said ☐

2 **Practise adding something extra to statements 1–4 below.**

Add:
- an example OR
- an extra idea OR
- a comment

Show by your pitch level when you are doing this. Use the extra information in the box below, or any ideas of your own. Listen to the examples on the tape.

1 In many countries the rainforests are being cut down.
2 Rainforests produce many things which are of benefit to mankind.
3 More species of animal life live in rainforests than anywhere else on earth.
4 There are many things we can do to save the rainforests.

1 In Latin America, Africa, South East Asia
2 Food, e.g. chicken, bananas, nuts, rice
Medicines, e.g. treatments for malaria and cancers
Drugs, e.g. for use in anaesthetics and surgery
3 In a few square metres of Brazilian rainforest: 700 types of butterfly, several hundred different kinds of tree
4 Refuse to buy tropical hardwoods, join environmental protection agencies, support reforestation projects

2 Animal life

Vocabulary *Fin, feather and fur*

1 **Look at the following groups of words, which are all connected in some way to animals. What do the words in each group have in common?**

| amphibian | bird | fish | insect | mammal | reptile |

| flock | herd | pack |

| domestic | pet | tame | wild |

| chick | cub | kitten | puppy |

| beak | claw | fin | hoof | horn | paw | tail | wing |

| coat | feather | fur | scale | skin |

| bark | buzz | grunt | hiss | howl | roar | squeak |

| breed | hatch | hunt | migrate | nest |

| bite | kick | lick | peck | scratch | sting |

| hunt | pat | poach | protect | stroke | train | trap |

2 **Give an example of one animal which you associate with each word.**

Reading *Strange but true*

1 *What is a hoatzin?*
What is a pig's favourite drink?

Read these two texts to find out.

Text A

In the swamplands and along the river banks of the Amazon and Orinoco there lives a bird that swims before it can fly, flies like a fat chicken, eats green leaves, has the stomach of a cow and has claws on its wings when young. It would not be out of place in Lewis Carroll's *Alice in Wonderland*, but it is real. It is called the hoatzin.

In appearance, the adult looks like a cross between a domestic chicken and a secretary bird. Male and female look very much alike with brown on the back and cream and rusty red underneath. The head is small, with a large crest on the top, bright red eyes, and electric blue skin. Its nearest relatives are the cuckoos. Its most remarkable feature, though, is not found in the adult but in the young.

Baby hoatzins have a claw on the leading edge of each wing and another at the end of each wing tip. Using these four claws, together with the beak, they can clamber about in the undergrowth, looking very much like primitive birds must have done. The hoatzin, however, could not be considered primitive. It is a highly specialised bird.

During the drier months between December and March hoatzins fly about the forest in flocks containing 20–30 birds, but in April, when the rainy season begins, they collect together in smaller breeding units of two to seven individuals. They build their nests about 4.6m above the river, an important feature for the survival of the young.

When danger threatens, in the form of a snake or a monkey, the young hoatzins – maybe three in one nest – dive over the side and into the river. They swim about under the water until it is safe to return and then, using their claws, haul themselves up through the branches and back into the nest. When they have learned to fly they lose their claws and escape predators not by swimming but by flapping off, in a rather ungainly fashion, to a neighbouring tree.

Text B

WHAT pigs really enjoy is a cool drink of orange squash, according to Professor Peter Brooks of South West Polytechnic in Plymouth, Devon. Piglets, however, prefer to drink milk shakes, especially chocolate and strawberry flavours.

Professor Brooks' research has a serious purpose, because pigs that drink the most have the biggest appetites. And pigs that like to eat are contented and perform well.

"Pigs have the reputation of being dirty animals," Professor Brooks, head of agriculture, said. "This is grossly unfair. They are intelligent, fussy and fastidiously clean."

His research showed that pigs drink most soon after eating and if they do not drink enough, cut down their food intake.

"They do not like drinking water that is dirty, or does not taste pleasant, any more than humans do," Professor Brooks said. "Persuading pigs to drink more makes them perform better, and we have found they like water with a slightly sweet and acid taste – just like orange squash." Professor Brooks insists pigs are the most intelligent of farm animals.

2 *Answer these questions by choosing the best alternative, A, B, C or D.*

1 What do baby hoatzins use their claws for?
  A swimming
  B climbing trees
  C finding food
  D fighting off enemies

2 What are we told about the way a hoatzin flies?
  A It is better at swimming.
  B It flies close to the ground.
  C It does not fly gracefully.
  D It does not fly in the rainy season.

3 According to the text, if pigs drink a lot, it makes them eat
  A more.
  B less.
  C anything.
  D too much.

4 Professor Brooks thinks pigs
  A are greedy.
  B are like humans.
  C have been misjudged.
  D are cleverer than most animals.

5 What do the writers of the two texts have in common? They both
  A write about wild animals.
  B write about recent research.
  C think they will amuse their readers.
  D think they will surprise their readers.

3 *Which would make the more interesting subject of a television nature programme: the hoatzin or Professor Brooks' research? Why?*

Grammar *The -ing form or the infinitive*

1 Some verbs can be followed by another verb in the -ing form, or by the 'to' infinitive. With some of these verbs there is no difference in meaning, whichever structure you choose, but with other verbs there is a change in meaning.

NO CHANGE IN MEANING

1 Some verbs which can be followed by either structure with no change in meaning are:
begin   continue   hate   like   love
prefer   start
Pigs that like to eat *are contented.*
They do not like drinking *water that is dirty.*

2 But only the 'to' infinitive, not the -ing form, is possible in these two sentences. Why?
Would you like to go *on an African safari?*
I'd prefer to study *the animals in Australia.*

3 We can say either:
Please help save *the panda from extinction.*   OR
Please help to save *the panda.*
But what comes after 'can't help'?

4 After 'make' in the active we use the infinitive without 'to':
The zoo keeper made *the chimpanzees* do *tricks.*
But what do we use after 'make' in the passive?
The chimpanzees were made ....

5 *You* need to brush *the dog.*
There are *two* ways of making this sentence passive. What are they?
The dog needs ....
The dog needs ....

CHANGE IN MEANING

1 After verbs like 'see', 'hear', 'watch', if we use the -ing form we show that the action continued happening for a period of time:
I once watched *a bear* pulling *apart the luggage inside my tent.*
If we use the infinitive without 'to' we show that the action was short and completed:
I heard *the bear* grunt *when it found some biscuits.*

2 After 'remember':
What is the difference in meaning?
I remember camping *in the Yellowstone National Park. I didn't* remember to lock *all my food in the car boot out of the way of bears. I* remember seeing *a grizzly bear for the first time. I was so excited I didn't* remember to take *the lens cap off my camera.*

3 After 'stop':
What is the difference in meaning?
I sneezed and the bear stopped to listen. *I* stopped breathing *for a second, but the bear didn't notice me.*

2 Put the verbs in brackets into the correct form: the -ing form, the 'to' infinitive or the infinitive without 'to'.

LION FOR SALE: GOOD WITH KIDS
Saladino de Souza Gonzalez takes advantage of the fact that in Brazil the law allows people (1 keep) lions at home. 'People's homes need (2 protect) from thieves,' says Mr Gonzalez. 'With a lion for a guard a thief may enter, but he won't leave!' Mr Gonzalez started with three lions ten years ago, and at the moment he manages (3 breed) three lion cubs a year, but he would like (4 expand) the business. 'I don't remember ever (5 have) trouble selling one,' he says. He advises owners (6 let) their lion (7 run) freely in the back yard at night. Owners like (8 hear) it (9 walk) up and down when they are in bed; it helps them (10 sleep) more soundly. 'A lion is no problem with children as long as the animal is bought when young, and you remember (11 feed) it regularly,' he says. Maria Conceicao de Oliveira is a satisfied customer: 'I just can't help (12 smile) when I see my little girl (13 play) with Mikey, our lion. I only regret (14 not buy) another cub at the same time.'

Writing *Different composition types*

Write one of these compositions (120–180 words).

1 Describe a visit to a zoo and one particular animal that impressed you.

2 Describe three ways in which humankind makes use of animals.

3 A child has asked you to tell him/her a story about an animal that saves the life of a person. What story do you tell?

4 The factory opposite your house has a guard dog which barks all night. Write to the manager to complain.

5 A friend has written to tell you about his/her fear of one of these animals: spiders, mice, snakes or sharks. Write a reply trying to persuade your friend that he/she has no need to be frightened.

3 Concrete jungle

Speaking *Near and far*

1 **Which of these two places is more similar to where you live at the moment? In what ways is it similar?**

If you lived in these places, what would you find:
- strange?
- frightening?
- beautiful?
- interesting?

What skills do you think you would need to survive in each?

2 **What do you need in the place where you live to make you feel happy and comfortable? How easily could you adapt to living somewhere else?**

Reading *Away from their homes*

1 **Work with a partner to do this activity. Read one text (A or B) each. When you have read your text, discuss with your partner:**
- where the visitors were
- how the new place was different from what they were used to
- what specific problems they faced

Text A

The writer is describing a journey he made with two native guides through the jungles of Borneo.

John Bong and Tingang Na knew from the moment I pulled out my map that I had very little idea what I was getting myself into.

They were right. Nothing had prepared me for the terrain through which we slowly travelled. The rainforest felt magical and enchanted as long as I was sitting still, but the moment I began walking it became an obstacle course of steep razorback ridges, muddy ravines, fallen trees, slippery buttressed tree roots, impenetrable thickets of undergrowth, and a confusion of wildly twisting rivers running in every direction. All of this was in the shade of the interlocking branches of giant rainforest trees. I became disoriented. I exhausted myself trying to remain upright. It was futile.

The week we spent in each other's company made me realise how helpless and dependent I was: I had no jungle skills, and as a result, my admiration for John and Tingang Na grew each day. Their uncanny and seemingly effortless ability to live off the jungle filled me with excitement and wonder. This was a feeling that would never leave me. A piece of thin bark placed between two small river rocks became a drinking fountain; a leaf plucked off a certain tree, folded double, and sucked on to create a vibrating sound, would call the inquisitive barking deer (Muntiacus muntjak) to within shotgun range; a vine known as *kulit elang*, when pounded and dipped in water and scrubbed on our ankles, would keep leeches from climbing up our legs. As we advanced through the rainforest, fruit trees laden with loquats, giant grapefruit, durians, mangosteens, guavas, rambutans, and jackfruit appeared at regular intervals, and it rarely took more than an hour to set up camp and collect food. It was so easy – in the company of experts. On my own I would have died of hunger.

Text B

The writer is an anthropologist who brought four wood carvers from Torajaland, Indonesia, to London to build a traditional house in a museum.

Personal documentation had been a major difficulty. It is very hard to get travel papers for a man who does not even know how old he is. The forms that needed to be filled in seemed perversely ill-adapted to carvers living up a mountain in Indonesia. Telephone number? Educational certificates? Income in money? Even remembering names and ages of all children defeated the younger men. They worked out that one had eight children and one seven, but did not know their ages or even relative order of birth. That was the sort of thing only women knew.

Nevertheless, quite suddenly, they were here in an English 'hot season' with the wind and rain howling outside the house. It seemed only fair that, as I stayed with them in Torajaland, they would stay with me in London.

From the start they were amazingly adaptable. As carvers, they were used to the idea of working away from their homes and families. The problem with some novelties lay precisely in their being assimilated to something Indonesian that they already knew. While it is normal to stand in an Indonesian bathroom and simply throw water over yourself, in an English bathroom the consequences can be disastrous. While there was no problem about turning taps on, they would never remember to turn them off, since in Torajaland, water simply gushes eternally from a bamboo pipe.

Certain concessions had been made towards the Torajan way of life. It would be easier for me to change than to ask them to. Beds were unpleasantly soft. They preferred mattresses on the floor. Instead of spreading themselves around the house, they all slept in one room. 'If we had a nightmare and slept alone, who would comfort us?'

We travelled to the museum every morning by underground train. They liked that a lot and rapidly became masters of it. Initially, Nenek had difficulties with escalators. Although he could run over a greasy log bridge in Torajaland, where I would have to get down and crawl, he found it hard to cope with staircases that moved or the motor skills involved in standing up in a moving train.

2 *Choose the best answer (A, B, C or D) for the questions on your text.*

Text A

1 How did the writer find being in the jungle?
 A boring
 B difficult
 C frightening
 D relaxing

2 The writer says he respected John Bong and Tingang Na because they
 A showed him how to use his map.
 B stayed with him for a week.
 C could survive in the jungle.
 D worked hard to find food.

Text B

1 Why was it difficult to get travel papers for the visitors?
 A They lived a long way from a government office.
 B They could not remember how much money they earned.
 C The forms asked them questions they found strange.
 D The authorities did not want them to travel.

2 When they lived in England, the visitors had to get used to
 A using a different type of bathroom.
 B being away from their families.
 C sleeping in their own rooms.
 D sleeping on mattresses on the floor.

3 *Work with your partner to choose the best answer (A, B, C or D) for this question.*

One difference between the visitor in Text A and the visitors in Text B is that he
A didn't have to adapt completely to his new environment.
B was delighted by some things in his new environment.
C was soon able to look after himself.
D found nothing similar to his old environment.

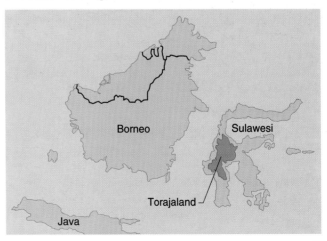

Grammar *Impersonal 'it'*

1 *How could you rewrite these sentences beginning with the impersonal subject 'It'? You can find the answers in the reading texts.*

1 Setting up camp rarely took more than an hour.
2 A man who does not even know how old he is can't get travel papers easily.
3 They would stay with me, which seemed only fair.
4 In an Indonesian bathroom you normally stand and simply throw water over yourself.

How could you rewrite this sentence using the impersonal object 'it', and beginning 'He ...'?

5 Coping with staircases that moved was hard for him.

2 *Finish each of the sentences so that it means exactly the same as the sentence printed before it. Each one is about a man who returned to England after living in an African village.*

1 'I haven't lived in England for two years.'
'It ....
2 Getting used to the English way of life again took him a long time.
It ....
3 Choosing food in a huge supermarket caused him great difficulty.
It ....
4 It was hard for him to resist cream cakes.
He found ....
5 He couldn't throw away empty bottles or paper bags.
It was impossible ....
6 His friends had continued their lives without him, which upset him.
It ....
7 He found it difficult to make polite conversation at parties.
Making ....
8 It was ages before he felt at home.
He ....

Speaking *Telling a story*

Prepare to tell a story on one of the following topics. You will need to include in your story a mixture of narrative, description and perhaps opinion.

See if you can keep talking for one minute. When you have finished, find out if other people have had similar experiences.

1 A NEW SCHOOL/JOB
How was it different from what you were used to? What aspects of the rules or systems were unfamiliar to you? How easily could you find your way around?

2 A NEW NEIGHBOURHOOD/COUNTRY
How were people there different from what you were used to? How long did it take you to find out where all the things you needed were? What did you miss?

3 A NEW FAMILY ENVIRONMENT
Who were its members? Relatives or friends in another town? A family where you stayed while working or studying away from home? Your in-laws? How were their habits different from what you were used to?

4

Exam skill *Composition*

You have $1\frac{1}{2}$ hours for Paper 2, Composition. In that time you have to write two compositions of between 120 and 180 words each. You have a choice of four composition topics. The topics may be a description, a story, a letter, a talk or an opinion composition. There will also be a fifth topic on the optional set books (see Unit 8 Lesson 4).

Stages in exam composition writing

1 CHOOSE
Choose the two topics you think you can do best. Do not attempt a topic if you are not sure what is meant.

2 PLAN
Make a paragraph plan. Make notes of the ideas you intend to include in each paragraph. Make sure you follow the instructions exactly.

3 WRITE
Most people do not have enough time to write their compositions out twice, that is, to do a rough copy and then a clean copy. If you make a good paragraph plan, it should not be necessary to do a rough copy as well. It does not matter if you cross out words in your composition, as long as you write clearly. Remember to keep to the word limit.

4 CHECK
Check what you have written carefully.

Timing

It is important to watch the clock so that you finish both compositions in the $1\frac{1}{2}$ hours. You should spend about the same time on each one. How many minutes would you spend on each of the above stages?

Skills needed

1 All types of composition:
 – good paragraph organisation
 – good linking of ideas

2 Description:
 – good use of a range of appropriate vocabulary

3 Telling a story:
 – making clear the order in which events happen through the correct use of tenses, and the use of time expressions

4 Letter:
 – using the appropriate layout for both informal and formal letters, and suitable opening and closing phrases

5 Talk:
 – using appropriate 'spoken' language, formal or informal as required

6 Opinion:
 – expressing your ideas clearly
 – using linking phrases to show the relationship between your ideas

7 Set books:
Revise Unit 8 Lesson 4 if you want to do this option.

A composition might be a combination of more than one type, for example a description in a letter, or a story as part of a talk.

PRACTICE COMPOSITION PAPER

1 hour 30 minutes

*Answer **two** questions.*
Your answers must follow exactly the instructions given and must be of between 120 and 180 words each.

1 Write a letter to a friend who used to live next door to you. Tell him/her about the family that has just moved into his/her old home.

2 Write a story which ends with these words: 'Safe at last. Thank goodness I had remembered to pack my English dictionary!'

3 'There's nothing I, personally, can do to stop the pollution of the world.' What do you say in reply to a friend who says this to you?

4 Watching television is a waste of time. Do you agree?

Test exercises

1 *Make changes and additions to these sets of words in order to write a complete letter.*

José Menino 103
Santos
Brazil

2 January 1994

Dear Robert,

1 I be / Brazil / three months now and I really enjoy myself.

....

2 I go swim / New Year's Day, / be something I be not used / do!

....

3 It be supposed / be / cool summer this year but it be quite hot enough / me!

....

4 I like look / all / beautiful tropical trees and flowers.

....

5 I remember have indoor pot plants / England / never grow very big.

....

6 Here / same kinds / plants grow / enormous heights everywhere.

....

7 Fortunately / only snakes I see be / zoo.

....

8 I give you / impressions / people when I write next time.

....

Love to all the family from
Charlotte

2 *Complete each of the following sentences so that it means exactly the same as the sentence before it.*

1 We haven't heard from Nicola for ages.
It's ages ....

2 Don't wash the dog before we go for a walk: it's pointless!
It's not worth ....

3 It's a four-hour flight from London to Athens.
It takes ....

4 We've run out of cat food.
There ....

5 I'd rather not use disposable bottles.
I don't ....

6 'Why don't we go to the zoo?' said Gwen.
Gwen suggested ....

7 People say the climate is getting warmer.
The climate ....

8 In some places people believe a black cat brings good luck.
In some places it ....

9 The government should make industries pay attention to environmental problems.
Industries should ....

10 We must protect endangered animal species.
Endangered animal species need ....

3 *Complete each sentence with a word connected with* **animals**.

EXAMPLE: The Indian rhinoceros has one ..*horn*.., whereas the African has two.

1 In the tree opposite my window there's a bird's .... with four babies in it.
2 The hunters caught the leopard in a .... and sold it illegally to a zoo.
3 The burglar heard a dog .... behind the gate and decided not to break into the house.
4 The peacock's tail is made up of the most beautiful, long ....
5 The patterns on this butterfly's .... are like big eyes.

4 *Choose the word or phrase (A–D) which best completes each sentence.*

1 Plants suck up water from the ground through their ....

   A branches   B flowers   C leaves   D roots

2 The journalists were .... by the company's false statistics and so wrote inaccurate stories.

   A exploited   B interfered   C misled   D mistreated

3 In the geography class the students sat in small groups quietly .... the causes of acid rain.

   A arguing   B dictating   C discussing   D proposing

4 Environmentalists believe we have to .... up to the mess we have made of the planet.

   A face   B feel   C live   D stand

5 The Minister says the government is committed to .... the National Parks.

   A deserving   B preserving   C reserving   D serving

6 The Green movements .... in convincing world governments to protect Antarctica.

   A achieved   B fulfilled   C managed   D succeeded

7 Squirrels .... nuts in holes so that they will have something to eat in winter.

   A crack   B give   C grow   D store

8 I've been .... by a bee – have you anything to ease the pain?

   A bitten   B licked   C scratched   D stung

9 He saved himself from a difficult situation abroad by .... he couldn't understand the language.

   A begging   B cheating   C lying   D pretending

10 I've had enough of your complaints – .... you can cook the meals yourself.

   A in advance   B in future   C in the end   D in the future

15

Culture and tradition

1 Traditional stories

Speaking *Our culture*

You have been asked to design a set of five postage stamps to help promote the culture of your country.

Think of five different pictures to use on the stamps. Use these ideas to help you. Explain the reasons for your choices.

- a national dish
- the national costume
- a typical national handicraft
- a national monument
- a famous writer or musician
- a famous work of art
- an illustration of a traditional story
- a scene from a national celebration

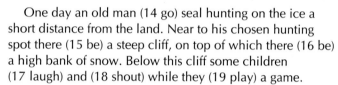

Grammar *Revision of tenses*

Read this traditional story from northern Canada. Put the verbs in brackets into an appropriate tense.

THE HUNTER AND THE CHILDREN

I (1 go) to tell you an Eskimo story. Nobody (2 know) how long the Eskimos (3 live) in northern Canada on the shores of the Arctic Ocean. Their life (4 be) usually very hard and although it (5 become) a little easier with the arrival of electricity and other modern conveniences, it still (6 dominate) by the harsh climate and the need to hunt for food. Before the time of supermarkets and imported food, in winter the only way to get fresh meat (7 be) by killing a seal. Seals (8 spend) most of their time swimming in the water under the ice but from time to time they (9 have) to put their noses through a hole in the ice so that they can breathe. This (10 be) the moment when a patient hunter could strike at the seal with his weapon, a harpoon. This story (11 be) about one of these hunters. You (12 sit) comfortably? Then I (13 begin).

One day an old man (14 go) seal hunting on the ice a short distance from the land. Near to his chosen hunting spot there (15 be) a steep cliff, on top of which there (16 be) a high bank of snow. Below this cliff some children (17 laugh) and (18 shout) while they (19 play) a game.

The hunter (20 wait) silent and motionless beside a breathing hole where he (21 see) a seal the day before. For a long time nothing (22 happen); then he (23 hear) the sound of a seal breathing. Just as he (24 raise) his harpoon, ready to strike, the silence (25 break)! The noise of the children playing at the foot of the cliff (26 distract) the old man and (27 warn) the seal, which (28 escape).

The old man (29 lower) his harpoon in a bad mood and (30 grumble), 'Those children! I wish they (31 not be) so noisy. If only they (32 not shout) just then. I hope the cliff of snow (33 fall) and (34 bury) them!'

Once more the hunter (35 wait) by the breathing hole. Again the seal (36 return). And again just as the hunter (37 go) to strike, the children (38 burst) out laughing and the seal (39 get) away unharmed.

The old hunter now (40 call) upon his magic powers. He (41 speak) to the spirits which (42 bring) bad luck: 'When the children (43 shout) again, send snow to bury them!'

Suddenly an avalanche of snow (44 fall) from the top of the cliff and (45 swallow) the children. Their cries (46 hear) for a long time, but gradually they (47 grow) weaker until at last everyone (48 be) silent.

When the parents of the children (49 realise) what (50 happen) they (51 want) revenge. Just as they (52 go) to catch him, the old man (53 call) upon his magic powers one last time and (54 lift) himself into the air. The parents (55 watch) him rise into the sky and turn into a shooting star. On a clear night, if you (56 look) carefully, you still (57 see) the old man running away across the sky.

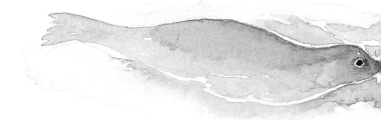

Listening 🖭 *A faraway kingdom*

1 **Listen to an expert talking about traditional folk stories from all over the world.**

As you listen check whether the speaker makes the points below. Mark Yes (✓) if the point is made by the speaker and No (✗) if it is not.

	YES	NO
1 The story teller doesn't tell you exactly where the folk story takes place.	☐	☐
2 People like listening to stories about kings and queens.	☐	☐
3 Children are more interested in stories than adults.	☐	☐
4 The ideas in Eskimo stories are similar to those in Australian aboriginal stories.	☐	☐
5 Characters can be shocked at what they find in a secret room.	☐	☐
6 Clothes can have an effect on a character's life.	☐	☐
7 Folk tales express feelings that people would rather keep hidden.	☐	☐
8 The magic drum has power over human bodies.	☐	☐
9 Eskimos think 'The Magic Drum' encourages women to be independent.	☐	☐
10 You can't enjoy a folk tale unless you know what it means.	☐	☐

2 **Do you know any traditional stories which include any of these things?**

- an animal that helps the human characters
- a beautiful woman and her horribly ugly lover
- two brothers with different personalities
- a forbidden room with a frightful secret
- a magic piece of clothing

Vocabulary *Prepositions*

1 **Some adjectives, nouns and verbs are usually followed by a particular preposition. Look at Listening exercise 1 and underline the prepositions that come after these words:**

listen   interested   similar   shocked   effect

2 **Match these words with the correct preposition:**

> accustomed   afraid   apologise   clever
> different   filled   keen   laugh (v.)   prevent
> proud   quarrel   reason (n.)   related   rely
> succeed   sure   take part

> at   for   from   in   of   on   to   with

3 **Complete these sentences with the correct preposition.**

1 The hunter (1) .... the Eskimo story was not capable (2) .... living (3) .... peace (4) .... the community (5) .... which he belonged. He was good (6) .... hunting but bad (7) .... understanding children's fun and games. The lesson (8) .... the story is that adults should not be unkind (9) .... children just because they have power (10) .... them.

2 Alternatively, the story provides a lesson (1) .... children. There is nothing wrong (2) .... noisy games provided they do not interfere (3) .... serious adult occupations. An adult will go away (4) .... children if they insist (5) .... making a nuisance (6) .... themselves. This will result (7) .... the children losing the benefit (8) .... the adult's company.

3 Congratulations (1) .... your engagement (2) .... Cinderella! I feel sorry (3) .... her sisters because they will be disappointed (4) .... the news. They have always dreamt (5) .... getting married (6) .... a prince like you. They will be jealous (7) .... Cinderella and won't be keen (8) .... seeing her installed (9) .... the palace. You aren't thinking (10) .... finding room (11) .... the sisters there as well, are you? You can depend (12) .... Cinderella to be nice (13) .... everyone and I'm sure she will forgive her sisters (14) .... their past unkindness.

2 Art and culture

Listening 🔲 *Chi wara*

1 *Listen to this conversation about one of these objects (a–c). Which one is being discussed?*

2 *Listen again and complete these notes on the carving in the collector's notebook.*

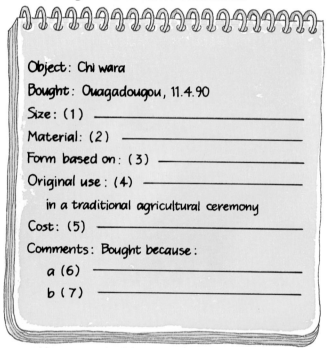

Object: Chi wara
Bought: Ouagadougou, 11.4.90
Size: (1) _____
Material: (2) _____
Form based on: (3) _____
Original use: (4) _____
   in a traditional agricultural ceremony
Cost: (5) _____
Comments: Bought because:
   a (6) _____
   b (7) _____

a   b

c

3 *If you had the opportunity, which of objects a–c would you buy for yourself?*

Grammar *Conditional sentences (4)*

1 *Which of these examples could you rephrase using:*

– 'if'?
– 'it doesn't matter'?

Provided you can do that, you should be able to find good things at reasonable prices.
It's quite quiet – as long as it's not market day.
It's impossible to work at the faculty, however hard I try.

What does 'suppose' mean in this sentence?
Suppose an artist asked to paint your portrait, what would you say?

2 *Rewrite each of these sentences so that it means the same as the sentence before it.*

1 Children can visit the gallery only if they are accompanied by an adult.
As long as ....

2 The museum will only be able to buy that sculpture if the government makes a contribution.
Provided that ....

3 I'm sure I'll never understand this painting, even though you keep explaining it to me.
However much ....

4 It doesn't matter what exhibition is on in that gallery, she always goes.
Whatever ....

5 Do you know what you'd do if you saw a vandal destroying a painting?
Suppose ....

Reading *Picture choice*

1 *Each of these works of art was chosen by someone as his personal favourite. Why do you think each was chosen?*

2 *Read these two texts to find out why. Then choose the best answer (A, B, C or D) for questions 1–4.*

Text B

Text A

Hiroyasu Ando, Japanese cultural attaché, on a writing-box at the British Museum

A box of pleasure

My favourite work of art in London has all the simplicity which the Japanese much admire; it is a writing-box in the collections of the British Museum, on display in the new Japanese Galleries.

It is made of lacquer, that most characteristic of Japanese materials, combining lightness, softness and durability.

In Japanese culture, writing is the most admired of all the arts and it is no surprise that the box, which contains inkstone, brush and other writing materials, should be the object of the most refined craftsmanship.

Like so many outstanding works of Japanese art and craft, this is an anonymous piece. But its style of decoration recalls the bold school of art of the incomparable Ogata Korin, whose painting and designs inspired craftsmen for

centuries after his death in 1716. The design of stylised pine trees, which so dominate the landscape of old Japan, is done in gold powder, with inlaid mother-of-pearl and silver, and is set against a huge full moon inlaid in copper. This suggests the season of late autumn, a season both beautiful and melancholy in our culture.

I also love the feeling of maturity in this centuries-old piece, which has been allowed to age gracefully without restoration.

In our hurried days, it is pleasant to gaze at this beautiful box and imagine the more leisured world of three centuries ago, when its first owner, whoever that lucky person was, placed it beside him before settling down to write a letter with brush and ink, which must have been a delight to read.

Kenney Jones, of The Law, finds ecological inspiration in a Constable

CONSTABLE's *Hay Wain* is so wonderful. I love most of his paintings, but this one makes me feel specially peaceful. I never tire of it, although it's an image that you see everywhere. They had one in my school, so it's been with me from day dot. I love its "naturalness". After all, these were direct observations from nature: he did endless sketches outside. But when it was exhibited in the 1820s, at the Royal Academy and Paris Salon, it was its "naturalness" that caused a stir, a contrast to the idealised landscapes of an artist like Claude. But as Constable himself wrote to a friend, a few months after completing the painting, "the sound of water … willows, old rotten banks, slimy posts, and brickwork. I love such things. … As long as I do paint I shall never cease to paint such places."

When I look at Constable's painting I feel we should all do something to ensure that the countryside is not damaged any further by man. It was my good friend Peter Blake, the artist, who first opened my eyes to really "looking" at art, while painting my portrait for an album cover. It shows me the day after a party: I just look happy, the way I feel when I look at this Constable. One day it might just inspire me to start painting.

Kenney Jones was drummer with The Faces and The Who. His new band with Paul Rodgers, of Bad Company, is called The Law.

1 What do the two texts have in common?
A Both express the writers' concern for the environment.
B Both were written by art experts.
C Both are about famous artists from the writers' countries.
D Both are about works which show landscape.

2 In what way is the work of art in Text B different from that in Text A?
A It has no practical use.
B It was produced a century earlier.
C It shows the season of autumn.
D It is based on countryside the artist observed.

3 What does Hiroyasu Ando feel when looking at the writing-box?
A He regrets the fact that he is not in Japan.
B He admires the naturalness of the pine trees.
C He thinks about the life of an earlier age.
D He wishes he was the owner.

4 What does Kenney Jones feel when looking at The Hay Wain?
A He would like to become a painter himself.
B He can never see it too much.
C He thinks it would make a good album cover.
D He thinks Constable is a better artist than Claude.

Vocabulary *Describing an object*

1 *Sort these words into the categories below.*

> blueish   bright   circular   delicate
> diamond-shaped   huge   ivory   leather
> pale   rectangular   silk   square   stiff   tiny

OPINION
**beautiful   elegant   extraordinary
interesting   nice   refined   simple**

SIZE
large

SHAPE
pointed

TEXTURE
rough   smooth   soft

COLOUR
light

MATERIAL
**copper   ebony   gold   lacquer
mother-of-pearl   silver**

Add at least one new word to each category.

2 *Words have not only meanings but realities of their own (e.g. shape, length, pattern of letters, sound). They can suggest things like colour, temperature, weight, age. They can also remind us of a wide range of things (e.g. people, animals, objects, places, feelings).*

Choose three or four words from the lists above which you particularly like. Use the ideas given here to help you explain:
- what the words suggest to you
- why you like them

Speaking *My favourite work of art*

Prepare to talk about your favourite work of art. It could be a painting, a sculpture or any other object.

1 Say something about what it is and/or what it represents.

2 Describe it in terms of:
- its age
- its size and shape
- its texture
- its colour
- the material it is made of

3 Explain why you like it, describing the effect it has on you.

4 Mention:
- where it can be found
- the culture and the society it comes from

Choose what order to put points **1–4** in. When you have finished speaking, find out if others like your choice.

3 Celebrations

Reading *A traditional wedding*

1 *Talk about weddings in your country.*

- Who is responsible for the practical arrangements?
- Who is invited?
- Where does it take place?
- What do people wear?
- When does the groom first see the bride on the wedding day?
- How long do the celebrations last?

2 *Read this extract from a historical novel. It describes the wedding day of Ibrahim, an important official at a Middle Eastern court, to Muhsine. How different is it from a wedding in your country today?*

3 *Choose the best answer (A, B, C or D) for questions 1–5.*

1 When Muhsine arrived at his house, Ibrahim first
A welcomed her male relatives.
B visited her in her rooms.
C went out to pray.
D introduced her to his friends.

2 When Ibrahim was taken to meet Muhsine, he felt
A excited.
B happy.
C uncertain.
D irritated.

3 When Muhsine met Ibrahim, she first
A showed him her face.
B accepted his present.
C spoke to him.
D took his hand.

4 What thought filled Ibrahim's mind while he looked at Muhsine?
A She was beautiful.
B He liked her hands.
C He didn't know her at all.
D She looked very tired.

5 How did Ibrahim feel when he went back to the feast?
A angry
B ashamed
C curious
D pleased

Now the day, so long awaited and so meticulously prepared for, had come and nearly gone. His house had been full to bursting from first light. Muhsine's younger sisters, her cousins and friends and aunts, had arrived early. He had heard them chattering and laughing and the rustle of their wedding finery as they made their way to the harem[1] to await the coming of the bride. She came at last, carried in a chair beneath a baldachin of rich brocade so that she still remained invisible, and accompanied by a noisy procession of musicians and male relatives and hangers-on. Even then he wasn't allowed to see her. He had perforce to go to the neighbourhood mosque with his friends – and what a lot of friends he found he suddenly had! And what a fool he felt, although normally no one enjoyed being the centre of attention more than he. But at last, on his return, he had been escorted, with a great deal of good-humoured pushing and shoving, to the door of the harem. Some woman (he had no idea who she was) had taken his hand and led him up to a motionless figure draped in rose brocade.

Later, when he thought about it, he was compelled to admit that all he had felt at that moment had been impatience to get the whole thing over. He was tired, he had expended too much emotion on – what? He didn't know, but he did know that it had not been attended by fulfilment or anything like it. Afterwards he remembered her hand, small, olive-skinned, perfect, with its oval fingernails and henna-tinted palm. It emerged from the draperies and rose to her head and drew back the silk veil. Well, she was beautiful, no doubt about that, but she was also a complete stranger. While she took his hand and kissed it and murmured something, he didn't hear what, he thought about that. The perfect face that had been revealed to him was empty of meaning for him, except that he thought he could detect signs of strain around the large, black eyes. Well, he could sympathise there; and suddenly he remembered that something was expected of him. He fumbled in the folds of his sash, and finally brought out his gift of one perfect pear-shaped pearl. Since she seemed as bewildered as he, he pressed it into her hand.

Then it was all over and he had to return to the selamik[2], there to endure the curious or sly glances from his friends, and to remember that in his confusion he had forgotten that he should have embraced his wife when he gave her the pearl. Now, no doubt, she must think him a complete boor. He felt embarrassment rise, and took out his handkerchief and mopped his brow. Ibrahim, my friend, he admonished himself, control yourself. Remember who you are, and never let it be said you were demoralized by a woman.

The wedding feast, of which he could eat little, seemed to last forever and he longed to escape from it, even if it meant making himself agreeable to this strange girl …

[1] the private rooms in the house
[2] the reception area in the house

4 *If you could have attended this wedding, what advice would you have given to the couple?*

Listening 📼 *A traditional festival*

1 *Listen to this extract from a radio programme in which the speaker describes a traditional festival. Fill the gaps in the box with the information you hear.*

Festival: The Palio

Place: Siena, (1) .... of Florence

Dates: (2) .... and (3) ....

In honour of: (4) .... , the patron of the city

Celebrates: Victory over an army from (5)................. in (6) ....

Central event: A (7) .... run round (8) .... of Siena

2 *Listen to the programme again. Sort the photos (a–e) into the order in which the events they show take place. Number the photos 1–5.*

a

☐

b

☐

c

☐

d

☐

3 *If you could go to this festival, who would you like to take with you?*

Speaking *A celebration*

1 *Prepare to talk about a celebration. It could be either:*

- private or public
- national or local
- traditional or modern

In your description explain:
- what it celebrates
- when and where the celebration takes place
- the setting and some of the typical activities
- what you enjoy about it
- what a foreign visitor might like about it

2 *Talk about your celebration. Then find out if others have been to a celebration like it.*

e

☐

4

Exam skill *Practical matters*

1 Answer sheets

Paper 1
You will have a question paper and a separate answer sheet on which you record your answers. Look at the example on page 192. Read the instructions on it to see how to fill in the answer sheet.

Paper 3
You will write your answers on the question paper.

Paper 4
You will have a question paper and a separate answer sheet (see page 192). Write your answers on the question paper while you listen to the tape. At the end of the exam you will be given time to copy your answers on to the separate answer sheet.

2 Materials to take to the exam

Pencil, rubber, pencil sharpener, pen, watch.

3 Instructions

Follow all instructions carefully.

4 Timing

Allow yourself enough time to do each question. Do not leave any questions unfinished at the end of the exam. Keep an eye on your watch, and leave yourself time for checking.

5 Relax

Even though it is difficult, try and approach the exam feeling relaxed.

Test exercises

1 Complete this passage. Use only **one** word in each gap.

Since its beginning in 1976, the popularity of the Hong Kong Dragon Boat Festival has steadily increased, attracting teams of rowers from around the world.

The (**1**) .... of Dragon Boat racing dates back to (**2**) .... fourth century BC. At (**3**) .... time there was a minister called Qu Yuan. Although he (**4**) .... much loved by the people, the King dismissed him (**5**) .... his high position. Some people (**6**) .... that unfriendly government officials had had a part in (**7**) ....

Unhappy and lonely, he wandered (**8**) .... the countryside writing poems about (**9**) .... love of the country and its people. (**10**) .... , unable to put (**11**) .... with life any more, he committed suicide by drowning (**12**) .... in the Mi Lo River.

It (**13**) .... said that local fishermen (**14**) .... out in their boats to save him. But they (**15**) .... So, to prevent his body from (**16**) .... eaten by fish, they beat the surface of the (**17**) .... with their oars (**18**) .... threw rice in the river.

(**19**) .... Hong Kong today the death of Qu Yuan is celebrated (**20**) .... year in the Dragon Boat Festival. The scene of the fishermen racing out to save Qu Yuan is repeated in the form of Dragon Boat races.

2 *Complete each of the following sentences so that it means exactly the same as the sentence before it.*

1 It didn't rain as much in June as it did in May.
In May it rained ....

2 He hasn't ridden a bicycle for three years.
He last ....

3 The other actors didn't like working with her because she always forgot her words.
If ....

4 'Paul, let's go to the carnival in Rio,' said Kate.
Kate suggested ....

5 Arguing with the boss isn't a good idea.
You'd ....

6 After a kiss from the princess the frog would become a prince.
Provided ....

7 The bad weather is destroying the young fruit trees.
The young fruit trees ....

8 She wears dark glasses so that the sun won't hurt her eyes.
She wears dark glasses to prevent ....

9 Don't blame me if the car won't start.
It's not ....

10 'Why did you come in late last night?' my father said.
My father asked me ....

3 *Choose the word or phrase (A–D) which best completes each sentence.*

1 The prize is given on the .... of the class teacher.

  A approval   B honour   C praise   D recommendation

2 If my plan to get a grant to study in Paris comes ...., I won't be here next term.

  A along   B off   C on   D round

3 .... you register with the authorities first, you can visit every part of the country.

  A Apart from   B As long as   C Except   D In addition to

4 The optician advised the student .... her glasses regularly.

  A should wear   B wear   C wore   D to wear

5 Stop pinching me – you're .... me!

  A damaging   B harming   C hurting   D wounding

6 She has a .... accent. Otherwise you'd never know she wasn't English.

  A brief   B low   C short   D slight

7 If you hadn't .... my advice you might have passed the exam.

  A ignored   B missed   C omitted   D quarrelled

8 The young man was very .... towards the old musician, taking care that he had everything he needed.

  A disrespectful   B respectable   C respectful   D respected

9 You .... have brought me a present – still, it's very generous of you.

  A didn't need   B mustn't   C shouldn't   D wouldn't

10 The success of her journey across Siberia .... me to go there too.

  A appealed   B encouraged   C fascinated   D undertook

11 The woman who had the heart attack is now out of .... and is expected to recover fully.

A breath   B control   C danger   D reach

12 Could you hurry up, please? We .... our meal half an hour ago.

A asked   B demanded   C ordered   D requested

13 The grey horse started the race badly, but soon managed to .... the leaders.

A back out of   B catch up with   C go in for   D look out for

14 A new model of this microwave is expected to be .... sale within three months.

A at   B in   C on   D to

15 It takes a long time to get .... malaria.

A across   B down   C over   D through

Speaking *End of course*

You and your partner have won a school competition for being the most hard-working English students of the year. The prize is a free trip to one of the festivals below. But there are four conditions to accepting the prize. You must:

1 Say what you plan to do with your English after the course has finished.
2 Link the festival to an aspect of your English studies.
3 Take part in the festival in some way.
4 Produce evidence of this when you return.

AUSTRALIA
Oct 7: Henley-on-Todd Regatta, Northern Territory – boat race down the dry bed of the Todd River through Alice Springs. Competitors cut holes in the bottoms of their canoes and run. The organisers even insure against rain.

CAYMAN ISLANDS
Oct 21- 27: Cayman Islands Pirates Week Festival – the islands celebrate their seafaring history with parades of lavishly costumed pirates, treasure hunts and a ball.

THAILAND
Nov 11-13: Loi Kratong, Chiang Mai – under the full moon the Thais float small, lotus-shaped banana- leafed boats containing lighted candles, burning incense, flowers and small coins, in honour of the water spirits and to expiate the year's sins. Festivities also include folk dancing and spectacular firework displays.

AUSTRIA
Nov 15: St Leopold's Festival, Klosterneuberg – a 200-year-old tradition dedicated to St Leopold who founded the town church in the 12th century. In the church stands a vast wooden barrel which can hold up to 56,000 litres of wine. Every November 15, it is filled to the brim, allowing the good people of Klosterneuberg to refresh themselves and take part in sliding over the barrel, a custom thought to hark back to ancient fertility rites.

Loi Kratong Festival

Discuss:
– which festival you will choose to go to
– how you will fulfil the prize conditions

When you have finished, explain what you have decided. Who has the most interesting ideas?

IF ONLY I'D SPENT MORE TIME ON MY READING!

Appendix

UNIT 5 LESSON 1
Reading *Questionnaire*

To find out how healthy and fit you are, give yourself marks in this way:

1	YES = +40	NO = −10	**8a**	+40
2	YES = −10	NO = +10	**b**	+10
3	YES = +10	NO = −10	**c**	−10
4	YES = −20	NO = +20	**d**	−20
5	YES = +20	NO = −20	**e**	−30
6	YES = +20	NO = −20	**f**	−40
7a	YES = −20	NO = 0	**9**	YES = −10 NO = 0
b	YES = −10	NO = 0	**10**	YES =+20 NO = −20

Do your points add up to a plus (more healthy) or minus (less healthy) score overall?

If you scored +100 or more, you are already taking most of the right steps for health and fitness. Well done, and keep up the good work!

If you scored −100 or worse, you seriously need to change your lifestyle. Start today!

If you scored between +100 and −100, have you thought about how you could improve the way you look after yourself? Perhaps more exercise? A more careful diet?

UNIT 5 LESSON 2
Speaking *Advice*

Student A

You have just had your leg put in plaster, and it has to stay like that for at least three months. You are not sure if you can carry on your normal life. You are especially worried about:
- essential everyday activities (e.g. washing yourself)
- getting to school/work
- getting enough exercise
- your social life

Ask Students B and C for advice:

e.g. *I can't get on a bus like this! What can I do?*
How can I go and meet my friends at the weekend?

UNIT 6 LESSON 3
Writing *Description of a place*

The descriptions on page 75 could be completed like this:

a The first thing I noticed about the room was its warmth and light. A gently hissing oil lamp brought out the cheerful red and gold in the carpet. The furniture was old, but it looked solid and comfortable. Everything had been newly dusted and polished, and the clean smell of polish mixed with the scent of freshly cut flowers. There were some well-used books in a bookcase and a basket of knitting on the floor. This was a room where people could relax after a hard day's work.

b The first thing I noticed about the room was a stiffly arranged vase of flowers, and a strong hospital smell of disinfectant and polish. The vase was exactly in the middle of a white lace

tablecloth on a round table. On either side of the table there were two old-fashioned brown chairs. Behind each chair there was a gloomy picture in a heavy frame. I did not dare to touch anything in case I made a dirty mark or moved something from its correct position. The only sounds in the room were the little rustling noises I made as I tried to find a comfortable position in one of the hard scratchy chairs. It was not a room to relax in.

UNIT 8 LESSON 3
Writing 🔲 *Telling a story*

One evening Colin Blake rang his wife in north London. He said he was just leaving work, but that he was going to the pub before he went home.

One hour later he was waiting for a train in King's Cross underground station. Suddenly two policemen hurried along the platform. 'Everyone must leave the station immediately,' said one. 'There is a fire!'

Going up the escalator, Colin smelt smoke. As he got to the top, a ball of fire rushed towards him with a deafening roar. He could hardly breathe and his hair and clothes were on fire. He threw himself desperately back down the escalator. At the bottom someone turned a fire extinguisher on his flaming clothes.

By this time the emergency services were dealing with the situation. Colin was helped out of the station and into an ambulance.

He was in hospital for 35 days. It was over a year before he recovered the full use of his burnt hands. But he was one of the lucky ones. Thirty-one people died in that fire.

UNIT 9 LESSON 1
Speaking *Asking politely*

Role card A – Job applicant

You are going to be interviewed in English for a job where it is important to be able to speak English.

1 Prepare to answer the sorts of questions you would expect at any interview (e.g. about yourself and your experience).

2 You will have the opportunity to ask any questions you like about the job. Prepare some polite questions now to ask the interviewer.

UNIT 10 LESSON 2
Speaking *Conversation skills (1)*

Student A

As you discuss each question, try to practise a different conversation skill:

Question 1	Inviting others to speak; showing you're interested in what the speaker is saying.
Question 2	Taking your turn to speak at the right moment.
Question 3	Keeping talking.

UNIT 9 LESSON 2
Speaking *Money and me*

1	YES	+1	**2**	YES	−2	**3**	YES	+2
	NO	−1		NO	+2		NO	−2
4	YES	−2	**5**	YES	−1	**6**	YES	+1
	NO	0		NO	+2		NO	0

If you scored:

4 to 8: You manage your personal finances well.

0 to 3: You're on the road to financial security. But there are still improvements you could make.

−1 to −4: You need to watch out. Things may be OK now, but if they start going wrong, you could find yourself in deep trouble.

−5 to −8: It looks as if you don't really care what happens to you. Fair enough, but what about your family?

UNIT 9 LESSON 3

Reading *What makes young people commit crimes?*

More and more people under the age of sixteen are involved in crime. There are many possible reasons for this.

Firstly, lack of discipline at home and at school could be the cause. Young people often grow up without any firm idea about the difference between right and wrong, because parents are too busy working to guide their children. At school also, teachers cannot control large classes.

Secondly, social conditions such as poverty and drug addiction are important. In some cities, London for example, there are groups of homeless teenagers who steal in order to eat. In other cities, such as New York, young drug addicts commit crimes so as to be able to buy drugs.

Finally, the police may also be to blame. They often ignore minor crimes. Consequently, many young people feel they can get away with things like theft.

In conclusion, there are many factors which have caused an increase in crime among young people. It is difficult to know which of them is the most responsible, or how the increase can be stopped.

UNIT 5 LESSON 2

Speaking *Advice*

Student B

Student A needs some advice. Listen to his or her problem. You are a very *optimistic* person, so make lots of suggestions which look on the bright side:

e.g. *Why don't you phone all your friends? I'm sure they'll want to help you.*

You could invite everyone to your house at the weekend. Then you won't miss the fun.

UNIT 10 LESSON 3

Writing *'For and against' composition*

What are the advantages and disadvantages of living in the same house as your grandmother?

I cannot speak about all grandmothers but just about my own. She is 78 and she has lived with us for five years.

The main problem with living with my grandmother is the generation gap. She criticises my choice in clothes, music and television programmes. I often feel embarrassed when she makes comments in front of my friends. Also, because she is old, she has some disgusting habits. She sniffs, and when she eats she often makes a mess like a child.

On the other hand, in spite of her annoying habits, she is a wonderful person to live with. Although she often criticises my behaviour, she always stands up for me in family arguments. She sews on my buttons and irons my shirts; when I am ill she brings me hot drinks and magazines. Although she cannot remember

what happened yesterday, she tells fascinating stories about life 50 years ago.

In conclusion, I cannot imagine life without my grandmother. Although the disadvantages of living with an old woman sometimes seem unbearable, the advantages are really far more important.

UNIT 9 LESSON 1

Speaking *Asking politely*

Role card B – Interviewer

You are interviewing someone for a job where it is important that the applicant should speak good English.

1 Ask the applicant politely to:
   – introduce him or herself
   – explain why he or she has applied for the job
   – say why he or she thinks they could do the job well

2 Say something about the job. After this, invite the applicant to ask any questions he or she likes. You can answer these as you like.

Prepare your questions now.

UNIT 12 LESSON 1

Listening *Logic problems*

There are two women in the Robinson family: the mother and her one daughter, who is the sister to each of her brothers.

UNIT 10 LESSON 2

Speaking *Conversation skills (1)*

Student B

As you discuss each question, try to practise a different conversation skill:

Question 1   Keeping talking.

Question 2   Inviting others to speak; showing you're interested in what the speaker is saying.

Question 3   Taking your turn to speak at the right moment.

UNIT 12 LESSON 3

Writing *A talk (2)*

Good morning. My name's Teresa; I'm your English-speaking guide. I'd like to welcome you to the Gold Museum of Bogotá. I hope you'll find your visit memorable.

As you know, our museum displays the richest collection of pre-Columbian goldwork in the world. You'll never forget what you see today. You'll marvel at spectacular wealth, and also at incredible craftsmanship.

Can you hear me at the back? Please feel free to ask me questions. I'll do my best to answer them.

Now let me outline our programme. First we are going to watch a short film. This will give you an idea of the historical background and introduce you to the techniques these ancient craftsmen used. Then we'll look at the exhibits, ending with a feast for your eyes in the famous treasure room. Now this room's walls are completely covered with golden artifacts of incredible beauty. You'll be dazzled, I promise you.

I'm afraid photography is forbidden. At the end of our tour you can buy postcards and slides in the museum shop.

I hope you enjoy your visit. Please follow me.

UNIT 5 LESSON 2

Speaking *Advice*

Student C

Student A needs some advice. Listen to his or her problem. You are a very *pessimistic* person, so you can only see trouble in A's situation. Advise him or her how to keep out of trouble:

e.g. *If I were you, I wouldn't have a shower. You might fall over. You'd better stay at home. You might break the other leg if you try and go out.*

UNIT 13 LESSON 1

Writing *A formal letter*

This is one way the letter on page 156 could be completed.

17 Clarence Road
London W14 9GP
18 February 1994

The Managing Director
The Technology Centre
135 Strawberry Hill
Twickenham TW3 9GH

Dear Sir,

  I am writing to complain about a faulty computer I bought in your shop, and also about your inadequate after-sales service.

  On Saturday 16 February *I went into your shop to look at portable computers. I decided to buy a Peony 386SX because your sales assistant informed me, incorrectly, it would be reliable.*

  When I tried to operate my new computer at home *it did not work. I have not dropped it nor mistreated it in any way. All that appears on the screen is a message saying: 'Error reading: Hard disk'. The instructions manual is totally unhelpful on this point.*

  I phoned your store *to ask for assistance early this morning, and again at intervals throughout the day, but I only got a recorded message. I am leaving the country at the end of this week so I do not have much time to sort out this problem.*

  I should be grateful if you could arrange either for a technician to come and put the fault right, or for a substitute computer to be delivered to me immediately.

Yours faithfully,

David Friel

UNIT 10 LESSON 2

Speaking *Conversation skills (1)*

Student C

As you discuss each question, try to practise a different conversation skill:

Question 1   Taking your turn to speak at the right moment.
Question 2   Keeping talking.
Question 3   Inviting others to speak; showing you're interested in what the speaker is saying.

UNIT 15 LESSON 4

Exam skill *Practical matters*

Reading comprehension answer sheet (extract)

Listening comprehension answer sheet (extract)